BODYBUILDING
A SCIENTIFIC APPROACH
FREDERICK C. HATFIELD, Ph.D.

Contemporary Books, Inc.
Chicago

Library of Congress Cataloging in Publication Data

Hatfield, Frederick C.
   Bodybuilding: a scientific approach.

   Includes index.
   1. Bodybuilding.   I. Title.
GV546.5.H38   1984   646.7'5   84-5817
ISBN 0-8092-5458-1

Published by Contemporary Books, Inc.
180 North Michigan Avenue, Chicago, Illinois 60601
Manufactured in the United States of America
Library of Congress Catalog Card Number: 84-5817
International Standard Book Number: 0-8092-5458-1

Published simultaneously in Canada by Beaverbooks, Ltd.
195 Allstate Parkway, Valleywood Business Park
Markham, Ontario L3R 4T8 Canada

CONTENTS

ACKNOWLEDGMENTS

v

To Joe and Ben Weider for the immeasurable impact they have had on the sport and science of bodybuilding.

To Bob Hoffman for his generous support and contributions to bodybuilding.

The IFBB, Weider Health and Fitness, and York all contributed immeasurably to the success of this book not only through their photographs but through their true dedication and concern for the future of bodybuilding. Without the aid of these organizations, and the men behind them, bodybuilding would most likely never have become what it is today.

And last, but by no means least, thanks to my loving wife, Joy, without whose love I would never have attempted to write this book at all.

PREFACE

Our lives are becoming both easier and more complicated, and the paradox is due to advances in science. Science has brought the moon within our range of exploration, but at a cost to society that is incalculable in terms of the complex issues such a venture inevitably creates.

So it is with sport. As science uncovers new technologies and methods of improving human performance capabilities, the lot of the athlete and coach is made more complicated. It is a price all athletes who aspire to greatness gladly pay.

The sport of bodybuilding fathered a new technology that has become a vital part of all athletes' training. The use of weights, or progressive overload in its infinite array of forms, builds bigger, faster, and stronger bodies. Just the thing for most athletes to help them improve at the respective sports. But bodybuilding is also an end in itself—not just a means of sport-performance improvement. Bodybuilding is one of the fastest growing sports in the world today, and its popularity is due, in large measure, to the wonderful health and fitness benefits that are derived from the bodybuilding lifestyle.

With the increasing popularity of bodybuilding there has been a plethora of books appearing on the subject. The growing Weider Library of Bodybuilding books (published by Contemporary Books, Inc.) contains practically the sum total of the **practical** knowledge compiled over the years on bodybuilding methods. There are at least 60 other books, most published during the past few years, on the general subject of bodybuilding techniques. However, there are no truly **scientific** books on the subject, a fact that is startling yet true.

It is odd that no one has ever taken the time to explain **why** an exercise should be done in the prescribed fashion, or **what happens** inside the muscle when one method of training is used as compared to another. Having been a college professor, it has always meant a lot to me to not only know what to do, but why I was doing it. In such a manner, my confidence in what I was doing invariably spurred me to greater accomplishments in athletics. I worked harder feeling assured that I was employing the most "correct" method science had to offer.

It is in this spirit that this book was written. You will not only know what the scientific approach to bodybuilding is, but why each method discussed is valuable. The physiological rationale for training and dieting methods, and the kinesiological rationale for the performance of each exercise are fully explored. This is perhaps the only book ever written in this fashion.

My introduction will trace the short history of bodybuilding back to its beginnings in 1939 when Bert Goodrich became the first Mr. America. Photos from both the Weider files and the York files make this the most complete pictorial history ever assembled under one cover. Comparisons of nutrition, training practices, lifestyles, and drugs are pointed out to explain the incredible difference in muscle size, density, and definition between the superstars of yesterday and today.

Parts I and II include the physiological and kinesiological rationale behind different training problems, methods, and exercises. The graphs, photos, electron micrographs of muscle tissue, and illustrations all add to the scientific authenticity of these important sections. Collectively they comprise the backbone of all bodybuilding practices.

Nutrition, the "infant science," is one of the subjects in Part III. Bodybuilders of today regard nutrition as just as important to ultimate success in their sport as is proper training. Nutrition becomes extremely important during the contest preparation phase of all bodybuilders' training cycle, and is discussed in detail along with the other scientific factors involved in precontest training.

Also included in Part III is a complete discussion of drug usage in sport—to many a tragic and paradoxical situation, considering that sport is, in its purest sense, supposed to promote health. This controversial topic is frankly and candidly discussed, and the anabolic and other preparatory substances bodybuilders use are listed and completely discussed for perhaps the first time in any book on bodybuilding.

Part IV is devoted to psychology. No athlete has ever tapped the true power of his or her mind to the fullest, and this portion of the book discusses methods that bodybuilders can use to enhance their mental state during training. Motivation, personality, and a host of other psychological and sociological factors can often be disruptive to a bodybuilder, and the research done in this area is presented along with practical suggestions.

Women's bodybuilding, as well as mixed pairs (couples) bodybuilding, has burst upon the scene and promises to become extremely popular throughout the world. The methods of weight training for women are, in practically every aspect, identical to those used by men, so the entire book is just as relevant to women as it is to men.

In all, this book represents a state-of-the-art description of the sport of bodybuilding—called by many the sport of the eighties. Whatever your bodybuilding goals, this book will help you to get there perhaps a bit quicker and more efficiently than others because it is based on scientific information rather than merely hand-me-down philosophies.

I wish you luck and good health in your sport, and—God willing—success on the platform.

Frederick C. Hatfield, Ph.D.

INTRODUCTION
A PHOTOGRAPHIC HISTORY
OF BODYBUILDING

The first **Mr. America** contest was held in 1939, but that isn't to say that bodybuilding started then. Since time immemorial men of strength have been the focal point of fables, songs, poems, and art. The ancient Greeks immortalized Hercules by casting him in stone. His statue remained the ideal by which those who followed him in time were judged—both from the standpoint of strength as well as physique.

During the early 1900s, physique exhibitions were popular additions to Olympic weightlifting contests. In fact, photo contests were sponsored by at least two or three different physical culture magazines—the most memorable one being that in which the legendary Charles Atlas claimed the title of **the world's most perfectly developed male.**

The classical ideals by which early physique artists were judged carried over into modern bodybuilding, and the first AAU physique contestants were judged at least partly on the basis of their athletic prowess. In fact this athletic ability requirement persisted into the late 1960s before being dropped.

It is hard to pinpoint the time at which bodybuilding began to be regarded as a sport, but it certainly appears to be connected with the fact that the early bodybuilders had to be successful athletes as well as well built. All sorts of arguments, both pro and con, have been advanced regarding the place of bodybuilding in the world of sport.

The fact that early bodybuilders were required to be athletes as well as bodybuilders seems, on the face of it, to be an argument against calling bodybuilding a sport—the athletic requirement seemed to be a feeble attempt at justifying the concept. But in time the bodybuilding community came around, and determined that bodybuilding could stand on its own merits as a sport.

Sport or not, bodybuilding as an art, as a science, as a lifestyle, and as a form of entertainment is here to stay, and the benefits (financial, self-satisfaction, notoriety, or health) can be substantial. Today, there are several million bodybuilders around the world, a fact which attests to its popular appeal and chances of survival as a sport, art form, entertainment medium, or whatever. The inception of bodybuilding into the 1981 World Games in California also lends strong support to the concept of it being a sport.

But it is not within the purview of this book to argue the pros and cons of bodybuilding in any regard. Those who have chosen to read this book are probably already convinced of the various benefits that can

Roland Essemaker,
Mr. America of 1939.

be derived from the practice of bodybuilding. Instead, this book focuses upon the scientific aspects of muscular development—how best to do it. And, this first chapter explores the differences between the training methods of the early bodybuilders with those of today.

The struggles that the forebears of the sport experienced in their quest for a perfect physique were not in vain, for they were the ones who gave impetus to the growth in popularity of bodybuilding as well as the development of the science behind it.

The Scientific Advancement of Bodybuilding Methods

There are several avenues that must be trod during the long trek to body perfection. The most obvious ones are:

- Training methods.
- Diet and nutrition.
- Ergogenic aids (such as **drugs, non-drug anabolic stimulators, training enhancers** such as ice, heat, massage or analgesics, and **meditation**).*
- Lifestyle factors (such as training time, vocational opportunities in related fields, and the increased popularity of bodybuilding).
- Trends in judging bodybuilding contests—what are the factors considered important to the judges.

Down through the years, the improvements, advances, and changes in the factors listed above have produced a distinctly different breed of bodybuilders from the early competitors of the late thirties and early forties. The photographs of the bodybuilding champions catalogued here attest to this difference. Greater mass, vascularity, muscularity, and attention to proportionment are all quite obvious as you peruse the pictorial history of the sport presented here.

It is a popularly held notion that the use of anabolic steriods (near the end of the fifties and on into the present day) is the major contributing factor in the startling differences in yesterday and today's bodybuilders. There is no question that steroids have indeed been a factor. However, far more than that are the great changes in training technique, diet and nutrition, and judging trends. Anabolic steroids help you grow more muscle mass, but continually increasing mass is not going to produce a champion bodybuilder! The "ripped" look and

---

*Part IV contains a complete listing of the ergogenic aids and practices currently in use by bodybuilders.

balanced proportions needed to win today's competitions come from proper nutrition and attention to training detail, not from use of anabolic steroids.

Further, the tremendous increase in the popularity of bodybuilding has created a mass influx of better talent into the sport. This same phenomenon can be observed in virtually any sport that is still growing.

Couple these factors with the fact that it was not in vogue to enter a contest "ripped" years ago (when much emphasis was given to athletic appearance), and you have what amounts to a strong case for explaining where bodybuilding has come from and what it is today. The answer lies in a collective view of the scientific and sociological changes which have taken place rather than in the narrow view that drugs are what produced the difference.

xii

Where Are Our Roots?

No explanation of where bodybuilding came from or where it is today would be complete without at least paying homage to those who laid the foundation upon which the art and science was later erected. By all standards, this foundation was laid by Joe and Ben

Text concludes on page xxviii.

John Grimek, 1940-41 Mr. America.

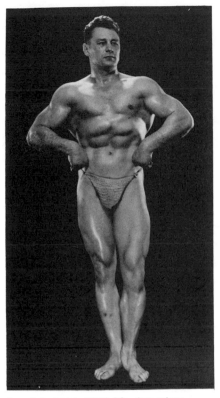

Frank Leight, 1942 Mr. America.   Jules Bacon, 1943 Mr. America.

Clarence Ross, 1945 Mr. America.   Alan Stephan, 1946 Mr. America.

Steve Reeves, 1947 Mr. America.

John Farbotnik, 1950 Mr. America.

Jack Delinger,
1949 Mr. America.

Ray Hilligen, 1951 Mr. America.

James Park, 1952 Mr. America.

Bill Pearl,
1953 Mr. America.

Dick DuBois, 1954 Mr. America.

Ray Schaefer, 1956 Mr. America.

Steve Klisanin,
1955 Mr. America.

Ron Lacy, 1957 Mr. America.

Tom Sansone, 1958 Mr. America.

Harry Johnson, 1959 Mr. America.

Lloyd Lerille, 1960 Mr. America.

AAU Mr. America Winners
1939 to Present

1939 Bert Goodrich[1] Roland Essemaker	1954 Dick Dubois	1970 Chris Dickerson
	1955 Steve Klisanin	1971 Casey Viator[4]
	1956 Ray Schaefer	1972 Steve Michalik
1940 John Grimek[2]	1957 Ron Lacy	1973 Jim Morris
1941 John Grimek	1958 Tom Sansone	1974 Ron Thompson
1942 Frank Leight	1959 Harry Johnson	1975 Dale Adrian
1943 Jules Bacon	1960 Lloyd Lerille	1976 Kal Szkalak
1944 Steve Stanko	1961 Ray Rutledge	1977 Dave Johns
1945 Clancy Ross	1962 Joe Abbenda	1978 Tony Pearson
1946 Alan Stephan	1963 Vern Weaver	1979 Ray Mentzer
1947 Steve Reeves	1964 Val Vasilef	1980 Gary Leonard
1948 George Eiferman	1965 Jerry Daniels	1981 Tim Belknap[5]
1949 Jack Dellinger	1966 Bob Gajda	1982 Rufus Howard (AAU)
1950 John Farbotnik	1967 Dennis Tinerino	Lee Haney (NPC)
1951 Ray Hilligen[3]	1968 Jim Haislop	1983 Jeff King (AAU)
1952 Jim Park	1969 Boyer Coe	Bob Paris (NPC)
1953 Bill Pearl		

[1] First Mr. America Contests (2 held).
[2] Only one to win twice (rules were changed after 1941).
[3] Only foreigner to win (South African).
[4] Youngest winner (age 19).
[5] Last open Mr. America Contest. AAU and NPC split thereafter with AAU retaining claim to Mr. A title and NPC conducting the National Championships thereafter.

**Ray Rutledge,
1961 Mr. America.**

Joe Abbenda,
1962 Mr. America.

Val Vasilef,
1964 Mr. America.

Bob Gajda, 1966 Mr. America.

Dennis Tinerino, 1967 Mr. America.

NABBA Mr. Universe Winners
(amateur and professional)
1947 to Present

1947 Steve Stanko (USA)*

1948 John Grimek (USA)*

1949 (no contest)

1950 Steve Reeves (USA)*

1951 Reg Park (So. Africa)*

1952 Mohamed Nasr (Egypt)*
Juan Ferraro (Spain)**

1953 Bill Pearl (USA)*
Arnold Dyson (England)**

1954 Enrico Thomas (USA)*
Jim Park (USA)**

1955 Mickey Hargitay (USA)*
Leo Robert (Canada)**

1956 Ray Schaefer (USA)*
Jack Dellinger (USA)**

1957 John Lees (England)*
Arthur Robin (England)**

1958 Earl Clark (USA)*
Reg Park (So. Africa)**

1959 Len Sell (England)*
Bruce Randall (USA)**

1960 Henry Downs (England)*
Paul Wynter (Antigua)**

1961 Ray Rutledge (USA)*
Bill Pearl (USA)**

1962 Joe Abbenda (USA)*
Len Sell (England)**

1963 Tom Sansone (USA)*
Joe Abbenda (USA)**

1964 John Hewlett (England)*
Earl Maynard (Barbados)**

1965 Elmo Santiago (USA)*
Reg Park (So. Africa)**

1966 Chester Yorton (USA)*
Paul Wynter (Antigua)**

1967 Arnold Schwarzenegger (Austria)*
Bill Pearl (USA)**

1968 Dennis Tinerino (USA)*
Arnold Schwarzenegger (Austria)**

1969 Boyer Coe (USA)*
Arnold Schwarzenegger (Austria)**

1970 Frank Zane (USA)*
Arnold Schwarzenegger (Austria)**

1971 Ken Waller (USA)*
Bill Pearl (USA)**

1972 Elias Petsas (So. Africa)*
Frank Zane (USA)**

1973 Chris Dickerson (USA)*
Boyer Coe (USA)**

1974 Roy Duval (England)*
Chris Dickerson (USA)**

1975 Ian Lawrence (Scotland)*
Boyer Coe (USA)**

1976 Shigeru Sugita (Japan)*
Serge Nubret (France)**

1977 Bertil Fox (England)*
Tony Emmott (England)**

1978 Dave Johns (USA)*
Bertil Fox (England)**

1979 Ahmet Enunulu (Turkey)*
Bertil Fox (England)**

1980 Bill Richardson (England)*
Tony Pearson (USA)**

1981 John Brown (USA)*
Robby Robinson (USA)**

1982 John Brown (USA)*
Eduardo Kawak (Lebanon)**

1983 Jeff King (USA)*
Eduardo Kawak (Lebanon)**

* denotes amateur
** denotes professional

xx

**IFBB Mr. Universe Winners
1959 to Present**

1959 Eddie Silvestre
1960 (no contest)
1961 Chuck Sipes
1962 George Eiferman
1963 Harold Poole
1964 Larry Scott
1965 Earl Maynard
1966 Dave Draper
1967 Sergio Oliva
1968 Frank Zane
1969 Arnold Schwarzenegger
1970 Arnold Schwarzenegger
1971 Giuseppe Deiana (Lightweight)
Albert Beckles (Middleweight)—overall winner
Karl Bloemmer (Heavyweight)
1972 Suetmisue (L)
Ed Corney (M)—overall winner
Mike Katz (H)
1973 Giuseppe Deiana (L)
Albert Beckles (M)
Lou Ferrigno (H)—overall winner

1974 Pierre Van Den Steen (L)
Ahmet Enunlu (M)
Lou Ferrigno (H)—overall winner
1975 Wilf Sylvester (L)
Robby Robinson (M)
Ken Waller (H)—overall winner
1976 Mohamed Makkawy (L)
Robby Robinson (M)
Roger Walker (H)
1977 Dan Padilla (L)
Roy Callendar (M)
Kalman Szkalak (H)
1978 Carlos Rodriguez (L)
Tom Platz (M)
Mike Mentzer (H)
1979 Renato Bertagna (L)
Roy Duval (M)
Samir Bannout

(LH)
Jusup Wilkosz (H)
1980 Heinz Sallmayer (L)
Jorma Raty (M)
Johnny Fuller (LH)
Hubert Metz (H)
1981 Ken Passariello (L)
Gerard Buinoud (M)
Jacques Neuville (LH)
Lance Dreher (H)
1982 James Gaubert (L)
Dale Ruplinger (M)
Ahmed Enunlu (LH)
Lee Haney (H)
1983 Herman Hoffend (Bantam Weight—1983 only)
Appie Steenbeck (L)
Charles Glass (M)
Chuck Williams (LH)
Bob Paris (H)

IFBB Mr. America Winners
1949 – 1977

1949 Alan Stephan	1964 Harold Poole	1971 Ken Waller
1950 - 1958 (no contests)	1965 Dave Draper	1972 Ed Corney
1959 Chuck Sipes	1966 Chet Yorton	1973 Lou Ferrigno
1960 Gene Shuey	1967 Don Howorth	1974 Bob Birdsong
1961 (no contest)	1968 Frank Zane	1975 Robby Robinson
1962 Larry Scott	1969 John Decola	1976 Mike Mentzer
1963 Reg Lewis	1970 Mike Katz	1977 Dan Padilla

Wilf Sylvester,
1975 IFBB Mr. Universe (Lightweight).

Robby Robinson,
1975-76 IFBB Mr. Universe (Middleweight).

Ken Waller, 1975 IFBB Mr. Universe
(Overall-Heavyweight).

Mohamed Makkawy,
1976 IFBB Mr. Universe (Lightweight).

Danny Padilla,
1977 IFBB Mr. Universe (Lightweight).

Roy Callender,
1977 IFBB Mr. Universe (Middleweight).

xxiv

Tom Platz,
1978 IFBB Mr. Universe (Middleweight).

Mike Mentzer,
1978 IFBB Mr. Universe (Heavyweight).

Samir Bannout,
1979 IFBB Mr. Universe (Light Heavyweight).

Ken Passariello,
1981 IFBB Mr. Universe (Lightweight).

IFBB Mr. World Winners
1962–1976

1962	Jose Castaneda Lence	1967	Rick Wayne	1972	Mike Katz
1963	(no contest)	1968	Chuck Sipes	1973	Ken Waller
1964	Jorge Brisco	1969	Frank Zane	1974	Bill Grant
1965	Kingsley Poitier	1970	Dave Draper	1975	Robby Robinson
1966	Sergio Oliva	1971	Franco Columbu	1976	Darcey Beccles

**Jacques Neuville,
1981 IFBB Mr. Universe (Light Heavyweight).**

**Lance Dreher,
1981 IFBB Mr. Universe (Heavyweight).**

Frank Zane,
Mr. Olympia 1977-79.

IFBB Mr. Olympia Winners

1965 Larry Scott, USA (Brooklyn, N.Y.)
1966 Larry Scott, USA (Brooklyn, N.Y.)
1967 Sergio Oliva, USA (Brooklyn, N.Y.)
1968 Sergio Oliva, USA (Brooklyn, N.Y.)
1969 Sergio Oliva, USA (Brooklyn, N.Y.)
1970 Arnold Schwarzenegger, Austria (New York, N.Y.)
1971 Arnold Schwarzenegger, Austria (Paris, France)
1972 Arnold Schwarzenegger, Austria (Essen, Germany)
1973 Arnold Schwarzenegger, Austria (Brooklyn, N.Y.)
1974 Arnold Schwarzenegger, Austria (New York, N.Y.)
1975 Arnold Schwarzenegger, Austria (Pretoria, South Africa)
1976 Franco Columbu, USA (Columbus, Ohio)
1977 Frank Zane, USA (Columbus, Ohio)
1978 Frank Zane, USA (Columbus, Ohio)
1979 Frank Zane, USA (Columbus, Ohio)
1980 Arnold Schwarzenegger, Austria (Sydney, Australia)
1981 Franco Columbu, USA (Columbus, Ohio)
1982 Chris Dickerson, USA (London, England)
1983 Samir Bannout, Lebanon (Munich, Germany)

WBBG Professional Winners

Mr. America
1967 Harold Poole
1968 Harold Poole
1969 Johnny
    Maldonado
1970 Rick Wayne
1971 Peter Caputo
1972 Bill Grant
1973 Chris Dickerson
1974 Warren
    Frederick
1975 Ralph Kroger
1976 Scott Wilson
1977 Don Ross
1978 Anibal Lopez
1979 Tommy Aybar

Mr. World
1971-75 Boyer Coe
1976 Tony Emmott
1977 Serge Nubret
1978 Anibal Lopez
1979 Tony Pearson

Mr. Olympus
1975 Sergio Oliva
1976 Sergio Oliva
1977 Serge Nubret
1978 Sergio Oliva
1979 Tony Pearson

Larry Scott,
Mr. Olympia, 1965-66.

Text continued from page xiii.

Weider, publisher of **Your Physique** magazine of the 1940s and founder of the International Federation of Bodybuilders respectively. The advances in bodybuilding listed earlier in this chapter would not have occurred without the organization (the IFBB) and the communication platform (**Your Physique** magazine) to sustain them.

Other magazines and organizations were, of course, on the scene during the early years. Most notably, Bob Hoffman's magazine, **Strength and Health**, and Peary Rader's magazine, **Iron Man**, were considerably influential in the growth and development of bodybuilding.

The Amateur Athletic Union (AAU) was also on the scene, and although often at odds with the IFBB (the classic power struggle), both contributed greatly to the sport. Today, both of these organizations still exist, and the IFBB clearly is the leading organization both from the standpoint of numbers of international competitors in its ranks as well as in producing the greatest bodybuilders. The AAU spent a short time in transition when they were ordered by the Congress of the United States to relinquish their control of amateur bodybuilding in this country. The National Physique Committee (NPC) was heir to the sport's governance from then on. However, as the sport grew in popularity and financial benefits became sufficiently prominent, the AAU saw fit to reclaim their control over amateur bodybuilding via maintaining legal ownership of the prestigious title, ''Mr. America.''

Now affiliated with the IFBB, the NPC began (in 1982) to run its own version of a U.S. National bodybuilding championship, calling it the NPC National Physique Championships.

If that isn't enough to confuse you—having more than one national championship—consider that the IFBB for many years (from 1949-1977) ran its own ''Mr. America'' contest, and that the WBBG did so as well until recently, relinquishing the title when the NPC lost its court battle with the AAU. New organizations spring up from time to time in protest over various conditions within the IFBB. There is even a ''Natural'' Mr. America contest, assumedly to protest the use of anabolic steroids by athletes in other organizations.

Being reasonably apolitical, my only comment regarding this state of affairs bodybuilding has gotten itself into is that as long as the best can compete against the best, it doesn't matter how many organizations there are. The result will be the same—one winner overall. Unfortunately, this has yet to happen.

PART I
BASIC CONCEPTS IN BODYBUILDING

With the advent of electron microscopy, scientists were, for the first time in the history of weight training, able to visually observe the effects of training on muscle cells. High reps with a light weight, it was found, produced changes in various components of a muscle cell that were totally different from those changes occurring from the application of fewer reps with heavier weights. Fast movements, slow movements, sustained movements, forced reps, rhythmic pumping, and other of the various types of training procedures common in muscle factories around the globe all became totally meaningful to the scientist armed with his trusty electron microscope!

Unfortunately, this information has not been passed on to the **practitioners** of the art. Bodybuilders everywhere still cling to the same old systems that their forebears told them were the best. They may be the best for certain aspects of bodybuilding, but certainly not for developing the entire muscle cell to its fullest capacity. There is a wealth of information in the scientific literature that would be of tremendous benefit to the aspiring bodybuilder—if only he (or she) could decypher it!

A few of the more germane bits of information buried in the sanctity of Academia's ivory towers is presented here in terms that I hope most will understand.

1

THE CASE FOR
HEAVY TRAINING

Some bodybuilders I know pay homage to "the pump" as though it were the product rather than merely a process. They spend year in and year out doing their curls or doing their abdominal crunchers with the same amount of weight, happily stopping after achieving a pump. These same misguided souls also happen to spend year in and year out in the ranks of the also-rans.

What has happened is that their muscles had long ago adapted to the stress of the weights they were using, and their nervous systems had also adapted to the lactate concentrations that signalled the pumped sensation they worshipped. Their continued use of the same level of stress in their exercises constituted a built-in ceiling beyond which they could not progress. Mediocrity set in.

Some learned the lesson of working through the pain barrier, and made a few more gains after that. But they were still using the same weight. The only thing that changed was their acceptance of, or ability to tolerate, greater levels of pain resulting from the lactic acid build-up in the muscles. The few added reps they were able to muster resulted in a few more cells being stimulated or a few more of each cell's components being increased, but their progress soon halted again, and they were once more forced to contend with being something less than championship caliber.

Ever hear of the **overload principle?** There are many ways of applying overload to a muscle. Increase the weight, increase the reps or sets, decrease the rest periods, increase the speed of movement, increase the speed with which the set is performed—there are many more ways. One of the most important lessons that you can learn as a bodybuilder is that each one of these methods of overload produce different results in the muscle cells! Forcing out more reps with the same weight is **not** the same kind of stress as adding more weight! And, going faster through a set is **not** the same kind of stress as decreasing the rest between sets!

It appears that the bodybuilders I knew were aware of the overload principle, but had a very narrow view of it. The word **overload** simply meant that one was going to make the muscle do something that it was not used to doing. The overload can range from severe to mild, and the muscle will eventually adapt to the level of overload being applied. When that happens, it is no longer overload, and greater stress must be applied for continued development to occur.

So, my poor, stalemated, bodybuilder friends should have added more weight as they grew stronger! You may ask, "what happens when you're lifting such huge weights that you can't possibly make gains any more?" Have you ever seen that happen? Many of my powerlifting friends are well past forty, and still getting stronger! And, I might add, **bigger!** The name of the game is to lift as heavy weights as you can and you'll continue to develop

Heavy vs. Light

So, what's heavy? What's light? Heavy simply means how much you can lift for a required number of reps. If your last rep in a set of twenty curls, for example, is an absolute maximum effort, then that's heavy! Light, on the other hand, means that you can perform the required number of reps without having to exert maximum effort on the last rep. Typically, bodybuilders will use a cutoff point in the number of reps that they consider light or heavy. For example, any set comprised of less than ten repetitions is heavy, and more than ten reps is light. For the sake of uniformity in our definition, let's accept the first definition offered as the proper definition of light and heavy.

There are some people out there who don't believe in heavy training. It's too dangerous and not productive in producing symmetry, definition, size—their excuses are endless, it seems, for not putting out the effort it takes to achieve championship status. Heavy is a relative concept! What was heavy for you five years ago isn't heavy now.

Upon questioning such people, however, I have found that their definition of "heavy" was not the same as mine. Heavy to these bodybuilders meant doing singles or doubles with a maximum weight. This kind of lifting has no place in a bodybuilder's training program, for it does indeed expose him or her to destructive levels of stress. Even powerlifters are learning that maximum singles in training do not help them get stronger over the long term. Most powerlifters have retreated, so to speak, to the 5-8-reps-per-set method for strength training, leaving the singles for the contest.

Since a muscle cell is comprised of many different components, each requiring a different form of stress for it to adapt, bodybuilders ought to include a wide array of techniques in their training. In so doing, they will not fall into the same trap as my misguided friends did, and wallow in the mire of mediocrity year after year. High reps, low reps, fast movements, slow movements, continuous tension movements, forced reps, cheat movements, iso-tension exercises, and everything between ought to be performed to force all of the cell's components to grow. And, importantly, they should all be done such that the last rep in every set is a maximum effort!

Let me become a bit more specific for a moment, and illustrate what I mean by engaging in holistic training.

The table below lists the major components of a muscle cell in order of their relative contribution to the overall size of the cell. Each component has a specific function to perform, and by overloading that function you will force that component to develop in size or quantity—

Muscle Cell Components' Contribution to Overall Cell Size and Appropriate Stress Factors

Cell Component	Approximate Percentage of Cell's Total Size	Method of Overload
myofibrils	20%–30%	strength 6–12 reps
mitochondria	15%–25%	endurance 15–25 reps
sarcoplasm	20%–30%	strength and endurance
capillaries	3%– 5%	endurance plus continuous tension
fat deposits	10%–15%	rest & diet
glycogen	2%– 5%	diet
connective tissue	2%– 3%	strength
other subcellular substances	4%– 7%	strength and endurance plus rest & diet

this is the way our body "protects" itself from destructive stress. By varying the stress you will insure that maximum growth and development is achieved. Performing the same reps and sets with the same weight year in and year out will never allow you to achieve your potential.

6   Holistic Training

The muscle cell is a very complex entity. No single method of training can force an adaptive process to occur in all aspects of the cell. If only one or two cell components are forced to adapt (i.e., to become larger) that means that the rest of the cell is remaining as it was prior to training. To maximize cell size, then, a wide variety of stressors must be applied to the cell. In this way, a greater number of the cell's components will develop. **Holistic training** is looking at the whole cell rather than just a part of it.

Before delving into some of the methods of training that are now known by scientists to produce maximum muscular size, consider some relevant facts about a muscle's capabilities for size increase. Mild exercise generally improves the size of a muscle by about 10% above that which it was during its years of inactivity. A trained bodybuilder's muscles are as much as 50% bigger than they were prior to training. Holistic training procedures can improve a muscle's size by as much as 70% or more! Think of how much the average bodybuilder is leaving behind!

As a general rule in holistic training, those cell components which contribute most to overall muscle size are trained the most. Myofibrils and mitochondria, for example, comprise a good portion of the average cell—more than most other cell components. Therefore, they should be given greater training time. The photo on page 7 is an illustration of a muscle cell with many of its component parts identified.

The muscle cell is surrounded by an extremely thin membrane called the **sarcolemma.** Just beneath the sarcolemma are the cell's **nucleii.** Within the fluid portion of the cell are the **myofibrils.** The fluid is called the **sarcoplasm,** and is actually a gelatinous protein substance. The myofibrils are the cell's contractile elements, and are arranged in alternating columns of light and dark segments. The coloring is due to the relative density of the overlapping protein filaments within each myofibril. The short, thick filaments are comprised of the protein **myosin,** and are overlapped by the longer, thin filaments comprised of the protein **actin.**

Tiny organelles called **mitochondria** are found between the myofi-

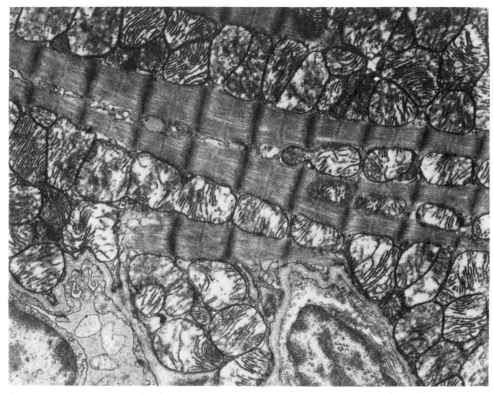

Electron micrograph of a human cardiac muscle. While skeletal muscles in man are nearly identical to cardiac muscle in basic structure, they do not possess such tremendous mitochondrial mass (the large, round bodies paralleling the fibers are **mitchondria**) as shown here. The **myofibrils** are the fibrous bands running across the photo. (**Courtesy of the University of Wisconsin Biodynamics Laboratory, Physical Education Department, Madison: 1980.**)

brils, and are responsible for the oxidative metabolism of the fibers as well as for the production of a chemical called adrenosinetriphosphate (ATP). Without ATP a muscle coud not contract. Indeed, it is the destruction of ATP (and the resultant build-up of lactic acid—the chemical "waste") that causes the famous "pumped" sensation that bodybuilders experience.

Other subcellular substances within the cell are of critical importance to the bodybuilder as well. The **sarcoplasmic reticulum** is a network of tubules running from the exterior of the cell to the myofibrils. Among other things, they assist in evenly distributing the nerve impulse which triggers muscle contraction. **Ribosomes** are responsible for the synthesis of protein molecules. **Myoglobin** (a red pigment) maintains the proper oxygen concentration in the cell so that the mitochondria can function properly. **Glycogen granules** are the "fuel" for energy and are stored in columns alongside the myofibrils for easy access. And, finally, many **enzymes** are present, each playing its vital role in the utilization of glycogen.

The most important facts for the bodybuilder to keep in mind when viewing the muscle cell are:

- All of these cell components take up space and therefore contribute to the overall size of the muscle.
- Each cell component responds to a different form of stress by adapting to that stress.
- Once the adaption has occurred, greater amounts of stress must be delivered for greater amounts of development. No increases in size can occur if the cell has already adapted to the level of stress being imposed.

In case you haven't recognized them, two of the most important principles of training are spelled out here. The **overload** principle and the **SAID** principle (SAID stands for "specific adaptation to imposed demands"). The overload principle is inherent in the third point while the SAID principle is the second point. Collectively, they relate to the concept of holistic training.

It becomes quite clear how bodybuilders must train after considering all of these components of a cell and what their respective functions are. You must train with a variety of methods. The greatest amount of size will be gained by training the myofibrillar elements.

Generally, performing high speed movements for about 15 reps and 4-5 sets is good for increasing the number of myofibrillar elements, but such training will do little for improving endurance or strength. By increasing the load to greater than 80% of one's maximum and performing 6-8 reps while still maintaining the high speed movement, strength and power can be increased as well as size. The increased strength will allow for continued progress, since greater loads can be handled thereby forcing greater levels of adaption. The high-speed movements are important because of the fact that the so-called "fast-twitch" muscle fibers are called upon and they have a greater capacity for hypertrophy than do the slower contracting fibers.

The white, fast-twitch fibers have a thicker nerve supply serving them, allowing for greater innervation. The red, "slow-twitch" fibers, on the other hand, have greater supplies of mitochondria and myoglobin (the red pigment gives them their deeper red color), and are better suited for submaximal loads and sustained work. To maximize the myofibrillar content of these red fibers, high-speed work is still going to be the rule of thumb, for they will adapt slightly to this kind of stress as will the white fibers.

The myofibrillar content of a cell is generally proportional to the cell's contractile strength. Similarly, a cell's endurance capacity is

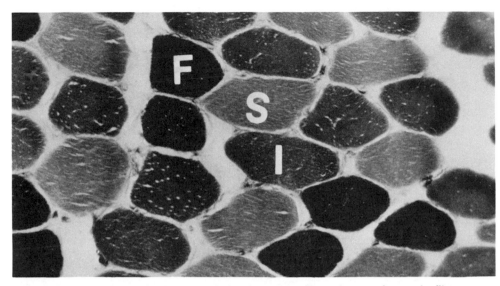

Electron micrograph of a human skeletal muscle. Three types of muscle fiber shown are: S (Slow-twitch, red fiber), F (Fast-twitch, white fiber), and I (Intermediate fiber). (Courtesy of Byrnes, W.C., "A comparison of the metabolic effects of breathing hyperoxic and normoxic gas mixtures during prolonged exercise." Unpublished doctoral dissertation, University of Wisconsin Biodynamics Laboratory, Madison: 1978.)

generally proportional to the number of mitochondria present. Using the lighter weights (about 60% of your max) for as many as 20-30 reps with slow, continuous tension will develop greater numbers of cell mitochondria as well as increase the extensiveness of the capillaries surrounding the cell—all of which take up space and contribute to overall size and vascularity.

The sarcoplasmic content of the cell appears to be regulated somewhat by the presence of the other cell components' development. As greater numbers of mitochondria or myofibrils are formed, the sarcoplasmic content of the cell increases. Furthermore, the sarcoplasmic content, as with all the other components of the cell, appear to be increased differentially depending upon what brand of anabolic steroid is used by the bodybuilder. More important by far, however, is the method of stress application the bodybuilder is using. No drug can do it alone, and whatever benefits there are in resorting to their use are often counterweighted with hazards.

Holistic training demands a **scientific** approach to training. It is no longer enough to follow in the footsteps of the great bodybuilders of the past. Too many new stars are on the horizon, each a bit more scientific in their approach to training than the last group. It is certain that the stars of the future will have to look to the whole muscle cell—indeed, the whole body—to gain entry to the winner's circle.

2
A SOLID FOUNDATION
FOR THE BEGINNER

Recall the biblical parable of the wise man and the foolish man. The wise man built his house on the rock, while the other foolishly built his house on sand. Ensuing wind and storm, we are told, washed the house on sand away. The house on the rock stood firm.

It doesn't take a wizard or a priest to apply this story to the sports world. Unless an athlete wisely builds a solid foundation of fitness before attempting to undertake the rigors of competition (with all the fury of wind and storm, albeit bodily stress and potential injury or failure), he, like the house build on sand, will inevitably be "blown away."

The question, then, is exactly what constitutes a solid foundation for the beginning bodybuilder? The answer is given in yet another question: What is it that the foundation must support? If we can assume that the foundation must be supportive of a massive physique and supernormal strength, and remain so for a period of many years, then the answer to the first question is quite obvious.

For the beginner, high-intensity training is out. Such training is overly taxing to the novice's relatively frail body, and injury or overtraining will be omnipresent. For the beginner, strength is essential, for the physiological changes that take place with increased strength are important in giving substance and support to the musculoskeletal system. The increased strength in the smaller (often overlooked) synergistic and stabilizer muscles will make it possible to achieve greater overload on the major muscles later on. This is good, for such increased stability and support will, together with the improved overload capabilities, further increase strength and size in the years to come.

These two factors—attention to overall bodily strength and attention to the superstructural muscles as well as to the larger, more visible muscles—are what the wise beginner must consider. Doing so will ensure greater progress as time goes by, and it will also stand as the single most important concept in avoiding injuries. Each of these factors deserves some elaboration here.

Strength

There has been much research into the area of improving strength. Scientists are generally in agreement that the following factors contribute to overall strength:

1. Muscle fiber arrangement (i.e., fusiform or penniform).
2. The number of muscle cells one can activate during the movement.
3. Enzyme concentrations in the muscle cell must be conducive to strong contracture.
4. The sensitivity of the Golgi tendon organ (a ''defense'' mechanism that shuts down a muscle that is contracting too hard).
5. The ratio of fast-twitch versus slow-twitch muscle fibers (the fast-twitch muscles have greater contractility potential).
6. Musculoskeletal leverage.
7. The coordination of movement stemming from the action of stabilizer muscles, synergistic muscles, and the primary muscles.
8. The number of myofibrillar elements in the activated cells.

Some of these factors are very complicated indeed. While some are determined by hereditary endowment (i.e., factors 1, 5, and 6), the others can be improved upon through proper training. Of greatest significance to the beginner is factor 8. A myofibril is a thin strand of protein within the muscle that shortens if stimulated. Thousands of these myofibrils acting together in each muscle cell give the overall muscle great contractility, or what we know as strength. And, what's most important, scientists now know the best way to increase the number of these little devils in each cell.

Observe the figure below. You will notice that the beginning body-builder's objectives range from about 60%-85% of his or her maximum effort (e.g., 1-RM). In other words, the number of reps in each set should range from approximately 6 or 8 to as many as 18 or 20. Strength will be improved most dramatically through the application of sets of 6 or 8 reps with about 80%-85% of one's 1-RM. The sets comprised of higher reps are not as conducive to strength increases because the intensity is not high enough. Instead, other components of the muscle cell will increase in size, quantity, or both—and they offer little to increased strength. Still, they are important for overall size.

On the other hand, engaging in training that involves fewer than about 6 reps is, in the long run, counterproductive to the beginner because of the potential for injury and overtraining, and also because the strength level will eventually "peak" with such training rather than progressing ever upward.

12

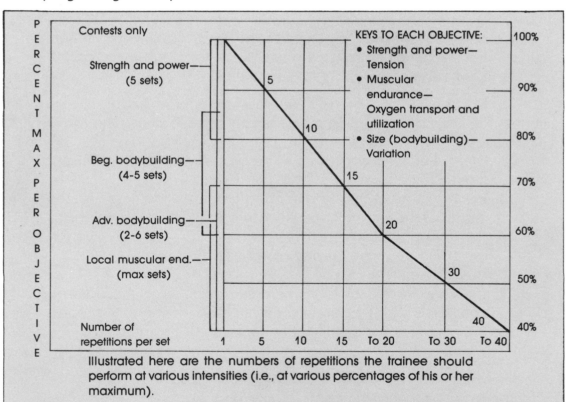

Illustrated here are the numbers of repetitions the trainee should perform at various intensities (i.e., at various percentages of his or her maximum).

Synergy among Muscles

The second factor—that of improved synergy and stability—requires that the smaller, superstructural muscles be strengthened along with the larger, more dominant major muscles. The following analogy explains why. Picture yourself attempting to jack up a car with the jack resting in sand. The instability of the jack will make it nearly impossible to hoist the car, even though the jack is plenty strong to do the job. The same is true for the body. Your muscles may be strong enough to lift a heavy weight, but unless you have good stability in the assisting muscles to aid the major ones (for greater control and coordination), you will invite injury and failure. The major muscles, the ones that are most visible and therefore most appealing to the average beginning bodybuilder, are important, but they will be given far greater potential for growth over the years if they have the help of the often nonvisible synergists and stabilizer muscles.

So, the training formula for the average beginning bodybuilder becomes clear: 4-5 sets of between 6-20 reps per set (giving greater time to sets of 6-8 reps). The exercises of choice should include both major movements such as squats, bench presses, and deadlifts, as well as more specialized movements such as full-range shoulder movements, groin strengthening, abdominal strengthening, and the like.

Most gym instructors will prescribe the "major" exercises for each body part to beginners. Their assumption is that since these are the basic exercises they must be suitable for beginners. They're only half right. The other half of the truth is that those small (but often extremely important) muscles will, if tended to from square one, give rise to greater potential over a greater number of years.

Training Tips for Beginners

After a couple of weeks of orientation to weight training, have an experienced, weight-training instructor assist you in determining what your maximum is for each of the exercises you will be performing in your training program.

Once you have established baseline strength levels in each of your exercises, set the limits with which you will be training at between 60% and 85% of your max.

You should be able to perform up to 20 reps per set at the 60% of max level and up to 6-8 reps at the 85% level.

13

At first, perhaps for about a month of training, stay in the 60%-70% range of maximum effort on each set, and perform about 3-5 sets per exercise.

After this "preconditioning" period, you can then safely and effectively begin to increase the intensity of your training by including sets in the range of 80%-85% of maximum intensity. In all, you should now be performing about two or three sets at low (60%-70%), intermediate (70%-80%), and high (80%-85%) intensity for each exercise you do.

For the first several months of training, it is probably going to be more effective if you work out three times weekly, hitting each exercise all three workouts. However, as you progress in strength and size, and your training becomes more intense, additional recuperation time is bound to become more important. At that point, begin training each body part only twice weekly. This will undoubtedly necessitate switching to a split routine, a system requiring more than three workout days per week. But, by the time you reach that stage, you can no longer be considered a beginner, so let's leave that discussion for the future.

In the beginning months of your training, you should perform basic exercises such as those listed in the table below. These basic exercises involve the major muscles of the body and consequently the major bodily movements as well. The major exercises are also important to bodybuilders because they involve the most visible and largest muscles that will eventually give you the appearance of a bodybuilder rather than just another person off the street.

Do not neglect the smaller, helping muscles (called **synergists**) or the stabilizer muscles. These important muscles, though generally not as visible or as strong as the major ones, are extremely important cornerstones in your foundation of fitness, as well as for the continued

14

Basic Exercises
pectorals (chest)—bench presses
quadriceps (thighs)—squats
trapezius (top of shoulders)—shrugs
rhomboids (upper back)—bent rows
deltoids (shoulders)—lateral raises
latissimus dorsi (outer back)—pulldowns
abdominals (belly)—crunches
gastrocnemius (calfs)—toe raises
biceps (upper arm-front)—curls
triceps (upper arm-back)—tricep extensions
erector spinae (lower back)—stiff-leg deadlifts

development of the larger, more visible ones. They, too, are listed in the accompanying table.

All beginning bodybuilders should perform their exercises slowly and deliberately through the full range of motion. This will ensure maximum early development and fewer nagging injuries.

Always remember that the overload principle should guide you in selecting the proper amount of weight. As you get stronger in each exercise, the amount of weight with which each set is performed should also increase accordingly. What used to be a 60% load will, in time, become only a 50% load. So, for continued progress, add weight as strength increases allow.

It is always advisable to train with a partner or two. This will not only provide "spotters" for safety and assistance, but will also add to the encouragement and incentive to train hard.

Bodybuilders in heavy training require plenty of sleep. Beginners who are not used to the rigors of serious training need at least 7-8 hours of uninterrupted sleep daily for maximum bodily growth and reparation.

3

HEAVY TRAINING AND
THE BEGINNING BODYBUILDER

Show me a beginning bodybuilder who can bench 500 pounds, and I'll show you a beginning bodybuilder who should train heavy! Really, now, did I say that? Let's start over.

Show me a beginning bodybuilder who is able to exert maximum force on the weight for 5 reps, and I'll show you a beginning bodybuilder who may someday bench 500 pounds.

What does **heavy training** entail? Can a beginner expect to be able to muster up **maximum** effort of the type that will produce great strength and size? And, more importantly, is it reasonable for beginners to even attempt to train heavy? This is a topic that has been kicked around a lot lately, and no one writing about it has been able to really put their finger on the true significance of the query.

What Is Heavy Training?

Most bodybuilders generally use the word **heavy** to describe the amount of weight that's being lifted in a given exercise. Little regard for who is doing the lifting is given, and even less for the exercise being performed. If all you can do is 1-2 reps, perhaps as many as 4-5 reps, then that's heavy. Or, at least it's considered so in general gym parlance.

The intensity of effort put into a max set of 3 reps is far greater for the experienced bodybuilder than it is for a beginner. This is a fact, because a well-conditioned muscle is able to receive a greater electrochemical impulse to that muscle. A beginner will have a commensurately weaker neurological response, even though the amount of weight being lifted is also less. The usefulness of this fact is that while an experienced bodybuilder is capable of exerting a high-intensity effort, a beginner has yet to develop that capacity.

17

Given this important distinction, what's heavy? For beginner and expert **heavy** becomes a relative term, and must be defined according to the exact circumstances in which it is being used. Heavy for the experienced bodybuilder signifies extreme effort being expended, whereas no comparable effort is within the capabilities of the beginner. Therefore, heavy for the beginning bodybuilder means with maximum effort given the limitations of neurological input. Because of this important distinction, however small you think it may be, there will be a totally different training effect for the advanced bodybuilder and the beginning bodybuilder, despite the fact that both are training heavy!

Heavy Training and the Experienced Bodybuilder

The expected outcome of heavy training for experienced bodybuilders is that, like most powerlifters (who often train with heavy weights for low reps), their physiques will become more massive and "dense" looking. While this is true, to a point, most advanced bodybuilders will be quick to add that other forms of training are just as important in achieving the finished look that wins contests. Mass or density alone are not the criteria for a contest-winning physique.

So, heavy training for experienced bodybuilders helps to improve density. That simply means that greater numbers of myofibrillar elements (the contractile portion of a muscle cell) are forced to grow. And, that growth gives the muscle a hard and defined look that cannot be achieved through any other training means. Of course, a by-product of increased cellular density is greater strength, much to the delight of both powerlifters and bodybuilders.

The improved strength level is critical to the bodybuilder because they can use heavier weights in all phases of their training thereby improving the quality of the overload they're imposing on their muscles. Size comes quicker with maximum overload, in both heavy as well as light forms of training.

Heavy Training and the Beginning Bodybuilder

The initial gains in size and strength a beginning bodybuilder experiences from heavy training are, of course, attributable in part to the increased number of myofibrillar elements within each muscle cell. In this, both experienced and beginning bodybuilders are the same. However, there is more to it than that, and the real key is in the **quality** of muscle contraction.

Inexperienced bodybuilders have not spent sufficient time under heavy iron to force the kind of adaption in the body that the advanced bodybuilders have. Motor pathways have not been fully developed to allow for coordinated muscle action in performing an exercise efficiently. The number of motor units that are functionally reachable is considerably less for the inexperienced bodybuilder than it is for the advanced bodybuilder. This means that the total output of force will be considerably less, too. Over time, these deficient functions will become more efficient, but it is a long, tedious process. Time is needed.

All of these deficiencies add up to one thing: beginners are not yet able to impose high-quality overload on their body's systems, including their muscular and nervous systems. As the quality of overload improves (with time, patience, and diligence) the gains will begin to materialize and, in fact, have a snowballing effect. As the ability to overload efficiently improves, the cumulative effect upon the musculature becomes more and more noticeable with each passing month of training.

Should Beginning Bodybuilders Train Heavy?

The gym soothsayers have spoken. A loud and outraged "NO!" is often heard in response to this question. "Heavy training predisposes the relatively weak muscles and tendons to injury," they chorus. "Start light, and over several months you can begin lifting heavy weight" is their standard advice.

It's not bad advice. It's a nice, safe way to go. And in the long run, you'll still get to your bodybuilding goals. **In the long run** sounds too ominous for my blood! How long? Years? Months? Almost every athlete I have ever met has been in a big hurry to get to the top. "Don't hold me back!" is their youthful (and healthy) attitude.

I submit that beginning bodybuilders ought to train heavy! I further submit that their inability to handle the kind of intensity that advanced lifters can (owing to their yet-to-be-developed nervous systems and strength levels) will act as the failsafe mechanism that will guard them from unnecessary injury. Beginners can indeed profit from heavy training, provided it is not the only kind done, and providing their heavy training is limited to sets of five or more reps. This will not only shorten the waiting time for strength to improve sufficiently to allow them to impose high-quality overload on their muscles, but it will also shorten the waiting time for the nervous system to adapt to the stress of heavy training as well.

On the other hand, performing heavy doubles and singles in training is potentially dangerous. Further, no real growth results from such training anyway. This, while indeed a form of heavy training, is not the best kind of training for any beginning athlete, whether you are a bodybuilder, powerlifter, or otherwise. Such training is limited in its value to periods before a lifting contest where getting the body used to the heavy weight is desirable. It has no place in any bodybuilder's arsenal of training techniques.

Powerlifters and Heavy Training

It is inevitable that bodybuilders, at some stage in their careers, test their strength. The opening lines of this section aren't as far fetched as you may have thought, considering the widespread worship of strength in the bodybuilding community. After all, what's the sense of **looking** strong if you can't also **be** strong? At least that's an implied value that permeates the bodybuilding world.

Powerlifters are strong people. Stronger as a group than bodybuilders. No argument. However, bodybuilders have only a passing interest in strength, since their ultimate goal is not that of a powerlifter's. While it is healthy for a bodybuilder to worship strength, beware that that is not your ultimate goal, and heavy benches (or squats, or whatever) shouldn't be performed except under extremely controlled conditions, if ever.

Lifting heavy implies intensity, and intensity implies concerted effort to a maximum degree. Powerlifters, advanced bodybuilders, beginning bodybuilders, and athletes in general all have different needs, training objectives, and training regimen. The word "heavy" must be incorporated into the basic fabric of all athletes' training philosophies, but never without the addendum that it is not to be regarded as a universal concept. **Heavy must remain relative**, always defined in terms of an individual's training objectives. And, it can produce different results, depending upon how it's applied as well as upon who applies it.

More Tips for Beginning Bodybuilders

Stay away from maximum singles, doubles, and triples in training during your first year.

Occasionally performing submaximum singles, doubles, and triples for the purpose of determining your current strength level is all right— but not more often than once per month, and only under very carefully controlled conditions.

You will realize faster gains in muscle density and strength by sticking with maximum sets of 5-8 reps, and also avoid the great risk of injury that comes with lower reps with heavier weight.

Holistic training—looking at all muscle cell components—will yield the best overall results for any bodybuilder, including beginners.

Beginners should concentrate on basic strength and stability first so that the ability to achieve a more stimulating level of overload is developed. The better the quality of overload, the faster the gains will come.

Basic strength is best achieved by performing 4-5 sets of around 6-8 reps in each of the most important exercises.

Always have a spotter work with you when doing particularly dangerous exercises—squats and bench presses are among the most dangerous—expecially when training heavy.

Your initial gains in strength almost always reflect motor learning, a reorganization of neuronal input to the muscles, rather than true muscle growth. This is good, since you will be encouraged initially, and be able to achieve a higher degree of overload very soon.

Great strength comes only with time and patience. Most research on the subject indicates that up to nine years are required before maximum strength levels can be achieved. So, don't be in a hurry, but stay diligent!

4

IS SINGLE-REP
TRAINING APPROPRIATE
FOR BODYBUILDING?

Great strength is recognized most often not by the feats one performs, but rather by appearances. Bodybuilders are strong-looking human beings, and most people naturally assume that they are indeed strong. This is justifiable and right, for by any standards of comparison, bodybuilders are among the strongest human beings on this planet. And, not just because they look it—they **live** it as well!

How many times have you walked down a crowded street and caught the glimpses of your adoring public? How often have you felt superior to them because of your great strength and muscular appearance? No doubt, many times a day if you are like the bodybuilders I know. To your public you have nothing to prove—your appearance says it all, and you recognize their admiration. But in the gym, quite a different yarn is spun! In the gym you are among your **peers!** In the gym there are others like you, all of whom have felt the tingle of self-satisfaction in the circumstance of physical superiority. After all, that's what bodybuilding's all about, isn't it?

In the gym you are no longer a **superior** human specimen. You are **normal.** "Oh, wretched me! Only normal! What can I do to display my superiority? How can I prove to these other bodybuilders that I am indeed worthy of their admiration and praise—just as I am worthy of the street folk's adulation?"

Not a normal response, you say? Guess again, fellow strength worshipper! It is not only typical, but totally normal as well. What's more, it's healthy! What's **not** healthy is the response that frequently follows—heavy training with singles! Heavy singles are nothing more than an outcry against being just average—wanting to be held in higher esteem than your normal pencilneck geek on the street—among fellow bodybuilders.

22

What's Wrong with Doing Singles?

Doing max singles may feed your hungry ego, but that's all they do. They do not contribute to greater strength, they merely test it. They do not contribute to greater size either. The reason that they don't is simply that overload is not being placed on the muscles involved for sufficient duration to force an adaptive response to occur. After all, how many max singles can you do in one set? Of course, only one.

Powerlifters often perform heavy singles prior to a contest for two important reasons: 1) they help in isolating or identifying problems that need to be eliminated before contest time, and 2) they prepare the body for the heavy attempt by some neurological mechanism not fully understood. However, **heavy** singles and **max** singles are two horses of a different color! Most bodybuilders like to do max singles once in awhile, particularly when their egos need to be fed. Powerlifters avoid max singles like the plague, because they know they'll get their chance onstage, where it really counts.

In all fairness to bodybuilders, I don't mean to put powerlifters on any pedestal. No indeed! In fact, every top powerlifter I ever met is, in one way or another, something of a frustrated bodybuilder! They want to look good, they want to look the part of a strongman, and they spend nearly as much time in front of mirrors as do bodybuilders. And, again that's good, healthy, and normal. It has never been surprising to me that bodybuilders are often something akin to frustrated powerlifters though—being strong and looking strong are generally parallel roads.

Bodybuilders should take the lead of powerlifters, and avoid doing maximum singles in training. Besides the fact that nothing good (except a satiated ego) comes from them, much harm can be done.

The Leading Cause of Weight-Training Injuries

The Consumer Product Safety Commission estimated that in 1979, over 35,000 weightlifting injuries required hospital care. They further stated that teenagers comprised half of the injured list, and well over half of all injuries occurred at home. Considering the tremendous popularity weight training and bodybuilding is enjoying, the injury statistics probably are doubled for the current year. And that's just in the United States!

It has been my experience that a great majority of the injuries I have either witnessed or heard of were a result of max single attempts. Second on the list are incidences of injury resulting during the last rep of an exceptionally heavy set of triples, when the fatigue factor is most debilitating. If you have ever tried a max set of three, you'll remember how the third one felt—rather like a max single. The same kind of feeling is generally not experienced when the reps per set are set at five or more.

A few inferences can be drawn from these points. First, the safest place to lift is in a gym where there are spotters and/or instructors. Second, the kind of ego display that forces one to attempt max singles is childish—the heavier the weight, the more **macho** a teenage boy feels. And, thirdly, the way to reduce the chances of injury is to stay away from max singles, particularly while training at home. For every injury you sustain, you have lost that much time, money, and effort, and attaining your goal is that much further away.

Are Singles Ever Recommended?

As pointed out earlier, doing submaximum singles is one method typically used by powerlifters in the final stages of contest preparation. Bodybuilders simply cannot profit from max singles, and neither can powerlifters. However, there is a way that singles can work for bodybuilders bent on doing them, and it relates to the phase in their yearly cycle when power training becomes important.

When your progress assessment dictates that greater strength and density are the most immediate goals for you, exceptionally heavy training can get you there quicker than any other method. However, heed the advice given earlier—stay away from max singles. Instead, sets of five reps should predominate, and the weight should be as heavy as possible. Most bodybuilders are able to handle in the vicinity of 85%-88% of their max for five reps.

After performing three or four sets of five reps, move up to the 92% range of effort, and perform a triple. Then, go to about 97% of your max and do a single—it should be well within your capability, and

24

Strength Levels for Average and 100–Percentile College Age Men for Selected Exercises and Weight Divisions*
(weights listed are 1–Rep with Maximum weight)

Weight Division	Group	Sit-Up	Curl	Upright Row	Standing Press	Bench Press	Squat	Bent Row	Good Morning
120–129	100%	70	107.5	120	155	170	255	185	215
	50%	40	80	90	105	120	160	120	165
130–139	100%	70	112.5	125	165	175	265	150	220
	50%	40	85	95	115	125	170	110	170
140–149	100%	70	117.5	130	170	185	275	205	225
	50%	40	90	105	120	135	180	130	175
150–159	100%	75	122.5	135	175	195	290	210	230
	50%	45	95	110	125	145	195	135	180
160–169	100%	75	125	140	180	205	305	215	235
	50%	45	100	115	130	155	210	140	185
170–179	100%	75	124	145	185	215	315	220	240
	50%	45	100	120	135	165	225	145	190
180–189	100%	75	130	150	190	225	325	225	245
	50%	45	105	125	140	175	240	150	195
190 & Up	100%	75	135	155	195	235	335	230	250
	50%	45	110	130	145	185	250	155	200

* Adapted from Hatfield, F.C. & Krotee, M. *Personalized Weight Training for Fitness and Athletics*, Kendall/Hunt Publishers, 1978. (Scores based on norms developed by Dr. Richard Berger on over 3,000 college men.)

remember that on any given day your max will vary. Wait 30 seconds and take 2%-3% of the weight off the bar, and do another single. Again, rest 30 seconds and remove 2%-3% more of the weight, and do another single. In all, a total of 5-7 "singles" can be done in this fashion, and the fatigue factor is compensated for by the lessening of the weight on the bar. Also, the fact that you've performed a total of 5-7 singles in rapid sequence has turned your workout into one that can indeed be of benefit to you for increasing strength and muscle density. Clearly, the reason is that now you have placed your body under adaptive stress for sufficient **time** to force an adaptive process to occur. You have also given the body the stimulation it needs for neurological efficiency to be increased.

This method may be just the answer for those of you who feel the need to test yourself or to show off in front of friends in the gym. At the same time, you have greatly reduced the chance of injury and turned an exercise for the raw ego into one that is beneficial.

How to Make Singles Work for You

Stay away from **maximum** singles because they do not help you get stronger or bigger. If you feel the need to do singles, follow this step-by-step program:

1. Warm up as usual for the exercise you wish to do singles in. (Usually, squats, bench presses, or deadlifts are the ones most bodybuilders like to test themselves in.)
2. Perform four or five sets of five reps at about 85%-88% of your maximum capacity.
3. Perform one set of three reps at about 92% of your max.
4. Perform a single repetition with about 97% of your max take 5-10 pounds off the bar, and rest for about 30 seconds.
5. Perform another single with the lighter weight and repeat the procedure for a total of 5-7 times. You will have performed singles with about 97%, 94%, 91%, 87%, and 84% of your max— enough work for one day!
6. Do not let such a training practice interfere with the more produc- tive sets of five reps—as they will get you to your goal of greater density and strength faster than any other method.

The above program for singles training should not be done more than once a month.

Care should be taken to have necessary spotters handy during singles training to avoid unnecessary injuries.

Be sure that the equipment you are using is safe and sturdy. Home gym equipment is typically not strong enough to handle heavy singles.

Use the information you have just gathered to more scientifically gauge your training intensity in future workouts—make every aspect of your training more efficient.

Everyone needs to have a healthy ego—it's what keeps us all going in our sport. But, avoid childish games or unnecessary ego tripping because not only is it potentially dangerous to do so, but it's one of the factors that turns people off—harmony with training partners and your peers is important to your ultimate success in bodybuilding.

5
HIGH-INTENSITY TRAINING

In every gym you've worked out at, you've seen the ugly grimaces of bodybuilders engaged in maximum effort under heavy iron. Too bad you couldn't look into the minds of these bodybuilders, for if you could, you would then be able to determine whether they were truly involved in high-intensity training. It is the mind, the controlling entity of the organism, that determines the degree of effort expended. It is not the level of ugliness to which one can contort one's face.

Intensity Defined

Webster defines **intensity** as having or showing the characteristic of strength, force, straining, or (relative to a bodybuilder's focal point) other aspects of his or her effort **to a maximum degree.** The words **intense** and **intent** both have the same Latin root, **intendere** ``to stretch out.'' If one is intent on doing something, he does so, by definition, with strained or eager attention—with **concentration!** That intensity of effort is largely a function of the mind is not this writer's opinion. It is true by definition as well as by practical usage of the word!

Not Everyone Can Train with Intensity

In the early years of your training, do you remember approaching a weight with determination? Your jaw was set, your mind narrowed to a laser-like focus, the adrenaline poured into your blood, and your training partners' screams reverberated in your subconscious. You were READY! Your mind and body were both saying, "GO!"

All the essential ingredients for intensity were there. You wedged your body under the iron, and with a Herculean effort, you lifted the weight from the racks. You stepped back and got set. Down you went. And, there you stayed!

What happened? Chances are it was that little bitty devil that resides in all of us saying, "No! Don't hurt me!"

The link between the mind and body is a strong one, and doubt (that little bitty devil) is stronger still. Until you master, or eliminate entirely, such disruptive anomalies of the mind, your training efforts will always be something less than maximal. Achieving this mastery over mind and body is possible only upon enhancing the intercommunication processes between the two.

The Mind-Body Link

Try to picture your brain and your bicep interconnected by nerves— much the same as a printed circuit might look. Within the brain are your memories and impressions of the way your body responded to that missed 150-pound set of curls you attempted last week. It was the first time you had tried such a heavy weight, and it felt heavy. Deep within your soul you knew that you wouldn't make it, and now that you've actually failed this same doubt response has been fortified.

In the bicep, at the very end where the tendon begins, you have tiny sensory mechanisms that are designed to send messages of stress to the brain. If the motor memory of past failures is equalled or exceeded by the strength of the sensory message coming from the working bicep, you will again fail. Your job, if progress is to be made, is to alter both the brain's response as well as the level at which the inhibitory response is initiated at the bicep muscle's tendon.

This sensory mechanism is called the Golgi tendon organ. It's excitation threshold (the point at which the weight is too great and an inhibitory message is sent) can be pushed back with proper training. So, too, can the motor memory stored in the brain be modified to ensure success.

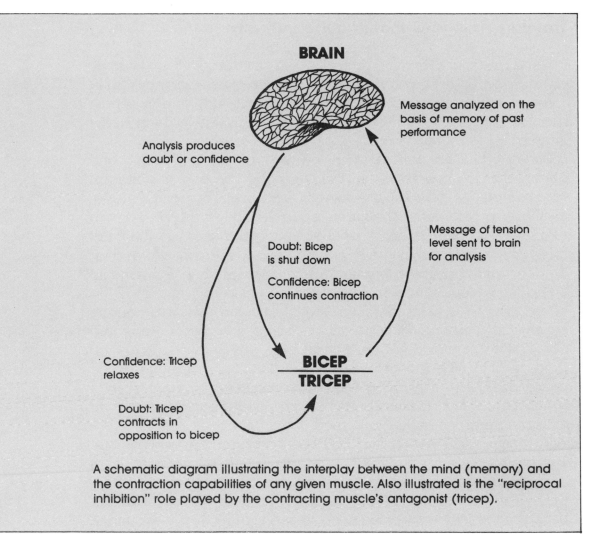

BRAIN

Message analyzed on the basis of memory of past performance

Analysis produces doubt or confidence

Doubt: Bicep is shut down

Confidence: Bicep continues contraction

Message of tension level sent to brain for analysis

Confidence: Tricep relaxes

Doubt: Tricep contracts in opposition to bicep

BICEP
TRICEP

A schematic diagram illustrating the interplay between the mind (memory) and the contraction capabilities of any given muscle. Also illustrated is the "reciprocal inhibition" role played by the contracting muscle's antagonist (tricep).

Success Begets Success

If you have never experienced failure under heavy iron, then the chances of doubt creeping in will be remote. And, if you have trained for years with heavy weights (without exceeding your capabilities but pushing them to the maximum), your Golgi tendon organs will not be stimulated to forward inhibitory messages to the brain. It sounds like a Catch-22 situation, but nonetheless it's true. Success will indeed beget success, and failure will beget failure.

When you have learned the very important lesson of avoiding failure while training, you will have attained the ability to train with intensity. Until that time, your efforts will be something less than maximal, and they will be something less than maximally beneficial.

Training Situations that Require Intensity

Some methods of training, to be truly effective, require high intensity on your part. Others do not. In fact, the injection of intensity may render some methods counterproductive! This is particularly true in certain sports-oriented training methods where speed is required—intensifying such rapid movements can easily result in severe injury.

During offseason periods when low-rep training for strength and density is emphasized, intensity becomes of paramount importance. For example, suppose you are doing five or six reps per set. Of course, the first two or three reps will require something less than maximum effort since fatigue has not diminished your capacity as yet. This is **not** the way to approach your sets! Each and every rep you perform must be done with maximum intensity! Further, maximum intensity should be applied throughout every inch of movement in each rep! Why? The effect that this kind of thorough intensity has on the Golgi tendon organ is such that disinhibition will, over time, take place. Repeated applications of maximum stress is the only way known to force the Golgi tendon organ to delay sending its inhibitory message to the brain. Such delayed inhibitory response results in increased strength of contraction. In turn, the increased strength yields greater size resulting from greater poundages being used.

During periods in your training cycle when higher reps with a lighter weight are performed, intensity is no less important, although for a different reason. High-rep training produces intolerable lactate levels within the muscle; and effort fails from fatigue. Doubt no longer becomes the inhibitory factor, since the weight isn't heavy enough to jeopardize your safety. Rather, fatigue does, and you must through extreme concentration, **will** the weight up. You must disregard the signals your pain sensors are sending to the brain. Concerted effort of this type will, over time, force a different kind of disinhibition to occur. Perhaps it is a greater electrochemical impulse that allows muscle fibers with higher excitation thresholds to respond. Perhaps it is a lowering of the excitation thresholds of these same hard-to-stimulate muscle fibers. It could also be both.

The point is that disinhibition will indeed occur, and the only way to force it to occur is to coax and intimidate your muscles into responding—and you have to ignore the pain to do it. It becomes a matter of mind over muscle. This kind of training must be learned—it is not an innate response, and neither is it easily acquired.

Like your low-rep training, the key to learning how to apply maximum intensity is to use as heavy weights as possible in each and every overload set you do, yet avoid failure like the plague! If your mind says, "No," you've succumbed. You've failed, go home! Come back to the gym tomorrow with a renewed determination not to fail. Make your mind say, "Yes," and then obey the command!

When a harmonious and synchronized link between your body and mind is established, you will experience gains in muscle size more rapidly than ever before. When you begin to realize the awesome power of the mind in controlling bodily functions, including its adaptability to stress, you will have learned what it takes to become a champion bodybuilder.

6
MUSCLE SHAPING

Does a bodybuilder have control over how a muscle will look after it has been enlarged? Will a bodybuilder's selection of exercises for a particular muscle make a difference in how that muscle will look? And, will one's choice of reps, sets, and cadence have any bearing upon the ultimate shape that muscle will assume? The vast majority of bodybuilders, be they beginners or superstars like to feel that they do indeed have control over how each of their muscles will look—as might the sculptor chiseling away at some inert piece of rock.

Despite the widespread insistence that muscle shaping is possible, careful scientific scrutiny of the problem reveals some very important considerations that tend to refute this belief. On the other hand, there are some techniques that can, if applied correctly, alter the appearance of a muscle. Such alterations in appearance are not of the type typically referred to as **shape** by bodybuilders, however, and the science behind such techniques are only now beginning to be understood.

The question of whether or not one can shape a muscle appears never to have entered the average bodybuilder's mind. It seems that it has always been taken for granted that one could do so merely by changing the angle or position of the weight, joint, or limb during the performance of an exercise. But the complete answer—the one afforded by studying what scientists have known since the advent of electron microscopy—affords us with nothing less than explosive implications regarding the way bodybuilders everywhere have trained for years. As you may have guessed, the answer to this question is rather complex, and many factors have to be considered, not the least of which is the principle of genetic predisposition or heredity.

Is a Muscle's Shape Determined by Heredity?

In the final analysis, after a muscle has been developed to its maximum, the shape of a muscle is genetically predetermined. Bodybuilders who have succeeded in developing all of the components of all the muscle cells in the biceps, for example, can only hope that the good Lord, in his infinite wisdom, gave him the genes necessary for the biceps to be well formed aesthetically.

The key concept in the above statement is whether the bodybuilder has indeed succeeded in developing all of each cell's components. There have been no laboratory tests offering conclusive evidence that an entire muscle's shape can be affected differentially by developing the myofibrils as opposed to the mitochondria within the individual cells, for example. But the concept nonetheless has a practical appeal that can be supported empirically.

Few bodybuilders have knowledge of the intricate workings of a muscle cell, and the true significance of the preceeding paragraphs may escape some. Let me elaborate on this point; it is quite important. Performing high reps with a light weight forces the involved cells to develop more mitochondria, the subcellular components responsible for the oxidative functions of the cell. It seems logical that the increased size and number of mitochondria will lend a shape to a cell that may be quite different than that achieved by doing low reps with heavier weights. Low reps with heavy weights forces the myofibrils to increase in number, leaving the mitochondrial mass relatively unchanged. Add to this potential difference the possibility that varying amounts of intracellular fluid may affect a muscle's shape, and you have what amounts to a reasonably strong argument for the notion that bodybuilders can indeed alter the shape of each muscle through training technique differences.

So, to answer the question of heredity being the only factor in determining a muscle's ultimate shape, the answer remains affirmative—with possible exceptions related to one's choice of training regimen. It is my opinion that whatever variability in shape one is able to accomplish through regimen selection is probably minute in comparison to the overall effect of hereditary factors, however. Still, the possibility exists, and the complete answer will not be forthcoming except through far more controlled laboratory analyses.

Can Different Exercises Shape a Muscle Differently?

The most pervasive view among bodybuilders is that by doing an array of exercises for a particular muscle, or by doing one or two exercises for a muscle to the exclusion of others, the shape of that muscle will be controlled. I'm not referring to reps, sets, or intensity here, just the actual movement performed.

This belief is not tenable, and has been responsible for improper training since bodybuilding began. Observe (in the accompanying diagram of a muscle's innervation) that the nerves entering a muscle branch out into **twigs.** Each twig terminates at the muscle cell and transports the electrochemical charge that causes each cell to contract. Not only do all of the cells serviced by the single neuron contract upon stimulation (called the **all-or-none** law of muscular contraction), but they do so at the same level of strength (impulse frequency). For bodybuilders concerned with **intensity** training, this basic premise of muscle physiology has vast implications. But, in considering shape training, the factor of greatest importance is the noncontiguity with which the fibers from each motor unit are arranged in the muscle.

It is impossible to isolate a border of a muscle, a small quadrant of a muscle, or the peak of a muscle's belly. Since the cells associated with each motor unit are spread all through the gross muscle, all portions of the gross muscle are affected similarly by a given exercise and therefore develop similarly. This is called the principle of **noncontiguous innervation.**

Using many variations of an exercise for one muscle in no way ensures more growth or different growth patterning than does performing the basic exercise. The many variations of an exercise may variably involve surrounding synergistic or stabilizer muscles, but the muscle in question receives no additional benefit beyond the overload being imposed. The shape of that muscle will not be affected by variations in the angle or position of stress application.

Does this mean that all a bodybuilder has to do is perform the basic movement, and rid himself or herself of the array of supplemental exercises for a given muscle? I suspect it does, if your goal is to improve

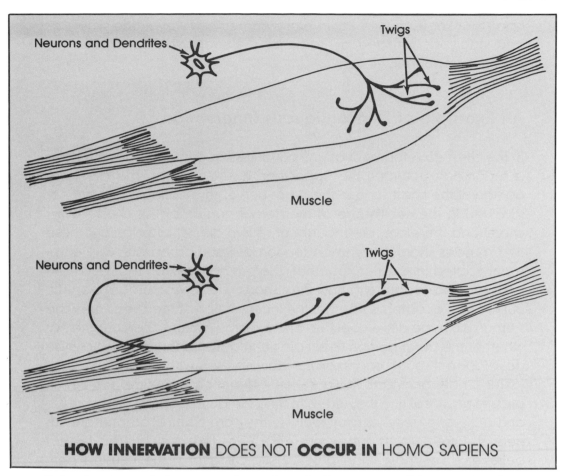

If shaping a muscle by means of exercise selection were possible, nerve input would have to be localized as shown above. If the above illustrations were a true picture, it would be possible to fill in the gap between the biceps and elbow (top) or it would be possible to shape just one border of a muscle (bottom). This is not how nature intended things to happen. The illustration below shows how muscles are **noncontiguously** innervated for **overall** growth and effect.

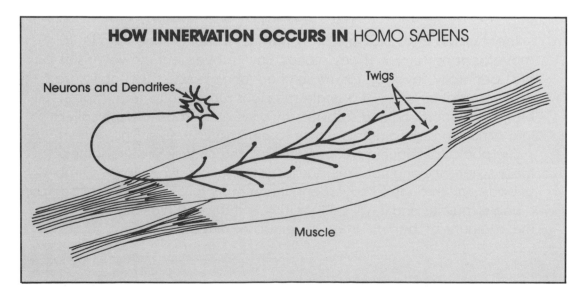

upon that single muscle. For overall symmetry, however, the synergists and stabilizers affected by some of the supportive exercises may become important.

An Example of Noncontiguous Innervation

The chest development of any advanced bodybuilder clearly shows a separation between the upper and lower portions. The clavicular portion of the chest (upper chest) has nerves stimulating it that are not involved in the contracture of the sternal portion of the chest (lower chest) and therefore, are thought of as two distinct muscles. But these two muscles share a common tendon of insertion, so are very commonly called into action together. There is no question that each can be exercised separately, and they should be for maximum benefit. But the real question is whether the inner portion of the chest (near the sternum) can be developed via one exercise moreso than another, or whether the outer portion (near the tie-in closer to the deltoid) can be developed through one exercise more so than with another.

The simple answer to this question is definitely no. Wide-grip bench presses may **feel** like they are affecting the outer portions of the chest, and close-grip benches may **feel** like they are causing greater growth near the sternum. But they are not. What the bodybuilder feels, I believe, is no more than physical stretching of tissue causing pain sensors in that area to respond. This physical sensation has nothing to do with the growth occurring there, and should not be thought of as an indicator of that particular exercise's area of effect.

The Complete Picture

The human musculoskeletal system is complex and allows for movement patterns in many planes. Each movement, however simple, generally involves far more than one muscle. The ability to achieve total isolation of a single muscle is functionally near impossible, since synergistic and stabilizer muscles are almost always called into action to assist a prime mover to perform any given movement.

The particular sequence of contracture, and contracture strengths of these synergistic and stabilzer muscles are what assist in guiding a limb or body part through a movement. The **primary** force may come from a single muscle, and it will be that muscle that most typically receives the majority of benefit from an exercise. Since the synergists and

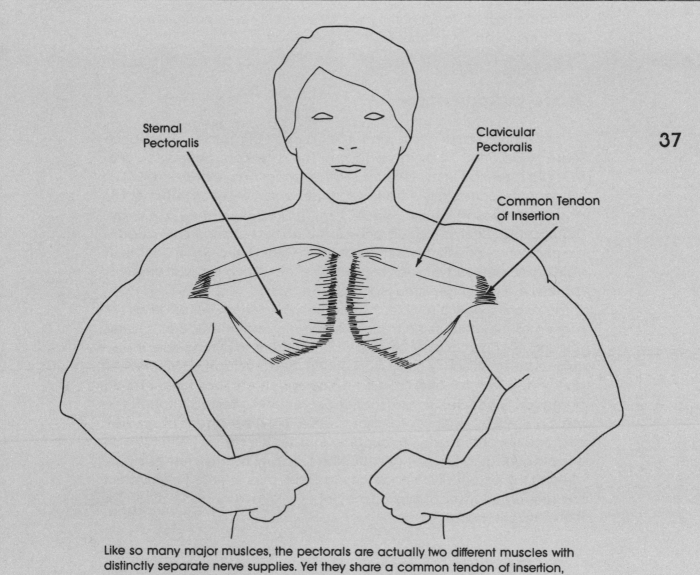

Sternal
Pectoralis

Clavicular
Pectoralis

Common Tendon
of Insertion

Like so many major muscles, the pectorals are actually two different muscles with distinctly separate nerve supplies. Yet they share a common tendon of insertion, making it difficult to achieve total isolation in weight training efforts.

stabilizers are being forced to direct the movement pattern in coordination with the prime mover, they also receive some benefit, albeit small.

The total picture, then, for any given exercise, is that the entire muscle receives growth or development stimulation from any exercise that requires its use. The exact amount of benefit derived will depend upon how closely that exercise is able to approximate an isolated movement, and the extent of the overload applied. Forcing that muscle through different rep/set/intensity systems may have variable effects on that muscle, but they will be primarily in appearance (**vis a vis** striations, etc.) as opposed to shape **per se.**

Shape vs Appearance

Vascularity, cuts, striations, and other aspects of muscle appearance seem to be affected by many factors. The most common factors are: (1) fluid retention in the cells and in the spaces between the cells, (2) fat deposits, particularly subcutaneous deposits, (3) blood volume, (4) glycogen stores within the muscle, (5) capillarization of muscle tissue, (6) **possible** external appearance fluctuations resulting from preponderance of myofibrils versus mitochondria within the cells, (7) length of training (older bodybuilder seem to be able to bring out striations moreso than younger lifters), and (8) heredity.

The exact shape a muscle assumes at any given level of development must be attributed primarily to heredity, with method of training offering only a possibility of shape alteration at minute levels. Shape cannot be significantly controlled during the developmental process, and even less so after complete development has occurred. In particular, a muscle's shape cannot be variably affected through the use of different exercises for that muscle; only the extent of synergy and stability afforded by surrounding muscles is affected. Alterations in the amount of synergistic and stabilizer activity has the net effect of altering the extent of overload on the entire muscle group involved in the movement, which may or may not be a favorable condition for the muscle in question.

What Is the Answer?

Concepts such as **intensity** and **muscle-shocking** techniques, or **forced reps, continuous tension** reps, **iso-tension** training—the list of training techniques is endless—all have validity, and will be explored in Part II. Each method appears to have merits lacking in the others, so all are assured of a place in one's training career. But they all pale in their importance next to the **return to basics** principle espoused in this section. It is not the answer. It is only a small part of the overall picture of a superstar's training, but a very important part nonetheless. Basic exercises are those which stress the muscle with minimal interference from surrounding muscles, and which offer a movement conducive to maximizing the benefits of overload. Each muscle has many different exercises that are quite good, but it would be a mistake to assume that what one misses the other will get. This **shotgun** approach to training a specific muscle simply has no valid base in scientific training, and is quite often the cause of bodybuilders entering states of overtraining.

39

7
HOW IMPORTANT ARE ISOLATION EXERCISES?

"Go to your room! You stubborn child!" Ah, how well I remember that favorite phrase of parents everywhere. It is typically used when parents mean to get their offspring to mend their ways. Sometimes it works and sometimes it doesn't. Isolating a normally gregarious child is a form of punishment that has both positive and negative effects.

What do you do to a stubborn muscle? Many unwary bodybuilders beat it into submission, expecting it to grow in response to destructive overload. The scientific bodybuilder, however, may try isolation techniques. Like the parent-child situation, isolation can work in forcing a muscle to respond favorably, but other beneficial factors may have to be forgone in the process.

Normally, the design features of bodybuilding equipment dictate the movement pattern through which the weight must be moved. That built-in movement pattern will generally lend each muscle or muscle group sufficient isolation from all other muscles to allow it to receive the benefits of overload. However, it isn't always so, and in fact just the opposite is true often enough to make it a serious problem in bodybuilding.

Definitions of Key Factors

Let's start by all speaking the same language. What do we mean by isolation, overload, intensity, duration, and the host of other terms used in describing weight training techniques? Those terms listed above are all interrelated—one can't be expounded upon without bringing all the others—and for me to explain how and why you should isolate a muscle forces me to describe all the other terms as well.

Isolation, to a bodybuilder, simply means that a single muscle or muscle group is being overloaded. Surrounding muscles, such as synergistic and stabilizer muscles, may also be involved, but a conscious effort is made to minimize their action in favor of the primary target muscle(s).

The degree of isolation can vary from **total** isolation of a single muscle to **partial** isolation of a muscle group (with synergists and stabilizers active) to **non**-isolation as in a coordinated movement such as the snatch in Olympic weightlifting. All of these degrees of isolation have their uses in bodybuilding, and it is important to know when to use each method and what the expected outcome(s) will be.

Overload is the term given to applying stress to a muscle or muscle group. The degree of overload can also vary, and can range from slight to severe. In all cases, it is assumed that the stress being applied is greater than what the muscle is normally acquainted. As the muscle(s) adapt to greater and greater levels of stress, the amount of stress that is required to constitute an overload situation becomes commensurately greater as well.

You have heard the old saying that a chain is only as strong as the weakest link. Well, the same can be said of a group of muscles. When a group of muscles act together to move a weight, it is the weakest of the group that determines the total amount of force applied to the weight. And, it is the weakest of the group that receives the greatest amount of overload!

The real significance of the above statement, which by the way is a fact of physics, is that it is **always** appropriate to overload, and the easiest way to do it is to isolate a muscle. It is not always the **best** way, however. And the reason for this lies in explaining the relationship among the concepts of isolation, overload, intensity, and duration.

The amount of **time** (duration) your muscle(s) spend under stress of overload proportions is as important as the overload itself in promoting muscle development. And the exact **measure** of overload (intensity) is as indispensable an ingredient in successful bodybuilding as isolation, overload, or duration. All of them must be considered in formulating a truly scientific and maximally beneficial training program.

When Is Total Isolation Best?

Many bodybuilders believe that the time to engage in strict isolation exercise is in the precontest stage. It is a widely held belief that a muscle or muscle group becomes more **cut-up** (or defined) through isolation techniques, and more **massive** through non-isolation or partial isolation techniques. I am not convinced that this is the case at all.

It may indeed be true that you can improve muscle definition in the latter stages of contest preparation by switching to total isolation movements, but that does not mean that the precontest period is the only time this should be done! In fact, it may be true that such a change in regimen just prior to a contest is the **worst** thing you can do! Curtailing mass training can cause you to **lose** mass, and what you think is an increase in definition may have been due to stricter diet rather than stricter isolation. I strongly believe that this is the case.

Alternatively, or perhaps concurrently, switching to strict and total isolation movements may have been the spark your training needed to pull you out of an overtrained state and back into a muscle-growth cycle once again. The Weider Muscle Confusion Principle applies here—"shocking" your muscles with a different form of stress or different method of contraction is often very productive in causing overtrained or stubborn body parts to respond with renewed vigor.

So, when is the best time to do total isolation exercises? I believe that your training should have a healthy mix of **all** forms of overload. The concept of holistic training holds the key to how you should train for maximum cell growth.

Holistic Training and Isolation

Every bodybuilder is familiar with the fact that each muscle cell is comprised of several different components. Each cell component serves a different function—mitochondria for endurance, myofibrillar elements for strength, robosomes for protein synthesis, capillaries for delivering nutrients and oxygen as well as removing wastes, and so forth. And each cell component will grow in size and/or number, but **only in response to a specific type of overload!**

Isolation exercises such as concentration curls, leg extensions, dumbbell flyes, and so forth (see the table on pages 44-45) often must be performed with extremely light weights because the isolated muscle is placed in a restricted leverage position necessitating the use of lighter poundages, and because the possibility of involving synergists and stabilizers to aid in the movement is effectively reduced or eliminated. Some theoreticians in the field of biomechanics argue that the loss of intensity that invariably occurs with total isolation exercises is inconsequential and that bodybuilders can still achieve maximum muscle growth despite the lighter poundages. Behind their reasoning is the notion that overload is overload, and as long as the individual muscle is taxed beyond its normal limits it will respond by developing.

43

I believe that this point of view is largely true, but in some instances must be modified. The reason for this belief is that I view intensity as an important element in developing strength, and with greater strength a bodybuilder can optimize the extent of overload for ever-increasing gains in size. Without occasionally injecting intensity into your workouts, your strength levels will fail to improve significantly to allow you to apply greater and greater levels of overload stress to the muscle.

Another reason why I think isolation must be tempered with considerations of intensity is that it is functionally impossible to achieve total isolation in the vast majority of muscles in the first place. For example, consider cross flyes, which is an isolation exercise for the pectorals. While the pectorals are contracting to draw the dumbbells upward and across the upper torso, the lats, triceps, deltoids, and several other smaller muscles are synergistically contracting both to assist in controlling direction of movement as well as to stabilize other body parts to make the flye movement possible. The same kind of multimuscle involvement occurs while doing leg curls, tricep pushdowns, lat pulldowns, and so forth.

Multimuscle teamwork is the way the human body works. To get specific muscles to develop you either have to completely isolate them, which is very often impossible, or you have to make them the weakest muscles in the group that is working. Only then will the isolated muscles receive the full benefit of maximum overload.

Even this is difficult to do in many cases. Sometimes it is necessary to engage the cumulative contraction of several muscles at a time because of the biomechanical impossibility of isolation. This is true in perhaps the majority of exercises, and includes such movements as squats, bent rows, military presses, and hyperextensions. In such cases, the greatest amount of overload is felt by the weakest muscle in the group, and the stronger muscles get commensurately less. If the muscle's strength is such that the load being moved doesn't tax the muscle at least to the arbitrary level of 60%-70% of its maximum, there will probably be little, if any, adaptive response. The intensity factor is just not sufficient for adaption to occur.

Examples of So-Called Isolation Exercises for Bodybuilders

Action	Exercise	Muscles (in order of their contribution to the action)
Shoulder girdle elevation	Shrugs (typically used for only Trapezius I)	*Trapezius I and II, Levator, Rhomboids*
Downward rotation of shoulder girdle and adduction of shoulder joint	Lat pulldowns (typically used for lat development)	*Latissimus dorsi, teres major, pectoralis major (sternal), rhomboids, pectoralis minor, posterior deltoid, biceps (both heads), coracobrachialis, subscapularis*
Shoulder joint horizontal flexion (accompanied by elbow extension)	Bench press (typically used for pectoralis muscles)	*Pectoralis major (sternal and clavicular), anterior deltoid, coracobrachialis, biceps (short head), subscapularis, triceps*
Elbow flexion	Curls (typically used for biceps development)	*Biceps brachii, brachialis, brachioradialis, pronator teres, flexor carpi radialis, flexor carpi ulnaris, palmaris longus, flexor digitorum superficialis*
Elbow extension	Tricep extensions (used for tricep development)	*Triceps brachii, anconeus, extensor carpiradialis longus, extensor carpi radialis brevis, extensor carpi ulnaris, extensor digitorum, extensor digiti minimi*
Trunk flexion	Crunches (done for abdominals)	*Rectus abdominis, internal and external obliques, psoas*
Trunk extension and/or hyperextension	Hyperextensions (typically done for erector spinae group)	*Erector spinae group (four different muscles), semispinalis thoracis, deep posterior spinal group (four different muscles)*
Shoulder joint abduction	Lateral raises (normally used for middle deltoid development)	*Middle deltoid, supraspinatus, anterior deltoid, biceps (long head), clavicular pectoralis major (arms above horizontal)*

44

Action	Exercise	Muscles (in order of their contribution to the action)
Hip joint extension together with knee extension	Squats (normally used for quadricep development)	Hip extension: *Gluteus maximus, biceps femoris (long head), semitendinosis, semimembranosis posterior fibers of the gluteus medius and minimus, lower fibers of the adductor magnus* Knee extension: *Quadricep group (rectus femoris, vastus lateralis, vastis medialis, vastus intermedius)*
Ankle plantar flexion	Toe raises (done for calf development)	*Gastrocnemius, soleus, plantaris, peroneus longus, flexor digitorum longus, flexor hallicus longus, tibialis posterior, peroneus brevis*

In each exercise listed, there are *prime movers* (muscles that contribute the major force) and *assistant movers* (muscles that only assist, because of their disadvantageous strength, size, or musculoskeletal arrangement). Each exercise listed effectively isolates the target muscle(s) to a degree that allows for maximum development. That is, the force that each must apply surpasses the critical threshold of 60%-70% of that muscle's maximum capacity by a sufficient margin to constitute adaptive overload.

If, however, that same exercise is performed with a heavier than normal weight, those stronger muscles may indeed be taxed sufficiently to promote growth. Sometimes the only way to perform such a bypass operation is to either **cheat** part of the movement or engage several synergists to assist by altering the movement pattern of the exercise slightly. A typical example of this kind of practice is seen in the bench press. By bringing the elbows in toward the sides slightly there will be greater emphasis upon the anterior deltoids and less upon the chest. Conversely, moving the elbows out to a position where they are perpendicular to the torso effectively reduces the anterior deltoid involvement and focuses more strictly upon the pectorals. Similarly, the wider the grip in the bench press, the less will be the triceps' role in the movement.

A New Perspective on Training

The only reasonable way to maximize the development of a single muscle is to arrange your exercise movement in a way that draws the two ends of the muscle toward the midpoint of the muscle's belly. This can be accomplished either by having the movement occur at the insertion end of the muscle, or, less commonly, at the origin end of the muscle. Typically, the insertion end of a muscle is located farthest away from the midpoint of the body, and the origin end is closest to the midpoint of the body. An example of this kind of dual movement function can be seen in abdominal crunches. Raising the torso accentuates the upper portions of the abdominal muscles (the abdominals originate on the lower ribs), while raising the pelvis accentuates the lower regions of the abdominals (the abdominals insert in the pelvis).

Then, in addition to the above contraction requirement, consideration must be given to the principles of overload and isolation (you must exceed the stress level that the muscle is used to), and the intensity and duration factors (the weight must be sufficiently heavy to force an adaptive response and it must be applied for sufficient time to cause the desired response). If these requirements are fulfilled then it makes little difference whether there has been total isolation or partial isolation. Development will take place. Mixing the types of movements often will have the net effect of variable levels of stress being placed on the muscle, and that's desirable because it fulfills the concept of holistic training. Variability is the key to maximum development, and you should remember that your muscle cells are capable of many different types of development, all of which will add to your size.

To totally complicate the whole picture, any given muscle may perform several different functions in human movement. For example, the biceps brachii consist of a long and short head. While they are prime movers in elbow flexion, the long head assists in shoulder joint abduction (as in lateral raises for the deltoids), while the short head assists in shoulder joint flexion (e.g., front dumbbell raises), adduction (e.g., lat pulldowns), and horizontal flexion (e.g., bench presses).

I mention this diversity of the musculoskeletal structure only to point out the fallacy of arguing for or against the effectiveness of total isolation movements. There are very few movements that can be termed total isolation movements, but again, it is of little consequence. The rules-of-thumb for exercise selection almost always are going to include the following concepts:

- Overload, isolation, intensity, and duration.
- Muscle contraction through the midline of the belly of the muscle for best isolation and overload.

- Contraction by keying on either the insertion end of the muscle or the origin end. Or, better yet, both.
- Use of a variety of exercises and overload methods throughout a training cycle, for **muscle confusion**—this improves overall responsiveness in the long term.
- Maximum overload is achieved when the force generated goes through the muscle's midline, and commensurately less tension (intensity) is achieved the farther the force line varies from the midline.
- To be effective, an exercise should supply enough isolation such that at least 60%-70% of the muscle's force generating capacity is exceeded.

Don't worry about achieving total isolation! Instead, concentrate on generating enough intensity for maximum overload for each muscle or muscle group. Then, apply it for sufficient time to stimulate growth.

8

HYPERTROPHY VS. HYPERPLASIA

For years scientists told us that genetic endowment alone would determine the number of muscle cells each of us would ever have, and that we could do nothing to increase that number. Now, they're not so sure. Imagine the possibilities: More muscle cells! Bigger muscles! Stronger muscles! Perhaps, but perhaps not. Let's take a closer look.

What Is Hyperplasia?

During the late sixties and early seventies European scientists discovered that the muscle cells of some animals adapted to severe overload by splitting in two. This compensatory response is called **hyperplasia**, and is generally accompanied by significant increases in the size of the surrounding muscle cells that didn't split. Needless to say, this discovery rocked the scientific community back on its heels. Subsequent research during the early and mid-seventies revealed the exact mechanisms that cause hyperplasia, but to this day scientists have been unable to determine whether such muscle cell splitting can occur in humans.

The Mechanisms of Hyperplasia

As a bodybuilder, you are no doubt aware that slow movements are a major source of the size-building stimulus in most training regimens. Iso-tension movements, peak contraction movements, continuous tension movements, and heavy-duty training methods all require relatively slow contraction speeds from the working muscles. The results of such training are what we all refer to as **hypertropy**—an increase in the size or quantity of various muscle components without an increase in the overall number of muscle cells. According to some recent studies, however, by engaging strictly in hypertrophy training, you may be robbing yourselves of the very stimulus that can promote hyperplasia.

A group of scientists working under the direction of Swedish exercise physiologist W. J. Gonyea discovered that a cat's muscle cells would undergo hyperplasia only if the cat were involved in a weight-training program that incorporated both high-speed and high-tension exercises.

So how does this relate to you as a bodybuilder? No one really knows, but some interesting possibilities exist. Some studies have used the electron microscope to observe the structural changes in muscle cells after exercise. This technique requires a **biopsy,** taking a plug of muscle tissue, freezing it, then slicing it super thin for microscopic examination. The typical hypertrophied muscle shows not only larger individual cells, but a closer packing of the cells.

Champion swimmers' deltoids were scrutinized by electron microscopy, and the findings of that study stand to this day as the most compelling argument for the occurrence of hyperplasia in humans. While the swimmers' total muscle size was obviously greater than the average person's, the individual cells comprising their deltoids were smaller and more numerous. The empirical conclusion drawn from this startling fact is that hyperplasia must have taken place in the deltoid muscles, giving them greater overall size and strength. Why the split cells did not achieve the level of hypertrophy possible in unsplit cells remains, for the moment, an intriguing mystery. Some scientists speculate that this inability to achieve a hypertrophied state resulted from each cell having only half the number of nuclei it had prior to splitting. The cells' nuclei regulate virtually all of their many functions, including their potential for growth.

What Can We Learn from Animal Research?

Cats, rats, and other animals are different than humans in some very important ways. For example, have you ever seen a heavily muscled laboratory rat? With few exceptions, animals seem incapable of developing the kind of muscle hypertrophy that humans can. It seems quite possible that compensatory cell splitting (hyperplasia) is their unique way of adapting to the stress of overload training.

Forget size for a moment, and consider muscle contraction speed. Rarely will you observe a slow cat! Animals that display muscle hyperplasia capabilities are generally faster afoot and in reaction time than humans, a fact that can be explained by comparing anatomical and histochemical differences between the respective species. Rats, for example, have eleven different kinds of muscle cells, whereas only three have been observed in humans. On this basis alone, the possibilities of movement speed, reaction time, contraction speed, muscular endurance, and other muscle functions are probably considerably greater in such animals than in humans.

These differences notwithstanding, the swimmers' deltoid study comes out more intriguing than ever! Is it possible to get those split fibers to grow larger? And if so, has that muscle's size potential increased in proportion to the increased fiber count? And, what about the strength factor? And the muscle endurance factor? Judging from the increased performance capabilities of the swimmers, hyperplasia seems to account for increases in all three areas of muscle function!

How Bodybuilders Can Promote Cell Splitting

Whether hyperplasia occurred in the swimmers' deltoids remains speculation. Conclusive evidence of hyperplasia taking place in human muscles will come only when scientists can observe the process taking place. For now, though, the empirical evidence is at least promising.

The studies that have been done with animals have clearly shown that hyperplasia can take place only if there is both sufficient intensity as well as movement speed. Unlike the average bodybuilder who performs primarily slow-speed exercises, swimmers engage in relatively fast limb speed movements against both weighted resistance as well as the natural resistance afforded by water. Since biopsies of bodybuilders' muscles have not shown the same structural alterations resulting from imposed stress as swimmers' muscles, it seems reasonable to conclude that if hyperplasia did indeed take place in the swimmers' deltoids, it was a result of their specialized training.

While slow movements with heavy weights produced increased size in certain laboratory animals, it also tended to result in losses in muscle contraction speed. No cell splitting was observed under these conditions. However, when the animals were forced to move quickly with the heavy weights, both size and speed were dramatically increased and cell splitting was observed.

If you want to maximize your chances of promoting hyperplasia, the evidence suggests that high-speed training is the only way to do it. There are many components to a muscle cell. Most have the potential to develop in size and number, but only in response to highly specific overload. Your job, as a bodybuilder, is to determine exactly what kinds of stress to apply to your muscles to promote such development in as many cell components as possible.

There is no doubt that you will find that a great **variety** of training methods must be incorporated to maximize muscle development. Promoting hyperplasia may become a part of the answer for bodybuilders of the future, but for now this interesting phenomenon remains only a possibility, leaving the old standby methods of hypertrophy training your primary concern.

Conclusions for the Experiment-Oriented Bodybuilder

Hyperplasia, the splitting of muscle cells, may be a reality, but present bodybuilding methods apparently don't promote it. Animal studies, together with research on champion swimmers, suggest that high-speed/high-tension exercise is the only way to promote hyperplasia.

High-tension/slow-speed movements make the muscles bigger, but they also tend to make it slower in contraction speed. Hyperplasia does not occur in animals engaged in high-tension/slow-speed training.

It is not known whether hyperplasia can increase the ultimate potential for a muscle's size in humans, or if it can take place in humans in the first place.

To derive the benefits of hyperplasia, bodybuilders should incorporate both traditional muscle-building exercises as well as the Weider Superspeed Principle which requires fast, explosive movements against moderate resistance for 10-20 reps.

9
MUSCLE SORENESS

How often have you heard this kind of discussion?

"Slept in the garage last night."

"Oh? How come?"

"Legs were too sore to climb the stairs."

"Really? What happened?'

"Did squats last night with Tom Platz."

Everyone who trains with weights or exercises for the first time in a few weeks or months experiences muscle soreness. Sometimes the pain can be debilitating to the point of exasperation. Not only can muscle soreness be painful, it can also cause unnecessary lost training time and tend to make you shy away from the exercise(s) that caused it. For beginners it can be the very excuse they needed to renounce their spa membership!

Probing the causes of this kind of delayed-onset muscle soreness has not been an easy task, and many theories have emerged over the years. As a bodybuilder, it will be of great benefit to you if you not only knew what caused this kind of debilitating soreness, but also how to treat it after the fact, or avoid it completely. Here are the major theories that have been proposed:

Muscle tissue tears. Minute tears in the actual muscle cell are, according to some scientists, the cause of delayed-onset muscle soreness.

Myofibrillar splintering. The actin and myosin strands that comprise each myofibril are literally "raked" across one another during eccentric (negative) contraction, according to one theory, thereby causing them to splinter and produce muscle soreness.

Muscle spasms. Reduced oxygen supply to a working muscle (called **ischemia**) produces pain and subsequent reflex contraction of a muscle; this, in turn, causes repeated bouts of ischemia and reflective contraction, producing muscle soreness.

53

Pressure changes and edema. Some scientists have advanced the theory that exercising after a layoff causes a build-up of certain metabolities in the muscle cell, which cause an increased osmotic pressure in the cell. This increased pressure is said to cause edema (water retention) and a subsequent stimulation of the pain receptors.

Connective tissue damage. Because of the presence of **hydroxyproline** (metabolite involved in the destruction of connective tissue) up to two days after exercise, scientists have theorized that delayed-onset muscle soreness may be caused by connective tissue damage.

Lactic acid accumulation. Lactic acid is formed during the process of muscle cell oxygen consumption. Its effect on muscle strength is immediately seen in that it causes muscle contracture to cease. Some scientists believe that lactic acid may be the cause of delayed-onset muscle soreness.

Which One Fits?

All of these theories seem to hold water at first glance. However, scientists are very clever people! A fact out of context, a chemical appearing or not appearing, or some other artifact related to the experimental procedure all have definite meaning to these intrepid sleuths from the Ivory Towers of Academe.

For example, consider the fact that almost no muscle soreness is experienced by those who engaged strictly in **concentric** types of exercises. This fact alone is justification enough to throw the pressure change theory out the window. Since the metabolic stress of concentric work is about 5-7 times greater than the eccentric portion of a given exercise, you would expect the metabolite build-up and accompanying soreness to be greater during concentric exercises. Such is not the case, and the theory can be discarded as untenable.

Scientists have removed plugs of muscle tissue (called **biopsies**) from post-exercise subjects and studied them under powerful electron microscopes for possible hints of cellular damage. No such damage has yet been observed, so the tear and splintering theories can also be put to one side.

Perhaps the most popular explanation for delayed-onset muscle soreness, and one that still persists among bodybuilders, is the lactic acid theory. Again, however, our clever scientists came through with convincing evidence to the contrary. They compared the levels of lactic acid in the blood during and after exercise as well as the levels of soreness in the muscles under study. An interesting twist was added to the experimental procedure, however, These factors were compared for subjects running on level ground and running downhill. Level running produced considerable elevations in blood lactate during the run, but produced little if any post-exercise muscle soreness. On the other hand, running downhill produced only minute lactate concentration changes but extreme post-exercise soreness. The major difference between level running and downhill running is that during downhill running the runner must continuously lower himself through eccentric muscle contraction to a considerably greater degree than his level running counterpart. This increased eccentric muscle activity is, according to exercise physiologist Dr. James Schwane and his associates, the reason for the increased post-exercise soreness, and lactic acid accumulation is not a factor.

So far, only two theories have emerged that in any way explain delayed-onset muscle soreness. The spasm theory holds water because static stretching of an exercised muscle reduces post-exercise soreness considerably. The stretching appears to relieve the muscle spasm, disrupting the vicious cycle that can often last for many hours after exercise. And, the connective-tissue-damage theory also seems to be capable of holding water. The chemical hydroxyproline was found to significantly increase in eccentrically worked muscles about forty-eight hours after exercise. This chemical is released when there is an imbalance of collagen metabolism (collagen is a fibrous protein found in connective tissue). Also, extreme pain was reported by all of the subjects in the experiment as being primarily located near the tendons of eccentrically exercised muscles.

What Causes Muscle Soreness?

The bottom line is that delayed-onset muscle soreness is probably caused by minute tears in the connective tissue of muscles, particularly nearer the ends of the muscles. It may also be true that continued spasms during the first few post-exercise hours causes local pain sensors to react. Due to the persistently reported fact that most muscle soreness occurs in eccentrically exercised muscles, it must also be concluded that such movements are to be avoided.

What Does This Mean to Bodybuilders?

As a bodybuilder, you no doubt have experienced such delayed-onset muscle soreness. You also know from experience that training hard despite such soreness not only results in continued soreness, but tends also to invite a state of overtraining and eventual staleness. It seems rather superfluous, therefore, to admonish you to avoid this kind of soreness to the extent possible, while at the same time not giving up any of your training time and abilities to engage in intense training.

Yet, despite the good sense such an admonition makes, most bodybuilders plod on, driving ever harder through the very pain they should be attempting to avoid. The common assumption seems to be that such pain is some sort of a signal—"no pain, no gain"—that growth is occurring. It is not. Indeed, this kind of pain is a signal that a **destructive** process is taking place. Growth and development slows down during such periods.

Another common fallacy among bodybuilders is that the pain they experience near the tie-ins between two muscle groups—for example, near the base of the bicep or near the armpit where the deltoid and pectoralis come together—is indicative that the exercise they are doing is going to help to develop that area in some sort of isolated or localized sense. It does not. The pain that is felt near the ends of such muscles is merely stretched or torn connective tissue, probably resulting from the eccentric phase of the applied exercise(s). Again, this kind of pain is a warning that a destructive process is in the works—it does not signal growth.

Avoiding Delayed-Onset Muscle Soreness

So, how do you avoid this kind of destructive process? By avoiding eccentric movements? **Certainly not!** By using only light weights? Of course not! Rather, by careful and progressive application of heavier and heavier eccentric movements, performed over a period of literally months and years, the ligaments and tendons, as well as the connective tissues near the tendons can be strengthened such that minimal pain, if any, will be felt after heavy training. Also, by careful application of pain-reducing modalities—such as stretching, heat, ice, recuperation periods, and proper nutrition—such trauma can be not only avoided, but be made to work for you rather than against you.

It is now a well-established fact that reverse-action training (eccentric or negative muscle contraction) is of considerable benefit to advanced bodybuilders. To avoid such training simply as a means of avoiding pain is not necessary. Here is what you can do to avoid the pain and discomfort of delayed-onset muscle soreness:

56

- After layoffs or periods of light training, work gradually into heavy lifting, and particularly if your movements involve eccentric muscle action.
- At first, try to avoid excessive negative movements, relying mainly on concentric movements. As strength increases, gradually add heavy eccentric work.
- After every workout, as well as before, you should do some light stretching of each muscle to be exercised for that day. Each stretched position should be static (do not bounce or ballistically stretch) and held for a period of several seconds, perhaps as much as a minute or two.
- Applying cold (ice packs) to the tendon areas has been shown to be effective in minimizing delayed-onset muscle soreness. This practice is recommended if such soreness becomes a persistent problem, but should be done immediately following the exercise.
- When soreness or lameness does occur, apply heat (hot compresses, shower massage, or whirlpool) to the affected area. And train very lightly until the soreness subsides, concentrating on blood circulation rather than attempting to achieve a "pump."

10
OVERTRAINING
THE SCOURGE OF BODYBUILDING

The line between adaptive stress and destructive stress is a fine one. Your bodybuilding efforts can only be maximized if you learn how to walk the gauntlet between these two states, never undertraining for fear of lost effect, and never overtraining for fear of injury, boredom, or diminishing gains.

Athletes from all persuasions refer to this kind of training as "the ragged edge." And, in most instances, the Weider Instinctive Training Principle is their only guiding light. Listening to your body's warning signals regarding states of under- or overtraining is reasonable. However, there are some other, perhaps more scientific, methods which can be employed to assist you in your efforts to stay on the ragged edge, or to avoid falling off it.

No bodybuilder is immune to overtraining. The tremendous number of variables involved in maximizing performance and training effect makes your training procedure a very complex puzzle indeed. More often than not, bodybuilders succumb to the effect of overtraining because of their powerful will to excel. This burning desire to win, to be the best, is healthy to be sure, but it must be tempered with wisdom and patience.

What Is Overtraining?

Much of the initial research into the effects, symptoms and problems associated with overtraining was done by Eastern European sport scientists. It has only been recently subjected to scientific scrutiny in the United States, a fact which explains why coaches and athletes the world over view American athletes as being perpetually overtrained in so many sports.

Eastern European scientists define overtraining as a condition in which there is a dip in performance or training effect, or a levelling off of performance or training effect over time. In other words, if an athlete has one or two bad workouts he is not necessarily overtrained. But, if this situation persists for four or more workouts, the chances are that the athlete is overtrained.

Overtraining results from an imbalance between the amount of stress applied to the body (or mind), and the individual's ability to adapt to it.

Types of Overtraining

The factors which contribute to overtraining are typically categorized as either **attitudinal** factors or **organismic** factors. Collectively, organismic factors relate to the body's inability to adapt to physical stresses that are applied. Usually these stresses are severe—more severe than the body can tolerate—and may accumulate slowly. Cumulative microtrauma is such that no single episode of superstressing the body has a pronounced effect, but rather show up after repeated bouts of superstress application. This is the most common form of organismic overtraining among athletes. It is probably the most pervasive form among bodybuilders as well.

Attitudinal overtraining. The more insidious enemy of the two is attitudinal overtraining. It is very difficult to diagnose and even more difficult to cure. Once the social, emotional, or psychological factors responsible for attitude problems have been identified, if indeed they can be identified, no less than major lifestyle changes are required to correct them.

Some of the factors bodybuilders should consider when attempting to uncover reasons for poor workout performance are as follows:

1. Cumulative microtrauma
2. Injury or illness
3. Poor diet
4. Drug-induced attitude problems
5. Academic problems
6. Financial problems
7. Familial problems
8. Sex problems
9. Personality conflicts with coach or others in the gym
10. Schedule or time problems

11. Poor facilities for working out
12. Facilities too cold or too hot
13. Monotony in training or lifestyle
14. Poor sleep habits
15. Lack of coaching
16. Lack of encouragement
17. Fear of success
18. Fear of failure
19. Strenuous job interfering with workout
20. Lack of clear or attainable goals in training

As you can well imagine, this list could go on endlessly. Factors 1, 2, 3, 4, 12, 14, and 19 are, of course, related to organismic overtraining, but can have as profound an impact upon your attitude as any of the others.

Make no mistake! Your attitude can make the difference between success and failure. Mental "burnout" is the common term used to describe attitudinal overtraining, and the symptoms are lethargy, lack of initiative, skipping workouts, sudden proneness to injury, loss of attention span, and other similar attitudinal aberrations. As must any wise bodybuilder, you must keep your goals foremost in your mind and selectively prune the inhibitory factors from your life, thereby allowing the fruits of your efforts to grow unimpeded.

Organismic overtraining. Two different types of physical overtraining are distinguished in the East European literature. They are: Addisonic overtraining and Basedowic overtraining. **Addisonic** overtraining, so named because many of the symptoms resemble those common in Addison's disease, is most commonly observed among older athletes, highly advanced athletes, and athletes who impose uncommonly high levels of stress upon their bodies.

Some of the notable symptoms of Addisonic overtraining are:

1. Slight overtired feeling
2. No increase in sleep requirements
3. Anorexia (loss of appetite)
4. No appreciable weight loss
5. Unusually low resting pulse rate
6. Hypotension (lower than normal blood pressure)
7. No change from normal metabolic rate
8. No change from normal body temperature
9. Increased diastolic blood pressure immediately after stress (over 100mm HG)
10. No apparent psychological manifestations

Because the physical changes resulting from Addisonic overtraining can be very subtle, it is very difficult to diagnose. Only complete recordkeeping of your workouts and performance, together with careful and systematic monitoring of the appropriate bodily functions, will allow you or your coach to effectively diagnose and prevent this kind of overtraining.

Basedowic overtraining, on the other hand, is more common and easier to diagnose. It occurs mostly among young, inexperienced athletes who are involved in explosive and strength-type sports such as sprinting, jumping, weightlifting, and powerlifting. It is also more common among less advanced and easily excitable athletes.

The East Europeans gave it the name Basedowic overtraining because many of the symptoms resemble some of those observed in Basedow's disease. Some of the more noteworthy symptoms of this kind of overtraining are as follows:

1. Easily tired
2. Increased sleep requirements
3. Reduced appetite (anorexial)
4. Weight loss
5. Increased resting pulse rate
6. Headaches more common than normal
7. Normal to slightly increased body temperature
8. Increased blood pressure (hypertension)
9. Reduced reaction time
10. Marked reduction in one's ability to perform skilled movements

Because many of the symptoms accompanying Basedowic overtraining are relatively pronounced in their deviation from normal, and because of the sheer number of symptoms that appear, it is a very easy condition to diagnose.

How to Cope with Mental Burnout and Overtraining

As a bodybuilder, your major training task is to impose the appropriate amount of stress on your muscles so that constructive processes are enhanced and destructive processes are avoided. Because of the often incredibly keen ego involvement required for success in bodybuilding, both physical as well as attitudinal overtraining are common among bodybuilders.

Those who choose to walk the gauntlet to bodybuilding success must first recognize the dangers that exist on either side. Overtraining can be as devastating to your future success as undertraining, and remaining on the ragged edge requires careful planning and constant

Guidelines on Avoiding Overtraining

1. Through careful planning, reduce the number of personal problems that may interfere with your training.
2. Develop a rational training regimen—one built on logic rather than ego.
3. Listen to your body! Follow the Weider Instinctive Training Principle, taking absolute care not to overstress your body.
4. Following the Weider Cycle Training Principle is the only way to ensure avoidance of cumulative microtrauma (small injuries becoming major ones).
5. Maintain harmony with your coach and training partners.
6. Find a gym that suits your temperament, your travel limitations, and your pocketbook.
7. Either learn to monitor your own bodily functions (such as heart rate, blood pressure, etc.) or find a sportsmedicine expert to do it for you.
8. Avoid training monotony by injecting a variety of exercise methods and systems into your training. But, whatever methods or systems you use, be sure that they are suitable in getting you to your goal.
9. Establish short-term goals—ones that are easily attainable—and you will find that your ultimate goal will soon be within your grasp.
10. Give your body all the help it needs to recuperate and develop. Sound eating and supplementing together with appropriate rest periods between workouts are essential features of wise and prudent bodybuilding.

monitoring of your body functions. Above are some guidelines that you can follow to ensure continued progress in your bodybuilding efforts.

How to Monitor Overtraining

Following the Weider Instinctive Training Principle may not be enough for some bodybuilders. Young or inexperienced bodybuilders may not have learned how to interpret body signals such as pain, overstress soreness, unwarranted fatigue, or other such symptoms of overtraining. In fact, many experienced bodybuilders never learn how to read their bodies. The ability to distinguish the pain that accompanies destructive stress from that caused by simple training must be **learned**—wisdom and patience are the best teachers in a case like this, and instinct alone is not sufficient.

Sport scientists the world over have used a number of techniques to monitor states of overtraining in athletes. These same techniques are generally suitable for use by bodybuilders as well, since overtraining symptoms know no sport boundaries. The most noteworthy ones are as follows:

1. Coach's subjective appraisal of athlete's attitude and mental approach to training and performance.
2. Monitoring heart rate both when at rest (upon arising from bed in the morning) and during recovery from exercise (how quickly your basal heart rate is reestablished).
3. Monitoring blood pressure both in the morning and following exercise.
4. Measuring the pH of your blood for signs of metabolic acidosis.
5. Measuring the changes that occur in your white blood cell count every two or three days.

Coach's appraisal. Most bodybuilders train alone or with a partner. Few have the luxury of good coaching. If you are fortunate enough to have a coach in whom you trust, however, put him or her to work! On at least a weekly basis, your coach should know not only the exact training load you will handle in each exercise, but he or she should also know your capabilities, and how far you are falling short of them. Your attitude, personal problems, mental set, and the host of other often overlooked mental and psychological factors may be the signal that a good coach can tune in on to help you avoid states of overtraining. In fact, it may not be a bad idea to have your coach brush up on the other methods of monitoring overtraining listed in this article, thereby freeing you to concentrate on your bodybuilding!

Heart rate. Upon arising in the morning, determine your heart rate by placing your fingers on the right side of your throat and counting the number of beats over a one-minute period. This will give you a good idea of what your basal heart rate is. Overtraining in the Addisonic sense will cause your morning heart rate to progressively become slower, and Basedowic overtraining causes it to become faster than normal. If there is a 15% change either way, you are probably overtrained, and should immediately enter a period of lighter workloads (fewer reps, sets, and exercises, and less intensity). If it takes longer than five minutes for your heart rate to subside to a basal level after an exercise, you are either out of shape aerobically, or you are overtrained.

Measuring your heart rate during exercise is an excellent means of determining whether you are training at the proper intensity. During periods of high-intensity training, your exercise heart rate should be in the range of 150-160 beats per minute (to be more precise, subtract your age from 220, and train at a heart rate equal to about 85% of that number). Low-intensity training periods require less stress on the cardiovascular system, and states of overtraining are not common under such circumstances anyway. As a rule of thumb, your exercise heart rate during low-intensity periods should average about 10-15 beats per minute slower than during high-intensity training periods.

Blood pressure. Blood pressure is expressed by using two numbers. The top number is the pressure against the arterial walls during the time the heart is forcing blood through them while the bottom number refers to the pressure against the arterial walls when the heart is at rest (between beats). These two numbers are called **systole** and **diastole**, respectively. A typically normal blood pressure may be around 120 over 85, for example.

You can determine your basal blood pressure by taking a reading each morning for a few weeks. The instrument used to do this is called a **sphygmomanometer.** They are inexpensive, ranging from $20.00 for the manual type to about $70.00 for the electronic models that are suitable for home or gym use.

During periods of Addisonic overtraining, your blood pressure may appear normal during morning readings, but following heavy training your diastolic blood pressure will generally increase by about 15%, exceeding 100mm HG. If this situation persists for a period of more than four workouts, you are probably overtrained, and should cut back on your training accordingly.

Basedowic overtraining, on the other hand, typically causes your morning (basal) blood pressure readings to increase by 15% or more. Such hypertensive states can also be caused by stress, illness, or various drugs (such as anabolic steroids), so be concerned, but don't confuse these conditions with overtraining.

Blood pH. The term pH refers to the level of alkalinity or acidity of the blood. Metabolic wastes and other cell functions can cause increases in the acidity of the blood, leading to what scientists call **metabolic acidosis.** This condition can cause muscle weakness and ultimately lead to overtraining, most likely of the Basedowic type. Some of the factors that can lead to metabolic acidosis are excessive sweating (dehydration and imbalance of bodily salts), impaired liver function, diarrhea (again, causing dehydration), vomiting (dehydration), and ketosis (resulting from the incomplete metabolism of fatty acids, carbohydrate deficiency, high fat diets, diabetes, and pregnancy).

As a bodybuilder, you should go over the preceeding paragraph again! Notice that the dietary pattern and sweating factors that cause acidosis are common in bodybuilding circles! Try to avoid these states through sound nutritional practices and replenishing body salts lost through perspiration.

You can monitor your blood pH with a simple litmus paper test, generally available through either prescription from your physician, or from your druggist. A blood pH test should be performed at least on a weekly basis. Your normal blood pH is generally around 7.4, and when it dips to 7.3 or less you are most definitely overtrained, have a horrible diet, or both.

White blood cell count. A drop of blood from a sterilized pin prick to the finger is all the blood you need to count your white blood cells. A microscope can be purchased for under $100.00. Place a drop of your blood on a grid slide, and visually count the number of white blood cells in the grid. During states of overtraining, your white blood cell count will diminish, often by as much as 15% or more.

Keep a training log. Carefully note symptoms of overtraining in your log as they appear (these symptoms were listed on page 60). Then scrutinize your training log each week for possible signs of prolonged levelling or decline in strength levels.

In conclusion, there seems to be no justification for bodybuilders to allow overtraining to occur. There are a number of methods available to monitor and detect such debilitating states, and just as many methods to avoid them altogether. The methods described in this chapter for monitoring overtraining are quite precise. They work and are in widespread use among athletes the world over, particularly in the Iron Curtain countries. However, I have found that avoiding overtraining in the first place is the best approach, and instinctive training together with cycle training should be given your utmost consideration if overtraining has been one of your problems in the past.

PART II
SYSTEMS AND TECHNIQUES OF BODYBUILDING

The preceeding chapters of this book should have given you a rational understanding of how muscles grow in response to training, and of the scientific principles behind them. This part of the book will attempt to explain how such training is to be accomplished in practical terms.

Over the years there have been literally dozens of successful systems of bodybuilding training, and hundreds of exercises used. Each had its advantages and disadvantages, and smart bodybuilders picked and chose from among them in an attempt to personalize their regimen. The successful elements of the various systems and techniques can invariably be traced to their adherence to the basic principles that will be presented forthwith.

Personalizing Your Training

You are unique. No one else in all the universe has training needs identical to yours. There can be no cookbook for the championship-bound bodybuilder that will tell him or her exactly what to do to attain the Olympia crown. Your only guiding light is science—a rational approach to training that first and foremost takes into consideration your uniqueness.

To complicate matters, during the course of a year's cycle, your training methods may change radically as a result of changing needs. States of overtraining, contest requirements, self-evaluation of physique requirements, and other situational factors numbering in the scores have to be tended to constantly. There is no such thing as a "system" that will always work for you or anyone else. Life is just not that simple.

Is there an answer? Indeed there is: Adherence to the basic principles! Whatever changes you make in your training, whatever route you choose, you can maximize your training efforts through careful application of the basic principles. Always personalizing your training will often require insight and diligence, but despite your uniqueness, you are biologically identical to the billions of other humans on this planet in many ways, and as such are bound by the same universal laws. Enough variation within the framework of these universal concepts is possible to account for your unique problems, and stepping out of that framework will invariably slow training progress.

The systems and concepts covered in Part II take these universal laws into account. None is perfect, for there is no such concept owing to the uniqueness of all bodybuilders. You will have to use your own intelligence and ingenuity to apply these universal laws to your training. The systems and techniques presented here are guides—only guides. They should be considered a starting point from which to grow in sophistication. And they are not inflexible. Change as your needs change.

11
SCIENTIFIC TRAINING AND DEDICATION

Webster's New Collegiate Dictionary defines two words in the above title in ways that are of great importance to all classes of athletes. Curiously, although these words are used freely by all, the true impact of their meanings seems to have escaped most.

> **Science** (noun)—the acquisition or possession of knowledge attained through study or practice; systematized knowledge as a sport or technique that may be studied or learned through the application of the scientific method.

> **dedication** (noun)—the act or right of dedicating to a divine being or a sacred use; self-sacrifice and devotion.

How many bodybuilders can you name that have, in at least a majority of instances, employed anything akin to scientific methodology in their training? And, how many do you know that are devoted to the point of self-sacrifice? Not in the egotistical or narcissistic sense of the word, for these words harken images of self-indulgence or self-gratification, rather, devotion to the point of self-fulfillment.

I know a few—just a few. Yet it is clear that the application of truly scientific training procedures will yield the greatest gains in muscularity, size, and symmetry. It is also clear that total dedication to the principles of science (often to the point of self-sacrifice) is the most efficient way of approaching the problem of employing the scientific method of training.

Science has come a long way since the days of DeLorme, Grimek, Reeves, and Parks. For example, consider the invention of the electron microscope. This incredible instrument enabled scientists, for the first time, to actually **view** the insides of a muscle cell.

They saw **mitochondria**—tiny organelles responsible for the oxidative functions of a muscle cell. They saw **ribosomes** at work manufacturing protein molecules. The tiny filaments responsible for the muscle cell's contractility, **myofibrils** were clearly visible for the first time. Many other cell components were observed. But what's more important to the practicing bodybuilder, these scientists actually were able to observe the effects of different kinds of stress applied to that muscle cell.

So, what used to be speculation in the old days became dogma! There is no longer **any** question as to how to increase the size, number, or quantity of a muscle cell's components through training. Yet, the bodybuilders who know this can probably be counted using fingers and toes.

This new body of knowledge grew in sophistication over the past few years until, today, a group of principles have emerged that stand as the guiding light for virtually all forms of conditioning. There are only six scientific principles, yet they encompass the sum total of man's knowledge about the effects of applying stress to the human body in such a way that constructive adaption occurs. Briefly, they are:

The Overload Principle. As adaption to stress occurs, progressively increasing resistance must be applied to ensure continued adaption.

The Isolation Principle. Overload will best be served if a muscle is isolated from all others; if it can't, the weakest muscle of a group that's acting will receive most of the benefit of overload.

The SAID (Specific Adaptation to Imposed Demands) Principle. Only those components of a muscle or muscle cell that are stressed beyond their normal limits (i.e., overloaded) will adapt. The muscle or cell adapts in highly specific ways to the demands (stress) imposed upon it.

The Simulation Principle. Where skill is involved, the movement patterns involved in the activity must be duplicated against resistance in order to facilitate motor learning of these skills (particularly important after spending much time in training muscles or groups of muscles in isolation).

The Disinhibition Principle. With appropriate overload, inhibitory mechanisms of the body (e.g., the Golgi tendon organ) will be altered to allow greater muscular force to be exerted before being stimulated to cause an inhibitory response. (All of the ramifications of this important principle have not been fully studied as yet.)

The Accommodation Principle. In many skilled activities, particularly those requiring fine eye-hand coordination, increases in body mass, strength, or speed as a result of heavy training may occur that will tend to alter or jeopardize these skills. Thus, to accommodate these alterations in one's body size or strength, distributed practice over the entire training period must be done to ensure maintenance of those vital skills.

It will become quite clear to bodybuilders that principles 1, 2, 3, and 5 are of **primary** importance, although all must be considered for competition on the posing platform.

Entire volumes of textbooks could be written on these principles— the cumulative knowledge contained in each is immense. I would like to concentrate on the third principle in this section, however, since it is this principle with which bodybuilders everywhere seem to have the greatest problem. For now, suffice it to say that any training program, whether it is for bodybuilding, football, tennis, or any other sport must, in the interest of scientific reasoning, be constructed with all of these principles in mind.

The Most Significant Principle

The SAID Principle was born from the knowledge gained from studies involving electron microscopy. All of the components of a muscle cell take up space; they all contribute to the overall size of a muscle. Since it is the main intent of any bodybuilder to maximize muscle size (within the bounds of maintaining a pleasing and symmetrical appearance), it would stand to reason that this principle is of primary importance to most bodybuilders.

After the initial year or so of beginning bodybuilding (when almost **any** kind of weight training program will yield gains in size) the gains begin to come more slowly. It is then that the aspiring physique champion must begin to employ all the tricks of the trade to progress. It will not do for this person to continue using a basic program designed to bring him or her to a level that is merely intermediate. If there is true dedication involved, most bodybuilders aspire to far greater heights than mediocrity. Enlarging as many of a cell's components as possible becomes of critical importance in progressing on to championship status.

Referring back to the graph on page 12, you will see that advanced bodybuilding requires heavy sets, light sets, high reps, low reps, explosive movements, slow movements, rhythmical movements, sustained contraction movements, and all the gradients in between. A great **variety** of movements, speeds, and intensities must be employed to ensure that each and every component of a muscle cell is being overloaded sufficiently for an adaptive process to be forced to occur. The key—the absolute key—to bodybuilding success is **variation**.

High reps and sets generally yield increases in mitochondrial mass within a muscle cell. Such mass will often account for as much as 20%-30% of the gross size of a muscle! Yet, high reps are often overlooked by advanced bodybuilders. Performing these high reps with continuous tension will force a greater number of capillaries to form. Thus, the vascular bed surrounding each cell becomes more prolific, thereby contributing to greater size. The fluid portion of a cell, comprised of a protein substance called **sarcoplasm** will also increase, contributing as much as 25%-30% of the muscle cell's total size.

And, lower reps with heavier weights will increase the number of myofibrillar elements in a cell, again to the tune of 20%-30% of the total size! Any one of these important elements' can very well be the deciding edge in top-flight competition. None should be neglected.

Fast (explosive) movements tend to affect the so-called "fast-twitch" (low-oxidative) fibers more than the red "slow-twitch" (high-oxidative) fibers. The slow-twitch fibers respond more to higher reps with a lighter weight and generally slower movements.

A Model Bodybuilding Program Designed to Maximize Gains in Muscular Size

One or two warm-up sets with each exercise (lighter weights) should be performed, as should a bit of stretching.

Sets	Reps	Weight	Method
1 & 2	4–6	maximum	Explosively, pausing between each repetition.
3 & 4	12–15	maximum	Moderate speed, with a relaxation pause between each repetition.
5 & 6	20–25	maximum	Perform each rep in a slow, sustained fashion (i.e., keep continuous tension on the muscle throughout the concentric and eccentric phases of the movement). No rest pauses through the entire set.

Stretch after training to avoid delayed-onset muscle soreness.

Limit the number of reps and sets you do to what scientific evidence dictates is most efficient. Too many bodybuilders are guilty of "over-training." They often will perform literally four or five exercises per body part and up to eight or ten sets per exercise! This is too much. Almost without fail, one or two carefully selected exercises per muscle will suffice, and up to six sets (done variably as described above) generally will yield maximum results. Overtraining only slows one down and precious time is lost recuperating or wallowing in despair.

A Model Training System

While each bodybuilder has his or her personal goals and individual requirements, the following "model" system of training may be a good starting point for many. The model on page 70 is simplistic, yet it embraces the scientific principles spoken of earlier. As you progress, refinement of the model will undoubtedly become necessary. Give it a try, and I am confident that the increases in size that you will experience will convince you once and for all that even a modicum of science and dedication will carry you a long way toward championship status.

12
THE SYSTEMS OF TRAINING

How should each exercise be performed? Fast? Slow? With rest pauses between reps or with continuous tension? And, how should the exercises be arranged in each workout. What should the intensity factor be? Should the weights used be 60% of your max? Should it be 70% of your max? Why?

Questions like these require careful analysis of your own progress, where you are in your cycle, when your next contest is, what your weak points are, your current percent body fat, your current level of fitness, and a host of other intervening variables. They all tend to dictate the training system of choice when viewed as a whole. That is, they should . . . under ideal conditions.

Oftentimes, the only guide you will have in choosing the appropriate training system will be your instinct. How a given training system feels can be important. Instinctive training must be carefully applied, avoiding at all costs the very real dangers and pitfalls of overtraining, undertraining, or unscientific training.

For an example of unscientific training, it is very common for a bodybuilder to feel that an exercise for the chest specifically affects the tie-in area near the deltoids. The feeling stems from pain sensors in that specific locale being stimulated from physical stretching of connective tissue. This condition does not signal selective growth occurring there, although it seems to feel that way. All it signals is connective tissue stretching. This is the kind of pitfall that can seriously delay championship status if allowed to continue over the long run.

The best advice is to stick to the basic principles, and to benefit from the successes and failures of generations of the bodybuilders who went before you. Perhaps the most comprehensive list of guiding principles for bodybuilders was compiled over several decades by Joe Weider, publisher of **Your Physique** (1940s), a publication that changed names several times over the past four decades, evolving into the most popular bodybuilding periodical today, **Muscle & Fitness.**

As publisher of a popular bodybuilding magazine, Joe Weider has always had direct access to the training regimen of the great stars. The creative genius of this man allowed him to unravel training techniques with scientific substance from amongst the ever increasing pile of misconceptions and ill-conceived training techniques so prevalent in the early day. What evolved over the years was a list of so called "Weider principles" that truly are representative of the state of the art of bodybuilding today.

The remainder of this section lists and discusses these principles from the standpoint of their scientific applicability.

The Set System

This method of training is perhaps the earliest form of training used for bodybuilding. Actually it is the first **systematic** form of weight training period! First used by Olympic weightlifters, a group of exercises (assumedly the most important ones for the major muscles of the body) is performed sequentially, with anywhere from 2-6 sets being performed per exercise. The set is performed using anywhere from 1-20 or so repetitions, and a rest is taken before progressing on to the next set. The rest is a complete one—allowing lactate levels in the blood to subside, heart rate to fall to a manageable level, and muscle ATP (adenosine triphosphate) to be replenished in sufficient quantities to allow for maximum contraction on the next set. It became popular to train this way back in the old days because of the Olympic lifting influence—maximum strength gains are possible with this kind of low-key approach to training. Heavier weights could be used because of the ample rest periods

It is still a popular way to train these days, but only among lifters (both Olympic style and powerlifters) and beginners in bodybuilding attempting to build a solid foundation for future training with higher intensity and sophistication. Not a bad way to begin, but certainly not the best for bodybuilding of championship caliber. Below is a typical set system workout.

As you can see, each major body part is covered, but only one exercise is used per body part, and little, if any, regard is typically given to different rep/set schemes, cadence per rep, muscle priority system-atizing, or other vital factors in successful bodybuilding. It is a beginner's system, and it is also a strength athlete's system.

74

Typical Set System Workout

Exercise	Sets × Reps	Rest Between Sets
squats	3 × 10	2–7 minutes
bench press	3 × 10	2–7 minutes
pulldowns	3 × 10	2–7 minutes
crunches	3 × 10	2–7 minutes
hyperextensions	3 × 10	2–7 minutes
bent rows	3 × 10	2–7 minutes
tricep extensions	3 × 10	2–7 minutes
curls	3 × 10	2–7 minutes
toe raises	3 × 10	2–7 minutes

Superset System

A **superset** is a big set. Typically two different forms of exercise combining are used to produce a superset. The first and most popular is the combining of two exercises for antagonistic (opposing) muscles (for example, biceps versus triceps). Pulldowns versus presses, bench presses versus reverse flyes, crunches versus hyperextension, leg extensions versus leg curls—these are the traditional combinations used to produce a superset.

The two opposite exercises are done back to back to produce one big (super) set. For example, when supersetting biceps and triceps, the system would consist of the following:

curls—10 reps (no rest)
tricep extensions—10 reps (rest 2-7 minutes

curls—10 reps (no rest)
tricep extensions—10 reps (rest 2-7 minutes)

. . . and so forth until the required number of supersets are completed.

Supersetting in this fashion is a step up the intensity ladder from the regular set system because of the greater effort required to perform each superset. An added benefit of this form of training is that symmetrical development of opposing body parts is facilitated.

The other form of supersets that has become quite popular in body-building circles is combining two exercises for different muscle emphasis from among the muscles of a single grouping. For example, bicep curls for the long head of the bicep (incline curls) are supersetted with preacher curls which have a more general growth effect. Or, incline bench presses for the clavicular portion of the pectoralis muscle group, followed by decline bench presses for the sternal aspect of the same group.

75

Trisets and Giant Sets

Ever progressing up the ladder of increasing intensity we started with sets, then supersets for opposing muscles, supersets for within-group muscles, and now trisets for within-group muscles with three different muscles in the group, and giant sets for within-group muscles with more than three muscles comprising the group.

To clarify, set system training emphasized the combined strength of all muscles within a body part. Supersets took into account two-muscle groupings such as biceps and pectorals. Trisets, on the other hand, apply to three-muscle groupings such as the deltoids, although many bodybuilders use trisets on one, two, three, and four-or-more muscle groupings. The same is true with giant sets, originally designed to fully develop individual muscles within groups comprised of more than three muscles. The quadriceps and hamstrings, as well as the upper back, are particularly well suited to this sort of training, as many muscles work together to produce individual movements.

The real trick in maximizing the benefits of multi-exercise sets for within-group training is to ensure that as complete isolation as possible is adhered to for each muscle within the group. For example, trisets used for deltoid development should, by definition, include lateral raises, inverted flyes, and front raises—the three heads of the deltoid (medial, posterior, and anterior, respectively) are stressed as independently of one another as is physically possible.

The table on page 76 is a listing of traditional combinations for set, superset, triset, and giant set training. It is not all-inclusive, but it will give you a good idea as to some effective ways of getting the most out of your multi-exercise sets.

Illustration of Progression of Effect Specificity for Single-Exercise and Multiple-Exercise Sets

Set System	Superset System		Triset System	Giant Set System
	opposing groups	within-group		
Upper legs and hips (regular squats)	quadriceps vs hamstrings (leg extensions and curls)	quadriceps from different angles (lunges and leg extensions)	quadriceps from different angles (lunges, leg extensions, and squats)	quadriceps from different angles (hack squats, lunges, side lunges, and squats)
Upper back (bent rows)	upper back vs chest (bent rows and bench press)	upper back from different angles (bent rows and shrugs)	upper back from different angles (bent rows, shrugs, and lat pulldowns)	upper back from different angles (bent rows, shrugs, lat pulldowns, and inverted flyes)
Shoulders (military press)	shoulders vs latissimus dorsi (presses and lat pulldowns)	deltoids from different angles (lateral raises and inverted flyes)	deltoids from different angles (lateral raises, inverted flyes, and frontal raises)	deltoids from different angles (lateral raises, inverted flyes, frontal raises, and presses)
Midsection (crunches)	abdominals vs erector spinae (crunches and hyperextensions)	lower abdominals vs upper abdominals (crunches and reverse crunches)	abdominals, obliques, and lower back (crunches, side bends left and right, and hyperextensions)	abdominals, obliques, lower back and intrinsic muscles of lumbar spine (crunches, side bends left and right, hyperextensions, and bent trunk twists)

Split System Training

If you are using set system training, chances are you have enough energy reserves to carry you through a complete complement of exercises for the entire body. However, when you progress in training intensity to the use of multi-exercise sets, such as superset, triset, or giant set training, it is very often impossible to maintain sufficient intensity of effort. It becomes, therefore, essential for you to do only some of your exercises on one day, and the remaining exercises on the alternate day. With set system training, it becomes necessary for you to work out at least six times per week, and often as many as twelve times weekly, depending upon the sophistication of the split employed.

There are many ways to split up a routine. The most common one is the popular **push-pull** system of splitting. The pushing muscles (triceps, chest, and shoulders) are exercised on one day and the pulling muscles the other (e.g., bicep, back). The midsection and legs can be alternately arranged on either the pulling or pushing day (or both) in a variety of combinations depending upon the bodybuilder's preferences, training priorities, or energy reserves.

Another commonly employed split is the one in which Monday, Wednesday, and Friday are devoted to chest, shoulders, and arms, while Tuesday, Thursday, and Saturday are for legs, back, and midsection. Within any form of split routine, set, superset, triset, or giant set training strategies can be employed on a discretionary basis.

The basic philosophy behind these two commonly employed splits is that the muscles that are related to each other (i.e., the muscles that can't be excluded from synergistically assisting in a movement) are exercised on the same day to ensure that they are given enough recuperation time between each workout. Then, the muscle groups that are not involved are exercised on the alternate day for the same reason.

Many creative methods of splitting a weekly workout program can be generated, and behind each one there should be a rigid adherence to the basic principles of conditioning, and the notion that the split is designed to yield greater energy levels for maximally intense, individual workouts. In this way, greater gains will be possible because of the improved overall quality of overload.

Aerobic Training

There are two periods in a bodybuilder's yearly cycle that may, out of necessity, require aerobic training. Both periods in the off-season, and just before a competition—are the result of allowing yourself to put on too much fat. Excess fat, of course, is the result of improperly balancing your caloric intake with your daily activity level.

The best two ways I know of for bodybuilders to eliminate excess fat is to either engage in circuit training for awhile or to engage in peripheral heart action training for awhile. Both systems of training have the net effect of increasing your basal metabolic rate so you can burn greater amounts of calories even while sleeping. Of course, a proper diet is also required for fat reduction to occur, but the entire process can be greatly facilitated through either of these two systems.

Peripheral Heart Action (PHA) Training

The PHA system was conceived by Chuck Coker during the early 1960s and stands out as the very best system of training I have ever come across for overall fitness. Nearly all of the various components of fitness are served, depending upon how the reps, sets, and sequences of exercises are arranged.

It is a very demanding system of training, designed only for those who are already considerably fit. Bodybuilders fall comfortably into this category. It consists of four sequences of exercises, with each sequence designed to encompass movements from every major body segment. The idea is to "shunt" blood up and down the body, taxing the cardiovascular function to a great degree (for improved metabolic rate and fat reduction).

An Example of a PHA Training System

Sequence 1	Sequence 2	Sequence 3	Sequence 4
partial press	pulldowns	bench press	bent rows
crunches	back raises	side bends left	side bends right
squats	leg curls	leg extensions	toe raises
tricep extensions	bicep curls	dips	shrugs

Perform the exercises in Sequence 1 for the required number of reps sequentially, and nonstop. Repeat the sequence two or three more times and progress on to Sequence 2, performing it as you did Sequence 1. Then, follow suit with Sequences 3 and 4 resting after each sequence only if necessary. Maintain your heart rate at 220 minus your age times .8. For example, if you're 20 years old, subtract 20 from 220. Then 200 × .8 is 160. Thus, 160 beats per minute is your exercise heart rate. Speed up or slow down your training pace accordingly to maintain this heart rate. You should not have to give up tonnage intensity (the amount of weight you use per exercise) for training speed intensity.

At the same time, however, each sequential body part covered in each sequence is getting sufficient rest between each bout that it can again respond with maximum strength. The fact that the heart is beating furiously and the respiratory rate is very high has little to do with your ability to bite the bullet and bear down on each rested body part. The result, of course, is improved strength, size, tonus, and cardiorespiratory efficiency.

An illustration of a PHA system (see page 78) designed to affect all of the major body parts, improve flexibility (sequences 2 and 4 are supermultiple sets of sequences 1 and 3, respectively), and, of course, metabolic rate for fat control (all sequences are done nonstop at about 150 beats of the heart per minute sustained rate).

Circuit Training

The main objective in a circuit training system is to complete all the exercises in the circuit within a target time limit. Emphasis, then, is on training speed intensity. As with PHA training, however, you must avoid giving up your training tonnage for the sake of speed through the circuit. Improve your training speed only if you are able to continue to use the same amount of weight (or more) than you were able to when you started.

An illustration of a typical circuit for use by bodybuilders is on page 80. Remember that the function of circuit training is to help alter your basal metabolic rate so you will be able to control body fat. Emphasis, therefore, is on the large muscles of the body, as exercising those muscles will more effectively affect metabolism. Notice that the exercise arrangement is such that no body part is exercised twice in a row. This, of course, is done to avoid undue fatigue slowing progress.

You must traverse the circuit in nonstop fashion, attempting to equal or better your established target time. Then, after a brief rest, repeat the circuit in its entirety. Repeat the circuit three or four times for a complete workout. One helpful suggestion might be to follow a variable pattern for each circuit as follows:

warm-up: stretching and light sets
first circuit: heavy, explosive set of five reps for each exercise
second circuit: set of 12-15 reps done at a rhythmic cadence with a rest pause between each rep
third sequence: set of 20-25 reps done very strict and with continuous tension kept on the muscle

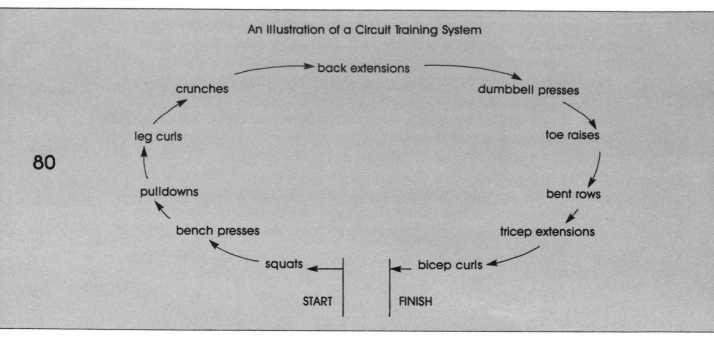

An Illustration of a Circuit Training System

In such a case, the target time concept can be thrown out the window in favor of quality training. What's given up, however, is maximum cardiovascular (metabolism increase) effect. What's gained is greater overall effect upon the muscles from the standpoint of the holistic training principle spoken of in the opening chapter of Part I. Since the circuit is still performed nonstop, however, it remains reasonably effective for fat reduction purposes nonetheless. Your choice of methods will depend entirely upon your own progress assessment.

Other Aerobic Training Methods

Many bodybuilders in training for a contest prefer to control body fat by running, bicycling, or other such aerobic activities. That's all well and good, but I personally don't feel that they're any better than circuit training or PHA training. In fact, they're probably not as good in the long run because much energy is spent on the running or cycling, robbing the bodybuilder of weight-training energy. His workouts suffer.

Circuit training and PHA training allow you to improve on your physique at the same time you're improving upon your fat-diminishing metabolic efficiency. There's no wasted energy. Still, cycling and jogging represent excellent means of speeding up your metabolic processes, and therefore cannot be ignored. The best way of doing it, is to maximize the benefits and, at the same time, minimize the wasted energy. The figure on page 81 shows how to do this.

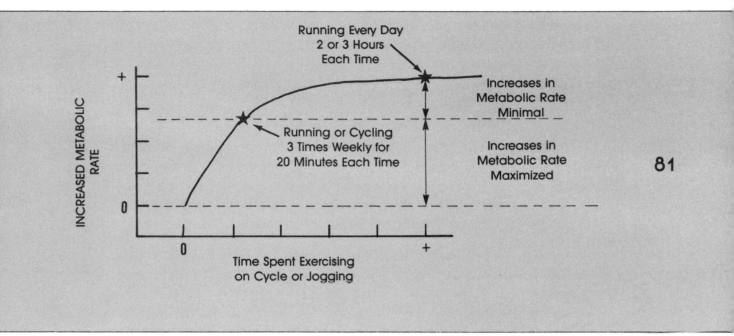

As you can see, the returns rapidly diminish over time, and those hearty souls who run every day for two or three hours are the champion marathoners. As a bodybuilder, you needn't go that far. In fact, it is absolutely counterproductive for your goals. Instead, cycling 3 times weekly for 20 minutes or so will give you all the fat-burning capabilities you need to maintain championship level muscularity—providing your diet and training are also adequate.

Helpful Definitions

Down through the years, there have been many techniques of training introduced to bodybuilders. Some came from the bodybuilding ranks (as for example, the Weider Principles) while others were gleaned from other sport disciplines. Some are beneficial for bodybuilders and others are only of minimal benefit. Listed here are some of the more noteworthy and most often referred-to techniques.

Training to Failure

Failing the last repetition in a set, you have, by definition, gone to failure. Through a set, lactate concentrations rise in the involved muscles, rendering them incapable of further contraction. Every set you do as a bodybuilder, whether you are doing sets of 5, 10, 15, or 20, you should use enough weight that if you were to do one rep more than the prescribed number, you would fail. That is appropriate use of the overload principle.

Heavy Training

82

The description of how to train (under Training to Failure, above) is the definition you should use for the word "heavy." Of course, doing single reps with a maximum weight is heavy, too, but for the bodybuilder such a practice is taboo because singles are counterproductive. In simple fact, all bodybuilders, beginners through advanced, should train heavy.

Intensity

Heavy Training, in the spirit of the definition offered in the preceding paragraph, implies intensity. You can make a set more intense by using maximally heavy weight per set, shortening the time it takes to do the set, or a combination of the two. Beginners find it more difficult to apply maximum intensity to their training, not because they aren't able to use maximally heavy weights, but they have yet to learn how to train through the pain barrier. As lactate concentrations rise, or as heart rate speeds up, effort becomes harder to apply. Total concentration as well as a learned response to fatigue signals that allow further reps to be performed (via greater neuronal input) allows advanced (experienced) bodybuilders to train past the point where beginners may falter.

The Pump

A pumped sensation is often experienced after a couple of sets of any given exercise. This sensation is the result of both blood engorgement and lactate increases in the muscle. It's a good feeling to many bodybuilders because they like the tightness of the pumped state, and because it is a signal to them that their set is forcing an adaptive process to take place. This belief is not always accurate, however. Worshipping the pump as if it were the end all-be all of a training set is not necessarily appropriate.

Low reps often do not produce as intense a pumped sensation, yet myofibrillarization occurs best with low reps (6-8 reps per set). Conversely, high reps (in the area of 20 or more) produce a monstrous pump, but little in the way of great strength results from such sets. Instead, capillarization and mitochondrial mass increases are produced.

Enjoy the pump, but don't use it as a guide to training effect. Perform your sets and reps as you know science dictates for maximum growth.

Forced Reps

After training to failure in a set, your partner may assist you in an additional 2-4 reps. The purpose of this practice is to push the muscle past the pain threshold that limited you in the first place. This practice eventually has the net effect, some believe, of lowering excitation thresholds of hard-to-stimulate motor units, thereby involving them in the exercise movement in ways that otherwise would never be possible. I tend to accept this as a good training practice, but certainly not to be used as general fare. The trauma experienced by the muscle with such intensity may catapult you into an overtrained state very quickly. Try it once a week or so, and limit its use to hard-to-develop muscles or lagging body parts.

Negatives

In an effort to further increase the intensity of effort, some bodybuilders use weights that they are incapable of handling, and have their partner stand by while they lower the weight. The partner assists them back to the extended position, and the weight is lowered again, the muscles fighting maximally against the effect of the overpowering gravity. This form of training causes considerable connective tissue damage, however, and should be used in a fashion similar to forced reps—for lagging body parts and never more than once per week.

Quality Training

This term has come to be defined by bodybuilders as meaning the practice of using shorter and shorter rest periods between sets. It is believed that by doing so, greater muscularity and definition can be achieved for precontest training. Of course, this belief is partly accurate, since shorter rest intervals have the net effect of keeping the heart rate higher for extended periods, thereby increasing overall metabolic rate. The improved metabolic rate, in turn, causes you to burn more calories thereby making it easier to control body fat.

However, I would like to add a new twist to the accepted definition. Quality training, as the name implies, should include doing everything right. Proper use of the basic principles of training, the right number of reps, sets, exercise selection, strict form—everything. Of course, all bodybuilders should strive for quality training. The old adage about comparing quality with quantity applies here. With quality training, you can achieve much more than you can simply by increasing the quantity of training.

Descending Sets

A form of single-sided pyramid training, the trainee begins by doing a set with a maximally heavy weight, and immediately progressing to the next set using a lighter weight, and so forth until several sets are performed, each with lighter weights than the preceding set. There is a lot to be said for this kind of high-intensity training. It is particularly effective for totally fatiguing a muscle group, and should not be used exclusively, since you will surely wind up in an overtrained state within a very short time.

Cheating Exercises

Swinging a weight past a sticking point and then, when leverage is more advantageous, finishing the movement with the target muscle, is called ``cheating.''

This technique should be used at the end of a set, when fatigue has made it impossible to the movement in strict form. However, you should not cheat the weight all the way through the movement, only past the sticking point. Swinging the weight all the way up defeats the purpose of the exercise. As with some of the other methods of improving training intensity (such as descending sets, forced reps, or negatives) this method of training should be used only for stubborn body parts and only infrequently. Once a week is plenty. You must avoid overtraining at all costs in order to keep your progress ever upward.

Rest-Pause Training

When emphasis must go toward building great strength, this is an effective means of bringing your strength level to a peak quickly. Some old timers call this form of training the California set system. It involves performing a near-max single, pausing for a brief 15-second rest, doing the single again, resting 15 seconds, and so forth until failure. Typically, up to 6-8 reps can be performed in this fashion, and will tax your body and soul to the ultimate. Frankly, I can't think of a single instance where this form of training should be necessary for a bodybuilder. Olympic lifters and powerlifters may find it invaluable for contest peaking but it really has little, if any, value to bodybuilders. Still, it's popularly used by some, and proponents claim that it helps them develop greater strength for better quality overload in other exercises.

Muscle Priority Training

Training the muscles that are most important, usually your weaknesses, is what muscle priority training is all about. This should be part and parcel of all bodybuilders' training practice. As weaknesses are eliminated, one by one, what's the end result? A physique with virtually no weaknesses!

Muscle Confusion

Like so many of the training techniques listed above, the Muscle Confusion Principle was developed by Joe Weider. Not that he invented it—he merely catalogued it and put it to the acid test, as he did with all the rest. The result in this case was that it is indeed possible to "confuse" a muscle action by introducing a slight variation of the same movement. In so doing, it is often possible to catapult a lagging muscle back into a full-growth cycle because new motor pathways were stimulated. For example, instead of always doing squats for the legs, try hack squats, lunges to the front or side, or leg presses. These exercises are essentially the same movement, but with different motor pathways to guide them. In so doing, you have not actually stimulated a different part of the muscle, like so many bodybuilders believe, but you have rekindled a need for further adaptation in the same muscles.

Compensatory Acceleration Training (CAT Training)

The CAT technique is actually the result of a mathematical model being applied to an exercise. Let's use squats as an example. You're performing a set of 10 squats. Because your muscles are fresh, the first seven reps are a breeze, and afford you with little adaptive stress. The first third of the remaining squats are the toughest since your leverage is poor in the bottom position. As you ascend beyond the bottom third of the movement, however, leverage improves greatly, and you can finish the squats with ease. So, only the first one third of the last three squats afforded you with sufficient overload to force and adaptive process to occur in the muscle. That relates to an efficiency percentage of only 3/30ths—or 1/10th! Virtually 90 percent of your efforts were wasted!

Now, wouldn't it be nice if you were able to improve that 10% efficiency rating to around 80% or 90%? Of course it would, for that would mean that you would be able to achieve the gains in one workout that it used to take you eight or nine workouts to accomplish! It is with great emphasis that I advise you that this improved efficiency can indeed be accomplished. Using CAT procedure, you can definitely achieve this kind of efficiency in many of your exercises. All you have to do is compensate for the improving leverage through a given movement by pushing harder and harder! Most bodybuilders let up on their effort at the point where leverage improves. This is not efficient. Through every inch of your range of motion, you should be exerting absolute maximal effort. Except, that is, right near the terminal point of the range, where it is necessary to slow the ballistic movement down a bit to avoid throwing the weight off your back or seriously injuring your muscle from the greatly speeded up movement.

Exercises such as squats, bench presses, and stiff-leg deadlifts are well suited to CAT techniques, but shorter range-of-motion exercises such as curls or lateral raises are not. When applying this compensatory acceleration to your exercise efforts, remember that it is the **mind** that controls effort. You must concentrate on maximum effort throughout the range of motion and on every rep in the set. With this kind of mental concentration you will improve the general quality of your training to an enormous extent.

13

HOW HIGH-TECH EQUIPMENT MATCHES UP TO OLD-FASHIONED HARD WORK

You are experiencing a period in history that has no precedent. High technology has opened a sort of Pandora's Box from which streams a never-ending flow of work-saving devices. Their consequences have changed the course of man's history. The very devices that were designed to save us effort gave birth to a new problem—man was becoming lazy and unfit from inactivity! Not to worry! New technologies were developed to get us back in shape with as little effort as possible!

Paradoxical? Perhaps. But the technology of fitness is both scientifically and practically valid. The fact is that if you're interested in lifting weights for firming up and strengthening the muscles of your under-used body, or achieving an Olympian physique, the easiest and most efficient way of going about it is to do it scientifically!

But this is also an age of specialization. Things have become far too complex for any single person to know very much about more than just a few things. When you enter the spa or gym, for example, you are confronted with a maze of contraptions that sparkle, whirr, clang, hiss, or grate. Each looks so different that it is immediately clear to even the most casual observer that the technology behind each is vastly different. Which one is best? And, for what?

The Science of Progressive Resistance Training

The machines that make you fit all have their advantages and disadvantages. It used to be that the only choice one had was to pump iron. Barbells and dumbbells were the only way to coax unused muscles into shapelier form and increased strength. As your strength grew, the amount of weight you were obliged to use to continue development also had to increase. That is the nature of progressive resistance. It is the basic tenet behind virtually all modern fitness technology.

It was an inevitable consequence of the dawning of the age of technology that machines were invented to better equip you with the wherewithall to apply progressive resistance exercises more efficiently. The early machines simply mimicked the physics of barbell and dumbbell training. Weight was hoisted with fixed lever systems or cable-and-pulley arrangements. Most of these early forms of training (machines and free weights alike) are still regarded as the most popular form of progressive resistance training to this day.

The technocrats who rule the fitness industry, however, being ever wary for new products to sell, have supplied us with some rather sophisticated machinery that is designed to make our quest for fitness ever easier and less time consuming! Many of the innovations given to us (whether we wanted them or not) by the denizens of the drawing board are, happily, very effective in these regards.

Let's explore some of the more noteworthy innovations in progressive resistance theory from a practical point of view. We can, I believe, decide for ourselves whether these contraptions are worthwhile.

The Four Technologies of Fitness

Exercise physiologists generally classify the various fitness machines into four general groups: (1) static resistance devices, (2) constant resistance devices, (3) variable resistance devices, and (4) accommodating resistance devices. Each group has its peculiarities, advantages, and disadvantages. All of them are quite effective, within their design limitations. But which are best for what?

Static Resistance Devices

When you pull or push against an immovable object, the muscles are forced to contract statically (without movement). The name given to this form of training is **isometrics.** As a viable exercise form, it is all but dead. Strength can be improved isometrically, but only at the specific angle at which the limb is positioned. This practical obstacle is generally too cumbersome with which to toil in a gym setting.

Constant Resistance Devices

When the muscle contracts and joint movement occurs, as in lifting a barbell, the degree of effort you put forth changes throughout the range of joint movement. Leverage changes, making the weight feel lighter or heavier, depending upon the position of the joint. This is called constant resistance training because the amount of weight doesn't change.

Variable Resistance Devices

To compensate for changes in leverage throughout any joint's range of movement, clever equipment designers found ways to vary the leverage of the machine to coincide with the body's leverage changes. If your leverage increases, the machine's leverage increases proportionately. Or, if your leverage decreases, so does the machine's. This important adjustment in design allowed the user to maximize the amount of stress placed on the muscle by the weight over the entire range of motion rather than just the weakest portion of the range as is the case with constant resistance devices. Cams and rolling levers are the two chief ways designers were able to accomplish this objective.

Accommodating Resistance Devices

The game of one-upmanship is never ending in the exercise equipment marketplace. Some manufacturers took the lead of the variable resistance device manufactureres and took the concept of full-range overload a step further. By controlling the speed of movement, they were able to greatly improve the quality of overload throughout the entire range of movement. This was done by using hydraulic systems, air systems, and clutch plates in tandem with flywheels. These methods have the net effect of reducing the ballistic characteristics of machine or barbell training to near zero, and also reducing the chance for error in compensatory leverage adjustments to near zero. In other words, the new accommodating resistance devices allow the user to apply maximum force against the resistance through the entire range of motion. Most of these accommodating resistance devices also have speed control capabilities. They can be adjusted to infinite gradations of speed ranging from very fast to very slow.

90

Machines vs Free Weights

Remember your first visit to the spa? Those shiny, complex arrangements of chrome, pulleys, and cams that people were sweating upon, you were told, were state-of-the-art muscle builders. They were impressive looking, weren't they? But were you given the truth or a sales pitch? (In the spa business, as elsewhere, truth and sales are not often coincident terms.)

Like most people nowadays, you had developed a reasonable level of sales resistance, and decided to pursue the truth. "Which is better for building muscle, these odd but beautiful contraptions or barbells and dumbbells?" you asked. The young instructor, of course, knew the answer—his jobs was sales, and he promptly replied, "Why, the machines are much easier, safer, faster, and efficient!"

Not entirely convinced, you pointed to the barbells and dumbbells over in the back corner of the spa, and asked, "Why do you have those here if machines are better?" The reply was startling. "Oh, those are for some of the more serious bodybuilders who train here."

What the Research Shows about Free Weights and Machines

Many of the research studies that have been conducted in recent years comparing barbell or dumbbell training with machine training (such as Mini-Gym, Universal, or Nautilus) was funded by the manufacturers of the machines. In the interest of being as objective as possible, these studies must be looked at with somewhat of a jaundiced eye. Millions of dollars in sales are at stake, and it wouldn't do for these equipment manufacturers to publicize any negative aspects of their products.

There was one study, however, that was significant by virtue of its objectivity. Jeff Everson, a doctoral candidate from the University of Wisconsin conducted a study in 1981 using identical twins as his

Advantages of Free Weights

1. Dumbbells and barbells are more effective in developing the smaller synergistic (helping) muscles and stabilizer muscles.
2. Free weight exercises more closely match the neurological patterns of associated sports skills because of joint kinesthesis, leverage similarities, and bodily involvement from a biomechanical point of view.
3. Barbells and dumbbells are more versatile.
4. Barbells and dumbbells are less expensive.
5. Barbells and dumbbells take up less space (for home gym use).
6. Greater overall strength can be achieved using barbells and dumbbells.
7. Power is improved more efficiently and to a greater extent through the use of free weights.
8. Other aspects of fitness, including size, flexibility, reduced body fat, and various anthropometric measurements are achieved more efficiently through the use of free weights.

Advantages of Machines

1. Certain machines are more efficient in maximally isolating a muscle or muscle group for more efficient overload.
2. Machines are generally safer than free weights —the weights are on slides and held in place by retaining pins.
3. For group use, some machines are more efficient in terms of space utilization (especially Universal machines).
4. Machines are easier to use, and therefore faster workouts are possible (less time wasted changing plates and waiting for spotters).
5. For the average fitness enthusiast seeking reasonable tonus and strength, machines generally prove to be more efficient because of the time factor (it's easier to get in a "lunch hour" workout).

Disadvantages of Barbell and Dumbbell Training

1. Training alone can be dangerous. The heavy weights can injure you if control is lost.
2. Barbells and dumbbells that are adjustable can come apart if care is not taken to secure the collars tightly.
3. Adjustments in weight from set to set require collars to be removed, plates affixed or taken away, and collars replaced—often a time-consuming and tedious ordeal.
4. For group use, barbells and dumbbells take up much space, and people milling around can make the area hazardous.
5. In certain exercises, it is difficult if not impossible to derive maximum isolation of a muscle or muscle group.

Disadvantages of Machines

1. All machines are not alike in every regard, but most are of the type that requires the moving of a weight along a predetermined path (or track), making it nearly impossible to derive synergistic or stabilizer muscle strength.
2. Machines which control velocity of movement (such as isokinetic machines), or vary the resistance over a given movement (such as Nautilus or Universal machines) have removed the "natural" aspect from the exercise, which many physiologists claim renders such machines less effective in developing strength and size. Neurological input differences is the chief reason given.
3. Because of machine construction constraints, it is generally impossible to achieve maximum velocity in training. The machines would either break, jerk about violently, or simply not accomodate such training. High-speed training is often a prerequisite in sport training.
4. Most machines are constructed to serve the average-size person. Very short or very tall people find it almost impossible to use many of the machines currently on the market, particularly Nautilus machines.
5. Machines tend to be in a price range beyond the means of home gym owners, and often beyond the means of commercial spas as well.
6. Many machines are so specialized that one would have to purchase several in order to get even a marginally effective workout—gym floor space permitting.
7. Space age appearances of many machines lull users into believing that high technology equals maximum efficiency in achieving fitness goals, a sentiment that is definitely not true. Nothing beats hard work in promoting fitness.

92

Effective Ratings for Each Type of Equipment on Selected Training Objectives
(on a scale of 1-10)

	Dumbbells & Barbells	Constant Resistance machines (similar to Paramount's)	Cam Machines (similar to Nautilus')	Lever Machines (similar to Universal's)	Hydraulic Machines (similar to Hydra-Fitness')	Clutch & Flywheel Machines (similar to Mini-Gym's)
Muscular size increases	10	8	7	7	5	5
Muscular strength increases	10	5	6	6	8	7
Explosive power increases	9	5	5	5	10	10
Sport skills carryover for the movement employed	9	5	5	5	5	8
Sport skills carryover for the velocity/acceleration employed	9	5	3	5	7	7
Quality of overload through the entire exercise set	6	6	7	7	9	8
Quality of muscular isolation	10	8	8	8	8	9
Overall versatility	10	6	5	6	5	9
TOTAL EFFECTIVENESS SCORE	73	48	46	49	57	63
	constant resistance		variable resistance		accomodating resistance	

research subjects. One trained with Nautilus equipment, and the other trained with free weights. The Nautilus-trained twin followed the instructions from the manufacturer (the same instructions you would receive at any Nautilus spa), while the other trained conventionally.

Both training methods produced positive results in strength, muscle size, body fat reduction, and muscular endurance. However, the free weights produced the greatest gains overall after 12 weeks of training.

It seems that the reason "serious athletes" most often choose free weights in their conditioning programs is explained in Everson's research findings. However, from a mere practical perspective, it seems that looking at each machine and each free weight exercise individually, rather than looking at an entire training regimen may prove more beneficial. After all, while one machine may be good, another may not be. The same can be said of different barbell exercises.

What Experience Shows about Free Weights and Machines

Machines have been a part of weight training for many years. As early as the 1920s, Eugene Sandow was selling wall pulleys to gyms. Practically every YMCA in the country that's over 50 years old has his pulleys affixed to the gym wall. There are movements that can be done on certain machines that cannot be duplicated with dumbbells or barbells, certainly not efficiently.

Leg extension/flexion benches, lat pulldown machines, wrist rollers, neck machines, and rowing machines are but a few of the machines that have been around for literally generations They have stood the test of time because they work. And, they work as well or better than free weights in many circumstances.

That machines have advantages over free weights is a matter of experience more than hard scientific research. But it is just as true, as Everson's study clearly illustrated, that free weights have many practical advantages over machines. The charts on pages 91-92 list some of the more noteworthy points of comparison.

I would like to point out that all champion bodybuilders use free weights as well as machines. While the majority of their workouts are performed with free weights, it has long been understood that in some instances machines are more effective than barbells and dumbbells. To be more explicit in regards to pinpointing the actual exercises that are best done with machines is impossible. Each bodybuilder and each athlete has his or her own peculiar needs, anatomical structure, and temperament. When you go to your spa or gym, experiment with both. Find for yourself which method feels better, and which method over time yields the best results. This kind of instinctive training has been the hallmark of those following the Weider system of muscle development for many years.

14

THE BIOMECHANICAL PRINCIPLES BEHIND THE MOST COMMONLY PERFORMED EXERCISES

The exercises that bodybuilders use in developing their individual muscles are regulated by biomechanical principles. The origin and insertion points of each muscle must be clearly identified, and the muscle must be forced to contract in such a way that the majority of stress is borne by the target muscle.

Surrounding muscles—synergists and stabilizers—will derive some benefit, of course, as it is functionally quite difficult (if not impossible) to achieve total isolation of single muscles. This is true because for any given muscle to work, others are needed to either assist or stabilize other body parts in the process.

Exercise Selection

The real trick in choosing an appropriate exercise for each muscle is to attempt to make it the weakest of those working. Then it will derive the fullest benefit from the applied overload. Typically, synergists and stabilizers are much stronger than the prime mover in an exercise, not because they are bigger—normally they are not—but because they have a more advantageous angle of pull (leverage). Thus, the larger muscle derives the major benefit of the applied overload.

Listed in each description for the accompanying major bodybuilding exercises are the practical considerations centering around how best to achieve maximum isolation and overload. Other muscles that act strongly as synergists or stabilizers are also listed, since they often become of interest to bodybuilders wishing to emphasis complete development of a body part. This concern is justifiable and is in fact critical in maximizing proportional development of the entire body. For example, performing only wide-grip, elbows-out, bench presses may be the best method of developing the pectorals, but if the upper and lower pectoral (clavicular and sternal portions) are not individually overloaded, full development is not possible.

As a final comment before delving into the various exercises, you should note that the exercises listed in this chapter are arbitrarily divided into groups. They are: chest, shoulders, arms, legs, midsection, and back. These six groups are used primarily because they represent the way most bodybuilding systems "split" the body up for each exercise session. While a more scientific method may be to account for each joint's action, doing so would become unwieldly in trying to sort out which exercises are best for which muscles—many muscles act on more than one joint. Those exercises listed are the ones that afford maximum potential for the corresponding muscle(s) to grow. Variations of each are possible, of course, and may be suitable for any of several individual reasons. However, as a starting point for size increases, the major muscles and their basic exercises are generally best.

Exercises for the Chest

Barbell Bench Press

For maximum isolation of the upper and lower pectorals, a wide grip (forearms perpendicular to the ground in the lowered position) and elbows out from the sides is best. Improved isolation for the upper (clavicular) chest or lower (sternal) chest can be achieved by lowering the bar to the upper or lower chest, respectively. Other muscles synergistically involved include the anterior deltoids and the triceps, both of which are activated to a greater degree by narrowing the grip and drawing the elbows closer to the sides during the movement. **(Photos on next page.)**

Dumbbell Bench Presses

This is a common variation of the barbell bench press, and is used when synergistic and stabilizer muscles are in need of strengthening or development. The requirement of having to balance the heavy dumbbells during the movement activates these smaller muscles and assists in laying a foundation of greater pressing strength. The fact that you cannot bench as much weight in this exercise as you can with regular bench presses is due to the fact that much effort is spent in stabilizing the unyieldly dumbbells.

Dumbbell Flyes

Flyes are at the top when it comes to isolating the pectorals maximally. Arm (tricep) strength is left out completely, except for some synergism from the biceps. Owing to the strict isolation achieved, much intensity is lost with this movement—lesser weight can be used—and is not the exercise of choice for strength building. It is a good supplemental exercise for the pectorals, however.

98

MUSCLES USED IN DUMBBELL FLYES

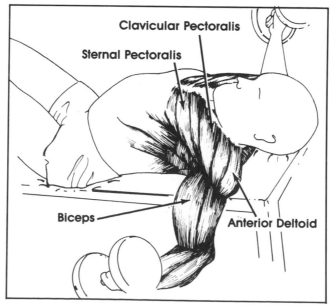

Clavicular Pectoralis

Sternal Pectoralis

Biceps

Anterior Deltoid

Cable Flyes

The effects achieved from this variation are generally identical to those achieved from dumbbell flyes. The advantage is that full contraction is made possible by being able to cross over. Because of this advantage, it is an excellent exercise and belongs in any body-builder's training program. No other basic chest exercise allows this kind of maximum contraction capability. **(Photo below left.)**

Incline Bench Presses

Inclines are designed to maximize upper chest development by stricter isolation. Variations include dumbbell inclines and cable in-clines, both of which have the advantages spoken of in the previous three exercises. For most bodybuilders, the bench angle of incline should be between 15 and 30 degrees. Above and below these angles there will be less emphasis on the upper pectoralis and more on the shoulders and lower pectoralis, respectively. The same precautions regarding elbow position and grip width apply here as in regular bench presses. **(Photo below right.)**

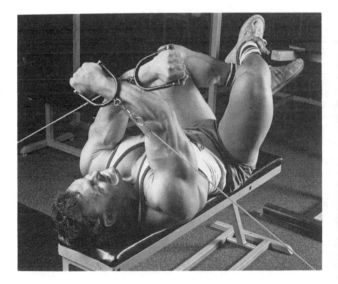

Decline Bench Presses

To achieve maximum isolation of the lower (sternal) pectoralis, declines work best. As with inclines, common variations include dumbbell or cable options. The most efficent angle of decline appears to be in the vicinity of 20-25 degrees for most people. Above or below this angle will selectively involve the latissimus dorsi or the clavicular pectoralis, respectively. Again, grip width and elbow position are the same as in regular bench presses.

100

Low Cable Crossovers

Using the lower cables on the cross-chest cable apparatus, begin with your arms in line with the cables, and pull them across your chest to a position in front of your face. This upward pull activates the clavicular pectoralis as well as (or perhps better than) conventional incline bench presses or incline flyes. Added benefit can be achieved by fully contracting the upper pectorals by crossing the arms in front of you (not shown here). Diminished leverage makes this an extremely difficult exercise, and much intensity is lost. Nonetheless, it is an excellent exercise because of the greater contraction possible and the isolation achieved. **(Photo below left.)**

High Cable Crossovers

As was the case with low cable crossovers, great isolation can be achieved for the sternal portion of the pectorals by pulling the handles down and across the chest to a position in front of the belly. Crossing over affords greater contraction capabilities, and therefore an excellent adjunctive exercise for chest development. **(Photo above right.)**

Pec Deck Exercise

This is an exercise rapidly becoming a favorite in many spas across the country because it is easy to do and safe. It also happens to be an excellent means of achieving a good balance between intensity and isolation for the entire pectoral structure. Machines that allow the user to do each arm separately also afford greater contractile range.

102

Dips

Notice the amount of stretch being placed on the pectorals of Tim Belknap in this picture. This exercise should be listed as a "compound" exercise since many muscles are involved—triceps, latissimus dorsi, anterior deltoids, and pectorals. However, it is a favorite of many body-builders for chest development particularly in the sternal portion, but must be done from an extremely low dipping position to be effective.

103

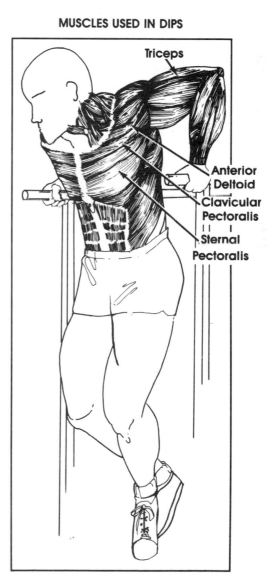

MUSCLES USED IN DIPS

Triceps

Anterior Deltoid

Clavicular Pectoralis

Sternal Pectoralis

Exercises for the Shoulders

Front Dumbbell Raises

104

Bending sideways first, the dumbbell is raised at arm's length to a position in front of the face. Then, after lowering the dumbbell, bend to the opposite side and repeat the motion with the other dumbbell. The purpose of bending to the side first is to more effectively isolate the anterior deltoid. Performing front raises from an erect position forces the anterior deltoid to pull at an oblique angle to the path of the dumbbell, rendering the movement less efficient.

MUSCLES USED IN DUMBBELL RAISES

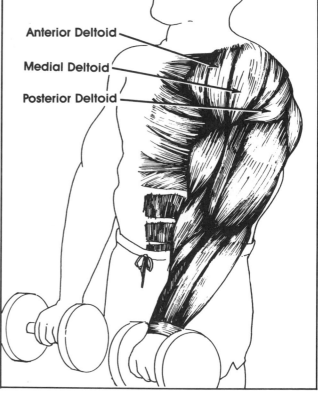

Anterior Deltoid

Medial Deltoid

Posterior Deltoid

Incline Dumbbell Raises

This is another extremely effective anterior deltoid exercise. The anterior deltoid is first placed at maximum stretch before the dumbbells are lifted, thereby improving the extent of contraction—the distance over which overload is applied, being greater, improves the quality of overload.

105

Seated Presses behind the Neck

All pressing movements overhead are really compound movements (involving more than one muscle group), but this exercise is a favorite of bodybuilders for both shoulder (mid-deltoid) development and serratus anterior development. The serratus are visible from the front, in the costal area below the pectorals, but they sweep around the torso and under the scapulae to insert along the medial border of these flat bones. Their function is to rotate the scapulae upward during the pressing movement as well as to hold the scapulae against the dorsal ribcage surface. The purpose for sitting down is to prevent unwanted backward lean, thereby improving the isolation on the delts and serratus.

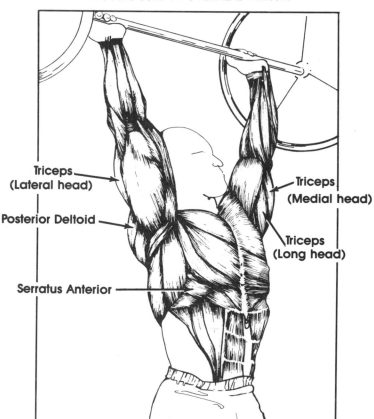

MUSCLES USED IN OVERHEAD PRESSES

Triceps (Lateral head)

Posterior Deltoid

Serratus Anterior

Triceps (Medial head)

Triceps (Long head)

Dumbbell Lateral Raises

Laterals effectively isolate the middle deltoids when done directly to the sides. Raising the dumbbells slightly in front or in back can also allow for development of the anterior or posterior deltoids, respectively while maintaining the central focus (overload) on the middle deltoids. The dumbbells needn't be raised above head height, as the deltoids stop working at that point—they have, by then, fully contracted—and the serratus anterior take over.

107

Cable Lateral Raises

Fast becoming the favorite middle deltoid exercise for bodybuilders, this movement simulates the popular lateral dumbbell raises, but is an improvement in that the starting position allows for maximum stretch on the middle deltoid before the upward movement begins. The beginning position should be from the opposite side of the torso and in front to completely stretch the middle deltoid. The cable is pulled directly upward from the side to a position even with the top of the head.

Exercises for the Back

Lat Pulldowns

The most effective way to perform pulldowns is in front—not in back as is popularly believed. The reason is that the insertion angle of the latissimus dorsi is most closely approximated by pulling to the front. Furthermore, the rhomboids and trapezius must work unnecessarily when pulling to the back, thereby "robbing" the lats of maximum effect due to the synergy afforded by the traps and rhomboids. The elbows should be drawn downward toward the sides for the pulldowns to be most effective. The bar needn't be pulled downward beyond the level of the chin, and backward lean should be avoided as doing so emphasizes muscles of the back other than the lats. A wide grip is necessary to minimize bicep involvement. **(Drawing on next page.)**

MUSCLES USED IN LAT PULLDOWNS

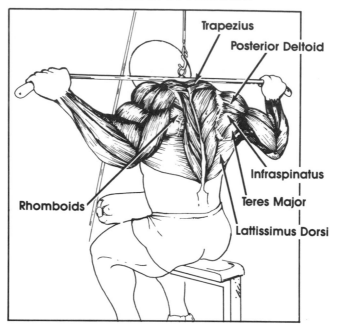

110

Trapezius

Posterior Deltoid

Infraspinatus

Teres Major

Lattissimus Dorsi

Rhomboids

Chip-Ups

This exercise is identical in all details to lat pulldowns. Weight can be added to increase the overload by wearing a power hook attached to a lifting belt, or by wearing a dip-chin belt with weights hung on it.

Long Cable Pulls

Also called **low rows,** this movement emphasizes lat development. It is perhaps the most often improperly performed exercise in all of bodybuilding, as too much low back or arm involvement is common. To perform the exercise correctly, the lats are placed at extreme stretch by leaning forward maximally to begin. Then, the lats are activated by drawing the elbows rearward and continuing the motion by drawing the elbows toward the sides. The involvement of the biceps and erectors of the lower back should be incidental during the finish of the movement. Emphasis should be given to drawing the shoulders backward as the elbows are forced backward and close to the sides to maximize latissimus action.

111

Close-Grip Chins

This movement should simulate, in all details, the action performed during long cable pulls. The body moves, however, rather than the handles. Added overload is possible through the use of a power hook or a dip-chin belt. Concentration is required to minimize bicep involvement in favor of lat contraction.

112

One-Arm Rows

Here is yet another exercise that should as closely as possible simulate the movement of low rows. A difference here, however, is that the lats are not prestretched as they are with close-grip chins or low rows. In addition to latissimus action, there is considerable posterior deltoid, infraspinatus, and teres major activity (just posterior to the shoulder joint). Because of these factors, I consider this exercise to be more fruitful as an upper back exercise than for latissimus development.

113

MUSCLES USED IN ONE-ARM ROWS

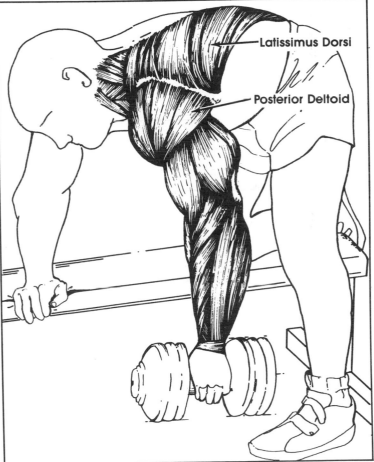
Latissimus Dorsi

Posterior Deltoid

Bent Rows

Like one-arm dumbbell rows, this exercise is ideal for upper back development. Since both arms act together, disallowing torso rotation as is the case with one-arm rows, it is also an excellent means of achieving rhomboid development as well as trapezius II and III development. Of course the lats are also involved.

114

Pullovers

The short-run gains with this movement emphasize lat development. The long-run gains, however, can be more important if you persist with the exercise long enough. The intercostal muscles are strengthened over time, pulling the ribcage outward slightly, thereby deepening the chest. To be effective, the dumbbell (or barbell) must be lowered far enough to achieve maximum stretch of the lats and intercostals.

115

Inverted Flyes

Trapezius II, III, and IV; rhomboids; teres major; and infraspinatus all assist the posterior deltoids in this movement. All are overloaded sufficiently to derive adaptive stress. The lats are kept out of this movement for the most part because the elbows are raised laterally rather than being kept close to the sides as is the case with one-arm rows.

Bent Rows with Wide Grip

The effect of this movement is identical to Inverted Flyes. Greater intensity can be achieved with this exercise than that possible with inverted flyes, however, and is therefore, a favorite upper back, strength-building exercise. Care must be taken to concentrate on minimizing action of the biceps in hoisting the weight.

117

Stiff-Leg Deadlifts

There is no better exercise for developing the lower back muscles, as great intensity is possible. The movement also strongly involves action from the glutei and hamstrings, all so-called "erector" muscles. The movement should be performed from a short platform to maximize erector prestretch, and the knees should remain slightly unlocked to avoid knee trauma.

118

MUSCLES USED IN STIFF-LEG DEADLIFTS

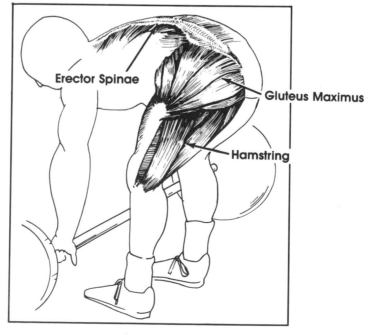

Erector Spinae

Gluteus Maximus

Hamstring

Back Extensions

Back when bodybuilders were foolish, unsophisticated, or both, this movement was called back hyperextensions. Going beyond a position of full extension (torso straight—not leaning back) invites undue trauma to the vertebral discs in the lumbar region of the spine. The erector spinae are stretched by leaning forward, and then are effectively isolated as the torso is drawn upward to a position of extension.

119

Good Morning

Good Night! would be a more appropriate name for this killer exercise! It is rather effective for low back development, but severely traumatizes the cervical spine (the bar rests heavily upon the neck). Still, because it affords great intensity (much weight can be handled), it remains an effective and popular exercise. I suggest using a thick padding on the bar to protect the neck.

Shrugs

The Trapezius muscle is subdivided into four distinct heads, called **I, II, III, and IV.** This upward shrugging of the shoulder movement effectively overloads Trapezius I, with some effect felt by Trapezius II, and less for Trapezius III and IV. Bent rowing movements are more effective for Trapezius III and IV.

Quarter Shrugs

This slight modification in normal shrugs (which are most effectively used for Trapezius I) maximizes the stress upon Trapezius II and III, while bending forward more fully involves Trapezius III and IV. To perform this exercise correctly, simply incline forward slightly, and shrug straight upward to a position located slightly behind the back of the head.

122

Exercises for the Midsection

Crunches

This movement is the Cadillac of all abdominal exercises. It completely isolates the target muscle. Great intensity is also possible owing to the great leverage advantage. As heavy a weight as can be held should be used here, and the movement is quite simply to try and touch your pelvis with your ribs—"crunch" the torso.

123

MUSCLES USED IN CRUNCHES

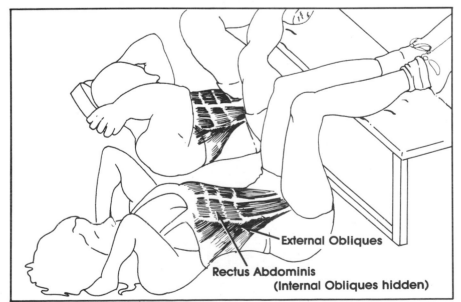

External Obliques

Rectus Abdominis
(Internal Obliques hidden)

Reverse Crunches

To more effectively stress the lower aspects of the abdominal muscle, some bodybuilders prefer to do a modified version of leg raises. Performing this movement as it is pictured here effectively eliminates action of the hip flexors (thereby protecting the lower spine from trauma stemming from action of the iliopsoas muscle), and maximizes the abdominal overload. To increase the tension, simply place the slant board at a more acute angle. The full movement is depicted here—do not lower the knees past the point shown as hip flexors become involved. Also, avoid ballistically swinging the knees upward, as this defeats the purpose of the movement. The object is to try and touch the ribs with the pelvis by ''crunching'' the torso.

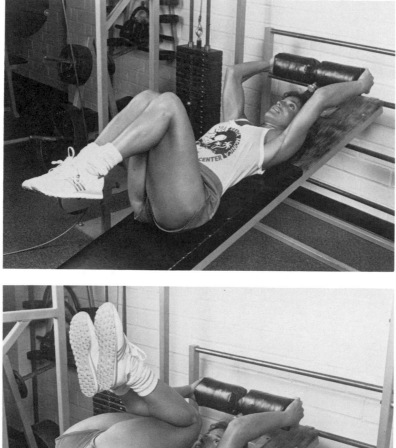

Roman Chair Sit-Ups

This is perhaps the most popular abdominal exercise, although I fail to see why. The combination of crunches and reverse crunches will give more development than any other abdominal exercise, and without the low back trauma received from Roman Chair Sit-Ups. Furthermore, greater range of movement by action of the abdominals is possible with crunches than it is with this exercise—unless you bend all the way back to a position where your head is near the floor, but that most certainly would be inviting serious lower back problems.

125

Side Bends

This is perhaps the most effective exercise for developing the obliques. Since current judging trends in bodybuilding require a wasp waist, however, many bodybuilders shy away from this exercise for fear of getting a thick waist. However, by strengthening the obliques, your waist will appear trimmer, not more bulky, because the tighter obliques will have a "girdle" effect. Long years of side bends may cause overdevelopment, but performing them occasionally (say, once a week) will insure a tighter and trimmer looking midsection. An important side benefit afforded by this exercise is that the quadratus lumborum is strengthened, thereby making the lumbar spine far less susceptible to injury.

Trunk Twists

Stabilizing the pelvis by sitting down, simply twist to and fro using a full-range movement. The movement is not what tightens the obliques; the act of stopping and restarting in the opposite direction offers the stress for development. The movement is merely ballistic with little in the way of adaptive stress. Maybe someday someone will invent a device to allow stress to be applied through the full range of the torso twisting motion. That would be desirable. As it stands, this exercise is marginally effective as a waist trimmer.

Exercises for the Legs

Squats

Squats are the king of all leg exercises, make no mistake! By squatting with an erect torso, great overload stress is placed on the quadriceps. There are many quad exercises—most of them good—but none allow the kind of growth and intensity as do squats. Putting a block of wood under the heels may be required to maintain an erect posture during the exercise.

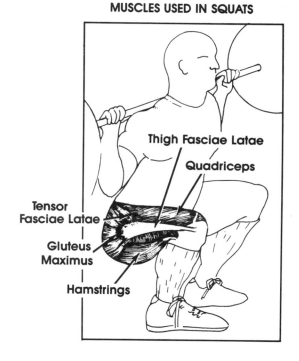

MUSCLES USED IN SQUATS

Thigh Fasciae Latae

Quadriceps

Tensor Fasciae Latae

Gluteus Maximus

Hamstrings

Side Lunges

This exercise is a killer, but quite effective in getting at the quadriceps from a slightly different angle. Of course, less weight must be used, limiting the intensity factor, but as an adjunctive exercise for leg development, it is excellent.

129

Front Lunges

This exercise is also quite effective as an adjunctive leg exercise, and is quite popular for not only quadricep development, but also used rather successfully in tightening the glutei.

Leg Extensions

If it's isolation you want, then this is the definitive quad isolation movement. The intensity factor prohibits this from being totally effective as a size builder—far less weight can be handled here than with squats. Many bodybuilders claim that its major benefit is derived from its ability to give greater separation (cuts) in the quads, but I personally think this is nonsense. Cuts are more readily observable when extensions are performed because the leg is tightened at full extension; that doesn't signal greater effect, however, and squats will give as much growth (and therefore separation) as any leg exercise. Nonetheless, it's an excellent adjunctive exercise, especially when the back or knees are sore and squats can't be done effectively. **(Photos and drawing on opposite page.)**

MUSCLES USED IN LEG EXTENSIONS

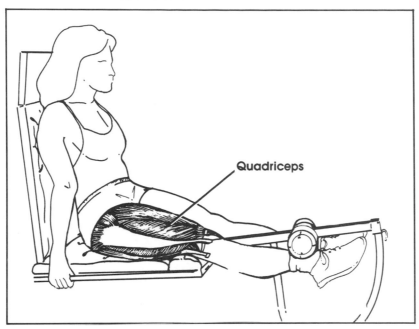

Quadriceps

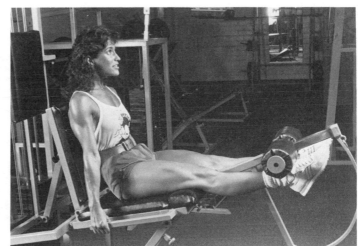

Hack Squats (Upright or Inclined)

Hack squats are an excellent means of achieving good isolation on the quadriceps and at the same time maintaining good intensity. Their true value is as an adjunctive exercise when the back is too tired or sore to allow full squats. Many bodybuilders feel that greater mass around the knee (the teardrop look for the vastus internus muscle) is more easily acquired with hack squats, but this claim seems spurious—regular squats are, in my opinion, just as stressful or moreso to all aspects of the quads as are hack squats.

Leg Presses

Here is yet another variation of squats, done upside down. It's a valuable adjunctive exercise that most appropriately is performed when regular squats can't be done effectively (for lack of a spotter or when the back is tired or sore).

133

Standing Leg Curls

The hamstrings are involved in regular squats and the many variations of squats. But, their action appears to be minimal, and are best developed by isolating them with this exercise. The leg bicep is a weak point with most bodybuilders, and this is the sure-fire cure for that problem.

134

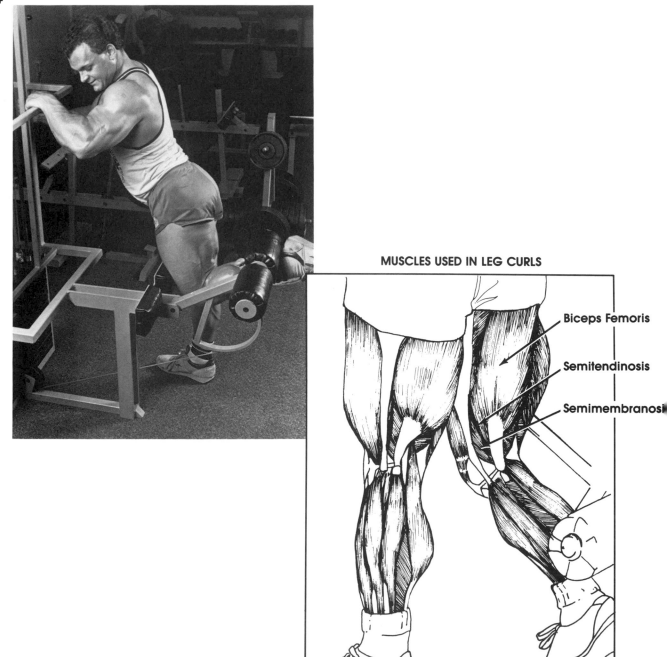

MUSCLES USED IN LEG CURLS

Biceps Femoris

Semitendinosis

Semimembranosi

Prone Leg Curls

This movement is functionally identical to standing leg curls, and whichever one you do is largely preferential.

Cable Kicks (Inward, Outward, and Backward)

Here is a group of leg exercises that has long been underrated in their effectiveness. The adductors (inner thigh), abductors (outer thigh and gluteus minimus), and the generally neglected hamstring muscles that act upon the hip joint as well as the knee joint are all activated with these exercises—and rather effectively I might add. These movements have been popular with women bodybuilders, but are rarely performed by their male counterparts, though the reason for this escapes me. They would, I'm sure, prove just as effective for men as they have done for women.

136

Donkey Raises

This exercise is so named because one's partner rides, in donkey fashion, while the other exercises the gastrocnemius. It's a very effective calf exercise, as all fibers of the muscle (including those spanning the knee joint) are fully stressed, because of the bent-forward, locked-knee position. Full-range movement is more productive than shorter partial movements.

137

Standing Calf Raises

By altering foot positions (inward, outward, etc.) bodybuilders feel that different effects are received by the medial and lateral heads of the gastrocnemius. I personally don't think that this is true to a measurable extent, considering the origin and insertion points are not altered by foot placement. What may change, however, is the extent of synergy afforded by the flexor digitorum longus (under inner gastroc), and the tibialis posterior (deep under the gastroc and soleus). These muscles all are involved in plantar flexion of the foot at the ankle joint, as is the gastrocnemius. However, they all have different origins and insertions, and differential foot placement involves each to a greater or lesser degree during plantar flexion (as performed with toe raises).

138

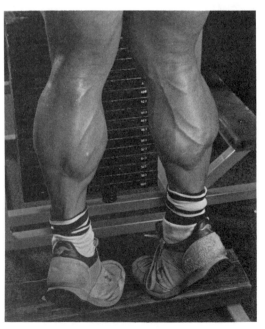

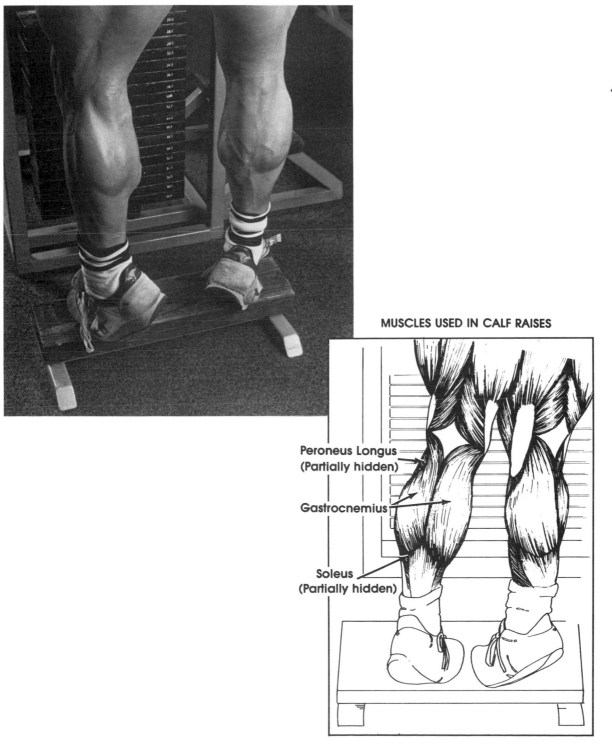

MUSCLES USED IN CALF RAISES

Peroneus Longus
(Partially hidden)

Gastrocnemius

Soleus
(Partially hidden)

Seated Toe Raises

This is the ''lazy man's'' calf exercise. No added benefit is derived by sitting down. In fact, much effect is lost because some fibers of the gastrocnemius span both the ankle and knee joints. And, sitting with knees bent gives the gastrocnemius too much slack for it to contract strongly. However, by disinvolving the gastrocnemius to the extent that it cannot afford the greatest amount of moving force in toe raises, you have effectively maximized the overload received by all of the other plantar flexors (listed under the description for standing calf raises). Thus, seated calf raises are a must for all bodybuilders.

Exercises for the Arms

Curls

The most basic and popular bicep exercise, barbell (or E-Z curl bar) curls is simple and straightforward. Just curl the weight up to the chest by flexing the biceps. The bends in the bar allow for a more comfortable grip, and it also keeps the contracting muscles' tendons in line with the insertion point on the radius bone to make the direct overload on the muscles more effective.

Alternate Dumbbell Curls

This is a popular variation of regular curls, and the freedom of movement afforded by individual dumbbells (relative to the tendon's points of insertion) make it a superior exercise for maximizing overload.

142

Concentration Curls

By resting the elbow against the inside of the thigh, you can effectively eliminate synergy from occurring, and make the movement more difficult because of the greater isolation on the biceps. Also, doing one arm at a time affords you with perhaps a bit more concentrated effort than having to concentrate on two biceps at one time.

MUSCLES USED IN CONCENTRATION CURLS

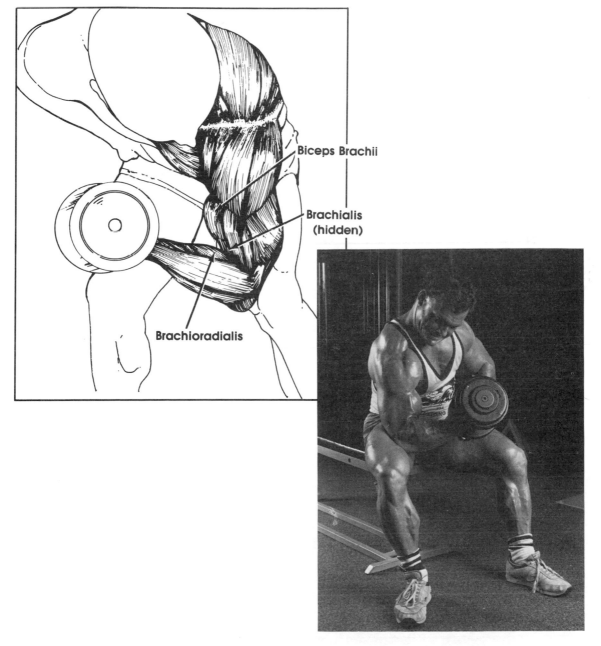

Biceps Brachii

Brachialis (hidden)

Brachioradialis

Preacher Curls

So called because the movement is performed over the edge of a lectern-style platform, great isolation is achieved on the biceps. It's quite similar in effect to concentration curls, except that most typically both arms are exercised together. They needn't be—a single dumbbell works just as well. An E-Z curl bar is most often used rather than a straight bar because it's more comfortable and also because the radius bone of the forearm (into which the biceps' tendons attach) is at a more natural position for maximizing overload.

Supine Cable Curls

This is an interesting variation of regular curls, affording you with very good action on the short head of the bicep. The long head is kept somewhat slack because of the forward position of the arm. The short head of the bicep is the inner head, and spans only the elbow, whereas the long head spans both the elbow and shoulder joints, and is located on the outer aspect of the upper arm.

145

Reverse Curls

This exercise is not as effective for the biceps as regular curls because the radius bone is situated in extreme pronation causing the insertion point of the bicep to be misaligned with the muscle. However, it does appear to be a more conducive position from which to exercise the brachioradialis muscle, which is an assistant flexor of the elbow and located on the outer aspect of the lower arm. **(Photo below left.)**

Cross-Chest Hammer Curls

This is a compound exercise, since it involves several muscles. The brachioradialis, the biceps brachii, the anterior deltoid, and the pectorals all are forced into extreme contraction using this unusual movement. Furthermore, the resting arm, because of the held-aloft position, forces the middle deltoid to work statically. It is a great premeet warmup (or pumping) exercise because of its diverse actions, but probably not a very effective training exercise. **(Photo below right.)**

Triceps Cable Push

This is perhaps the most effective all-around exercise for the triceps because of the extreme stretch that the long heads of the triceps are subjected to (the long head is the inside head of the triceps, and spans both the elbow and shoulder joint). The medial and lateral heads of the triceps only act upon the elbow.

Triceps Presses

Keeping the elbow joint fixed in space while the extension movement is performed ensures that there will be little synergy afforded by the pectoralis or anterior deltoid muscles. However, improperly performed, this becomes a modified close-grip bench press and is in such circumstances only marginally effective for the triceps (or anything else) because of the lost isolation.

Triceps Pushdowns

This exercise involves the lateral and medial heads of the triceps primarily. The long (inner) head also works, but since it is not prestretched as was the case with triceps cable push, it offers only moderate primary force during the movement, leaving the bulk of the work up to the two outer heads.

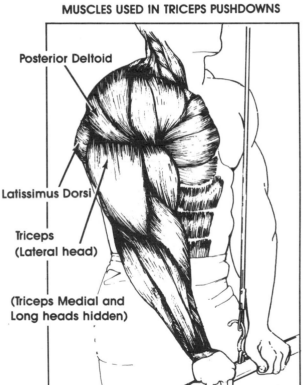

MUSCLES USED IN TRICEPS PUSHDOWNS

Posterior Deltoid

Latissimus Dorsi

Triceps
(Lateral head)

(Triceps Medial and
Long heads hidden)

French Presses

Similar to triceps cable pushdowns, this exercise forces the long head of the triceps into action very effectively. However, there is a common danger of allowing the elbows to drift away from their intended position against the side of the head, thereby allowing deltoid and serratus anterior muscles to synergistically assist in moving the load.

150

Weighted Dips between Benches

This is a popular exercise done primarily for triceps, but a great portion of the stress is also borne by the anterior deltoids. It is therefore classified as a compound exercise, and is only marginally effective as a triceps builder.

Forearm Curls

The flexor muscles of the wrist and fingers are located in the anterior portion of the forearm, with long tendons passing through the wrist and down into the fingers. Forearm size is achieved with this exercise; be careful to allow the fingers to initiate the flexion movement and the wrist to finish it. This will ensure that all the flexors located in the forearm are stressed.

Reverse Forearm Curls

To stress the extensors of the wrist, all of which are located in the posterior aspect of the forearm, perform the movement depicted here. It is a sister exercise to regular forearm curls, and complete forearm development requires that both be done.

PART III
DRUGS AND NUTRITION IN BODYBUILDING

155

No topics are more hotly debated and misunderstood among body-builders than are drug use and nutrition. These are the topics discussed in this portion of the book. My approach is one of the openmindedness and candor. I do not believe that a simple thing like controversy should disrupt the free exchange of ideas and philosophies in any sphere of life. That megadosing in a dietary sense as well as in a pharmaceutical sense has become a real problem in bodybuilding is common knowledge. Not so common, however, is a rational under-standing of the factors involved in proper dietary and pharmaceutical practices. In fact, you could say that this kind of knowledge is totally UNcommon!

I do not pretend to have the answers to your questions, and I frankly doubt that many others do either. So, accept what is written in this section as a discourse on some acceptably scientific information—you can then proceed to answer your own questions. Particularly those revolving around ethical issues.

15
DIET AND NUTRITION

A calorie is a measure of heat. The amount of heat that is required to
raise the temperature of one gram of water one degree Centigrade
equals one calorie. The caloric content of food is measured by how
much heat that food can produce when burned. The food we eat is
ultimately converted to glycogen and stored in the muscle to be
burned during activity. The enzymes located in the muscle, primarily in
the tiny organelles called mitochondrion, spoken of in Part I, are what
effects this metabolism of calories.

The specific speed at which calories are utilized by a person at rest
(e.g., lying in bed) is called basal metabolic rate (BMR). It is determined by age, sex, body size in area, body weight, and endocrine
function. The average BMR for a 20-year-old man is approximately
equal to 1 calorie per kilogram of body weight for a 24-hour
period. For the average 20-year-old woman, it is approximately .9
calories per kilogram of body weight for the same period of time.

Bodybuilders older than 30 will, due to a relatively lower BMR, use
fewer calories per day, but the differences are probably minimal if we
can assume that most bodybuilders are relatively similar in daily
activity levels. If such is not the case, then adjustments must be made
accordingly in one's computations.

Many charts and graphs have been generated in recent years that illustrate how many calories are burned when engaging in various types of sports or activities. The average person has come to believe that the significance of these tables is in the choice of activities, assuming that engaging in more strenuous activities requiring more calories is the best thing to do. The true significance is in the computation of one's caloric requirement per day, rather than using the table as a guide to activity. The table presented on page 159 is designed specifically for powerlifters and bodybuilders.

To understand the significance of the caloric expenditure table, let's look at an example. A bodybuilder weighing 181 pounds will, in a normal workout consisting of 5 sets of 8 reps with rest periods of about 5 minutes between sets, approximate the following calorie expenditure during the course of his workout:

Time per set	2 minutes
Average Heart Rate (HR) during set	150 BPM
Average HR during recovery	
1st minute	125 BPM
2nd minute	110 BPM
3rd minute	100 BPM
4th minute	98 BPM
5th minute	96 BPM
Average for 7-minute period × 118.43 BPM	
Average HR for entire hour of workout × 118.43	

By simple interpolation procedures, we can determine the approximate number of calories expended during the hour workout:

Calories burned during set	24.00
Calories burned during recovery	
1st minute	9.00
2nd minute	6.83
3rd minute	6.00
4th minute	5.80
5th minute	5.60
Average caloric requirement for 7-minute period × 57.23 BPM	
Average caloric requirement for 1-hour workout × 490.54	

Compare this figure to the number of calories expended during the course of an hour of running at a pace of one mile every seven minutes. The same 181-pound bodybuilder will burn in the vicinity of 1,000 calories.

Approximate K Calories per Minute Expended per Body Weight and Heart Rate for Men and Women

Body Weight lbs. & Sex	Heart Rate 100	125	150	175
100 M	2.75	5.75	8.75	11.75
F	2.48	5.18	7.88	10.58
114 M	3.75	6.75	9.75	12.75
F	3.38	6.08	8.78	11.48
123 M	4.0	7.0	10.0	13.0
F	3.6	6.3	9.0	11.7
132 M	4.5	7.5	10.5	13.5
F	4.1	6.75	9.45	12.15
148 M	5.0	8.0	11.0	14.0
F	4.5	7.2	9.9	12.6
165 M	5.5	8.5	11.5	14.5
F	5.0	7.65	10.35	13.05
181 M	6.0	9.0	12.0	15.0
F	5.4	8.1	10.8	13.5
198 M	6.5	9.5	12.5	15.5
F	5.9	8.55	11.25	13.95
220 M	7.25	10.25	13.25	16.25
242 M	8.0	11.0	14.0	17.0
275 M	9.0	12.0	15.0	18.0
300 M	10.0	13.0	16.0	19.0
325 M	11.0	14.0	17.0	20.0

If we can assume that our example bodybuilder is relatively sedentary other than during workout, he will burn about 1,980 calories at a basal activity level, and an average of an additional 500 calories just walking around, studying or other light activities during the day:

Basal requirement	1980
Workout requirement	490
Normal activity requirement	500
Total caloric requirement for a 24 hour period	2970

Reference to the table on page 160 will assist you in deriving a more accurate caloric requirement for your supplemental activities during the day.

The estimated energy requirements are based on a 154-pound man. You must add or subtract 10 KCalories per hour per activity for

Estimated Energy Requirements of Selected Physical Activities*	
Physical activity	Estimated K cal/Hour
Badminton	400
Basketball	560
Billiards	235
Bowling	215
Bull Session	90
Calisthenics	200
Cleaning	185
Cycling (easy pace)	300
Disco	450
Driving a car	180
Golf	340
Lying quietly (awake)	80
Playing cards	140
Racquet Sports	870
Running (7-minute mile)	950
Sitting in class	90
Sleeping	70
Studying/Reading	105
Swimming (steady pace)	500
Walking (normal pace)	180
Walking up stairs	300

*Adapted from: Krotee, M. and Hatfield, F. "The Theory and Practice of Physical Activity", Kendall/Hunt Pub.: Dubuque, 1979.

each 5 pounds that your own body weight deviates from the 154-pound baseline. Remember that due to differences in age, sex, and body area and weight, one's KCalorie count is only an estimate.

Determining your approximate daily caloric requirement will assist you in establishing a sound dietary regimen, particularly when you wish to gain or lose weight.

Weight Control

Fats, carbohydrates, and protein are the chief sources of calories in our diet. The calories one derives from these three sources are burned differentially. The energy to burn one gram of fat is 9.45 KCalories, carbohydrate 4.10 KCalories, and protein is 5.65 KCalories.

It becomes immediately obvious that fat constitutes a very concentrated form of energy, with carbohydrates being the lowest. It takes about 3,500 calories to make one pound of adipose tissue, with ingested fat being required in lesser amounts than protein or carbohydrates, respectively (by actual weight).

Gaining Weight

The human organism cannot biosynthesize muscle tissue any faster than about one half to one pound per week, with the lighter weight individual nearer the one half-pound figure, and the heavier individual nearer the one-pound figure. This gives us a clue as to how rapidly we can expect to gain muscle weight.

By computing your normal caloric requirement per day, and adding between 250 and 500 calories per day to your diet, thereby creating a positive caloric balance, it is possible to gain weight at the specified rate. However, there is virtually no way under the sun to ensure that the additional calories will be used in the manufacture of muscle tissue except through weight training. Weight training must accompany the increased caloric intake, or the result will surely be that fat (in the form of adipose tissue) is added to the body. The obvious moral of that story is that, in no case, should a bodybuilder strive to gain muscle weight faster than one pound per week.

If our 181-pound bodybuilder wishes to progress to 198 pounds, without sacrificing hardness, he must gain 17 pounds of muscle. This will take 17-34 weeks to accomplish, with the best guess being closer to a 30-week period since only the big men of our sport can gain muscle at the maximal rate, owing to their greater size. The table below is a

The Recommended Number of Weeks Required to Gain Muscle Weight

Present Lean Body Weight (in pounds)	5	10	15	20	25	30
100	10	20	30	40	50	60
120	9.5	19	28.5	38	47.5	57
140	9	18	27	36	45	54
160	8.5	17	25.5	34	42.5	51
180	8	16	24	32	40	48
200	7.5	15	22.5	30	37.5	45
220	7	14	21	28	35	42
240	6.5	13	19.5	26	32.5	39
260	6	12	18	24	30	36
280	5.5	11	16.5	22	27.5	33
300	5	10	15	20	25	30
Increase in Pounds Desired	5	10	15	20	25	30

guide for bodybuilders wishing to gain weight. It is assumed that the bodybuilder is on a very efficient bodybuilding program and a nutritionally sound diet.

Should you gain weight at a faster rate than what the table specifies, beware that the increase is not coming in the form of body fat. The tabled figures appear not to apply to women because of the difference between the sexes in their capacity to metabolize muscle mass. The male hormone **testosterone** is the key here, and the average woman's testosterone level is considerably lower than the average man's. The woman bodybuilder is well advised to constantly monitor her percentage of body fat during periods of positive calorie balance, to ensure that muscle is being laid down rather than fat. In fact, this is a good idea for men as well.

Losing Weight

Losing weight presents different problems than gaining weight. A **negative caloric balance** must be achieved in order to lose weight. That is, one must take in fewer calories each day than the number being burned. However, the problem is not so simplistic as counting calories. As with gaining weight, weight training is the real key to ensuring that the weight lost is not from the muscle mass, but rather from the fat.

For example, studies indicate that during the course of a fasting diet, 65% of the weight lost in the first ten days was lost from muscle breakdown, and only 35% from fat. It is necessary to maintain the integrity of muscle mass during the weight-loss period. The only way known to science to accomplish this is to train with weights during the period of negative caloric balance. The weight training program most desirable is a bodybuilder's regimen, and daily exercise is essential to ensure that a minimal amount of muscle is lost.

Again, as in gaining weight, the range of 250-500 calories per day is appropriately applied to this process. One should not attempt to lose more than half to one pound of fat per week. To attempt to lose weight at a faster rate exposes the bodybuilder to the danger of losing lean body mass as well.

Percent Body Fat

I have talked quite a bit on the subject of percentage of body fat. The question must have entered the average reader's mind as to what constitutes an appropriate level of body fat. The answer is that it varies from individual to individual, depending on factors such as one's yearly climate, activities engaged in, hereditary factors, and others. However, for male bodybuilders, there is rarely any sound reason for percentage of body fat to exceed 10% and for women 14%.

Clinicians recommend that adult men stay within the 10%-14% range, and women between 14%-18%. However, these figures are recommended as "good," and in no way apply to the serious body-builder.

163

Body Fat	Classification
1% – 10%	athletes – men
9% – 14%	athletes – women
10% – 14%	fit adult male
14% – 18%	fit adult female
20%	average men
20%	average women
20% – 22%	clinical obesity – men
25% – 28%	clinical obesity – women
28% – 30%	chronic obesity – men
35% – 38%	chronic obesity – women

These classifications are the recommended levels of body fat for the clinical interpretation of one's percentage of body fat. Chronic obesity is the point at which clinicians refer to the condition as a "disease."

Some fat is needed by the body. Fat acts in the insulation of nervous tissue, padding between the joints, lubrication for the space between skin and muscle, and padding from some of the vital organs. No one can live without some fat. However, far less is needed than the normal person generally carries.

Over the past 15 years, I have measured every college student entering my weight training classes, and have found that the averages are at the clinical obesity levels for both men and women at the beginning of the semester. By the end of the semester, the averages dropped to 15% and 21% for men and women respectively.

These fat losses are probably attributable to a number of factors—weight training, altered activity levels, changes in BMR, changes in diet, and changes in caloric intake.

Altering Basal Metabolic Rate

Earlier in this chapter, the notion was put forth that one's BMR controlled the speed with which calories were utilized. On numerous occasions, I have been approached by bodybuilders and other athletes who claimed that they couldn't gain weight (or lose weight) because their metabolic rate was too fast (or slow). We've all heard the same story. "I eat like a horse! Why can't I gain weight?" Or, I'm only eating one meal a day and stay away from all carbohydrates and fats! Why can't I lost weight?" Two problems manifest themselves in each of these examples. One is that the person is not eating in the right manner, and will be addressed in the next section of this chapter. The other involves the person's BMR. It can be altered, either up or down.

If one's goal is to gain weight, a reduction in BMR is called for, but only if there is a "problem" with gaining muscle weight. Under normal conditions (comprising the vast majority of cases), the bodybuilder wishing to gain weight can do so simply by following the guidelines in the previous section of this chapter. This method includes: (1) increasing caloric intake by 250-500 calories per day, (2) eating nutritionally sound meals, and (3) bodybuilding appropriately. With the "problem" gainer, the additional method of lowering BMR may be the step that'll make all the difference. It involves simply being lazy. The only calories being burned each day, other than those burned at workout, should be burned at the basal level. Engage in no other activity requiring increased caloric expenditure.

In the cattle industry, animals raised for meat are penned in rather than allowed to range, thereby reducing their caloric expenditure— and the amount of food that has to be supplied to them for growth. It seems odd that athletes haven't learned the same techniques as the cattle ranchers!

In Part I, I presented the mechanisms involved in muscle size, along with the functions of each. It was learned that the mitochondria are responsible for the oxidative functions of the body cell, and also contained a majority of the enzymes that collectively were associated with energy production. As it happens, increasing mitochondrial mass is the most efficient method of increasing one's BMR. Any method—be it running, swimming, cycling, or weight training—that increases one's heart rate to 80%-85% of one's maximum heart rate for about 15 minutes three times weekly is sufficient stress to force this adaptive process to occur. With the application of such stress, the enzymes responsible for metabolizing calories increase in concentrations, and the mitochondria increase in size and number. The result is that, whereas one's BMR may have been such that 1,900 calories were burned each day at a basal level, as many as 2,400 calories can now be burned!

**Recommended Heart Rates During
Exercise Designed to Alter BMR***

Age	Maximum Heart Rate	80-85 Heart Rate For Athletes
20	200	160-170
22	198	158-168
24	196	157-167
26	194	155-165
28	192	154-163
30	190	152-162
32	189	151-161
34	187	150-159
36	186	149-158
38	184	147-156
40	182	146-155
45	179	143-152
50	175	140-149
55	171	137-145
60	160	128-136
65	150	120-128

These heart rates are based on an average resting heart rate of 72 for men and 80 for women. To find your true maximum heart rate, use the rule-of-thumb of subtracting your age from 220.
*Adapted from: Bailey, C. "Fit or Fat?" Houghton Mifflin, 1978, pg. 24.

The recommended method of achieving this BMR change for bodybuilders is not running. Running tends to be traumatic to the joints, especially the hips, knees, and lower spine. The bodybuilders suffer enough trauma under the iron! I recommend swimming, or, if a pool isn't available, try stepping up and down from a bench for the 15-minute period—far less trauma to the joints results from this method than from running, since the full weight of the body is not constantly hammering away at the joints. Cycling is also a good method.

Exercising in this manner more than the recommended 3 times weekly for 15 minutes each time is not recommended for bodybuilders. First, it'll rob you of normal training time and energy, and second, the gains will not be worth the effort. On page 166 is a graphic example of the kinds of gains one can expect by exercising more or less than the recommended amount.

One can clearly see that beyond three times weekly the returns rapidly diminish, and become less and less with time. The trauma of the training will, at these higher levels, become counterproductive, and should only be engaged in by endurance athletes.

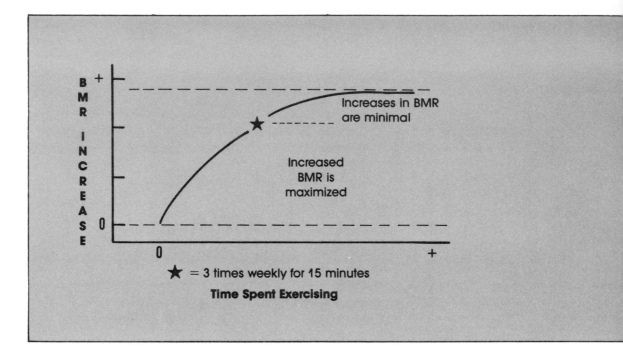

How to Eat

How one eats plays a vital role in whether fat is deposited, food is utilized maximally, and whether digestion is completed. Research dealing with rats (and later verified with human subjects) yielded some startling results. Rats were put on a diet consisting of fewer calories than they needed each day. Group one ate their calories in one big meal, and group two ate as they pleased all day. Both groups had the same number of calories given them daily. Thus, both groups lost weight. However, when returned to normal diets, the "one big meal" rats gained more weight than the rats that ate a little all day. Studies were made of the enzymes associated with the deposition of adipose tissue in both groups of rats, and it was discovered that the "one big meal" rats had ten times the concentration of these enzymes than did the other rats. The result was that they had "adapted" to the stress of famine by gearing their bodies to store fat. The same happens to humans who eat only one meal per day. In their efforts to lose weight, they are actually making themselves more prone to put on fat!

The human body interprets famine (fasting) as stress, even if the fast is only 23 hours long. It adapts to this type of stress by increasing the fat-storing enzymes. However, there's another reason that is more mechanical in nature. The body cannot accept all of the calories taken in in one big meal, and consequently must eliminate them or store them. The enzymes then take over in the storing process.

Eating four or five smaller meals (consisting of the same total number of calories per day as the large meal) will allow full assimilation of the calories, and therefore full utilization—no fat will be stored. This concept is important for all bodybuilders, including those wishing to gain weight, lose weight, or stay the same but get harder.

Another problem with how one eats is common in our society. That is the habit of snacking. Research tells us that complete digestion and assimilation of one meal takes roughly 3-4 hours. The digestive process involves a step-wise procedure of various enzymes and gastric juices being introduced as they are needed. As one completes its job, the next comes as the first is dissipated. And so forth until digestion is complete enough for assimilation to occur. However, if one snacks during this process, the original digestive enzymes are forced to enter, thereby negating the effectiveness of the ones already there. Digestion stops for the original food, and it often sits in the stomach for up to 72 hours before ever getting digested enough for assimilation! This kind of problem definitely interferes with one's attempt at gaining weight, since much of the food never gets into the system when it's needed. Further, it interferes with losing weight since much is stored in fat.

For the bodybuilders then, or anyone else for that matter, the appropriate method of eating appears to be to eat three meals minimum per day (preferably four or five). Each meal should be equally sized, calorie-wise, and spaced about 4 hours apart. No snacking is the general rule—not even milk. If you count calories, this method of eating is by far the most efficient method of gaining muscle weight, losing fat weight, or remaining the same weight while increasing muscle mass.

What to Eat

So far in this chapter, I have explored some of the factors involved in how much to eat and how to eat. I have also discussed a few ideas as to how to increase caloric expenditure. I will now direct my discussion to the problem of **what** to eat. As noted previously, one's chief sources of calories are fats, carbohydrates and protein. These sources for calories are derived from the food we eat. Foods are subdivided into groups as follows:

- Meat and egg group
- Bread, whole grain and cereal group
- Vegetable and fruit group
- Dairy group

Each of these food groups have fats, carbohydrates, and proteins in them to varying degrees. It, therefore, is advisable to include all of the food groups in each meal you eat. Further, this mixing of food groups happens to be the only method of ensuring that you are deriving the proper balance of vitamins, nutrients, and minerals from each meal. More will be said on this subject later.

168

Fats

One of the gravest injustices performed by the self-proclaimed "experts" on nutrition from among folks in our sport is that fat is bad, and should be avoided like the plague. In fact, fat is a vital part of sound nutrition. Fats are the richest sources of vitamins A, D, E, and K. The three so-called **essential** fatty acids, arachidonic acid, linoleic acid, and linolenic acid are essential to life itself. They cannot be manufactured by the body, and therefore must be derived from other sources.

The average American will consume in the neighborhood of 45% of his or her daily calories in the form of fat. It is an exceptionally concentrated source of calories, requiring roughly 9.45 Kcal of energy to burn one gram of it, in comparison to the 5.65 Kcal and 4.1 Kcal for proteins and carbohydrates.

Most of the best protein sources are high in fat content, so it is extremely difficult, if not impossible, to derive one's daily ration of protein without also getting plenty of fat. Fat comes in two forms, **saturated** and **unsaturated.** The American Medical Association informs us that about 23% of our daily calories should be derived from fats. This, assumedly, is due to the fact that much of the fat Americans consume comes in the form of saturated fats, which are not as desirable as are the unsaturated fats. The reduction from the common 45% to the recommended 23% should come from the saturated fats—the highest source of which is animal fats (meats, cheese, milk, and eggs). However, recent research emanating from Harvard University informs us that ingesting skim milk, for example, actually reduces the amount of cholesterol in the blood by as much as 17%. In fact, eggs, a high source of cholesterol, were once said to be bad for us in excessive amounts due to the cholesterol level. Eggs also have much lecithin, which, like cholesterol, is a "cousin" to the fatty acid family. Normally occurring lecithin aids in the breakdown to cholesterol such that it can be taken up by the cell and used as energy, rather than depositing on the arterial walls in the form of plaques.

It appears that, if one's diet consists of fats dervied from natural sources (unrefined and untampered with), that the body will accept and use them without problem. This is especially true if one's diet includes little sugar.

The best sources of fats are vegetables (unrefined, fresh oils), fish, nuts and seeds, dairy products, and eggs. Animal flesh is marbled with much saturated fat, and should be only a limited source of fats.

Since the weight training athlete rarely ventures into the aerobic pathway for energy, less fat is needed in his or her diet than might be the case for the average person or an athlete engaged in long distance training. It is therefore recommended that bodybuilders limit their fat intake to roughly 15% of the daily calories taken in.

Carbohydrates

Carbohydrates are formed by various combinations of carbon, hydrogen, and oxygen molecules. The three basic classifications of carbohydrates are **monosaccharides** (simple sugars, or glucose), **disaccharides** (sucrose), and **Polysaccharides** (starches).

Carbohydrates comprise the major portion of any nutritionally sound diet, with the recommended allowance for a bodybuilder being in the vicinity of 60% of his or her daily caloric requirement. The major source for muscular contraction during anaerobic activity (such as lifting) are carbohydrates. There has been much contradictory advice coming from our soothsayers and self-proclaimed experts on nutrition about carbohydrates. Closer scrutiny of the differences in the forms of carbohydrates is the answer.

There are, as indicated, three types of carbohydrates. There is a great deal of difference between these types of carbohydrates. While all types ultimately become glucose, a simple sugar, they do so at different rates. The complex carbohydrates become blood glucose very slowly, while the simple sugars like table sugar, milk lactose, and maltose, become blood glucose very rapidly. The simple sugars are actually a form of "predigested" sugar, and cause too rapid a change in blood sugar levels. All forms of horrors have been associated with the consumption of simple sugar, ranging from inability to utilize cholesterol to hypertension and even propagation of criminal tendencies! The FDA, a very conservative organization normally, was quoted as saying that if they knew 50 years ago what they now know about sugar, it would have been banned from the grocery shelves as a deadly poison!

Suffice it to say that it is the complex carbohydrates—in the form of vegetables, fruits, whole grains, and nuts—which are most desirable in one's diet, for they not only form the major source of energy, but also have many of the nutrients everyone needs. The so-called "starch" foods, like potatoes, corn, pasta, and the like are unduly scorned upon also. Sources such as these are also high in many nutrients, and both are good sources of fiber, which aids in the digestive process and in bowel regularity.

To illustrate the extent of differences between types of carbohydrates, let's look at a single kernel of corn. In England, nutrition experts used actual enzymes from a human digestive tract to break a corn kernel down into its component parts. It was found that 12% of the kernel was indigestible, being comprised of cellulose, hemicellulose, and lignin. Most people have noticed that kernels appear in feces; it is the outer layer of the corn, the roughage, that they see. The remainder of the corn's inside portion is comprised of sugars such as glucose, fructose, and sucrose, and also of starches. Taken as a whole, corn is much like all other cereal grains in that it is a relatively complete source of carbohydrates. Some of the benefits of deriving one's carbohydrates through such a source are:

- the roughage tends to reduce caloric value of the food
- the roughage gives some protection to the digestive tract
- the hard-to-chew roughage tends to discourage overeating
- necessary vitamins and minerals are derived as nature intended— together
- the simple sugars in the whole grains add some taste to the food, but are delayed from entering the bloodstream too quickly

If the average American (and especially athletes) were to limit their carbohydrate intake to complex forms of the food source, rather than eating so much refined sugar and sweets, the ingestion of carbohydrates would present no problems at all. Nutritionists and exercise physiologists recommend that people derive about 65% of their daily calories from carbohydrate sources. However, in light of new research indicating athletes' need for more protein, bodybuilders should limit carbohydrate intake to roughly 50%-60% of the daily calorie allowance.

Protein

Americans have been bombarded with slogans that fats and carbohydrates are fattening. Protein represents the only other calorie source. So, it is a natural conclusion that we should eat more protein, and less of the other two. This is, as has been pointed out already, totally erroneous. Calories are calories! And the body needs all three sources.

170

The generally accepted level of protein intake is about 15%-20% of one's daily calories. However, what kind of protein? Protein comes in an array of assimilability levels. Eggs are roughly 96% assimilable because they have a very equitable balance of the **essential amino acids** available. All other sources of protein are graded on assimilability according to that of eggs—eggs, then, are the standard by which all protein sources are judged. Milk is next highest, with an assimilability ratio of about 60%. Next comes the meats, ranging near 40%. Vegetables vary up to about 15% at best.

The assimilability ratio describes the extent of available amino acids that have been labeled **essential.** They are called such because they cannot be biosynthesized in the body. No single meal is worthwhile to eat, except for the calories, vitamins, and minerals derived from it, unless it has all of the essential amino acids. The protein content is literally wasted otherwise. Mixing foods often will ensure that all of the essential amino acids are derived in one meal, and that's desirable.

So, when the FDA recommends that the average person consume 15% of his daily calories from protein sources, you should ask "Which sources?" If 15% of your daily calories are derived from incomplete protein sources, this will normally necessitate consuming many more calories of protein foods than 15%. For example, if one's sources of protein are in the form of milk and meat (milk is 60% assimilable, and meat is 40% assimilable), the complement of these incomplete sources will generally tend to increase the assimilability ratio to something well above that of either when taken separately.

It is said that the average bodybuilder should take in about ¾ grams of protein per pound of body weight. This seems reasonable, but again, be sure that your protein is complete. This rule of thumb will generally average out to roughly 25%-30% of the bodybuilder's calorie intake being derived from protein sources, with a considerably smaller amount of those proteins being totally usable.

To summarize, the following ratios of calorie sources are recommended for bodybuilders in heavy training: fat (15%), carbohydrate (50%-60%), and protein (25%-30%).

Endurance athletes are well-advised to ingest a higher percentage of carbohydrates, as they are a more efficient calorie source. The same may be said of fats. Bodybuilders need slightly more protein for muscle reparation and muscle growth, but certainly not in excessive quantities advocated by our resident soothsayers.

Eating more protein causes formation of a highly toxic ammonia in one's system called **urea.** This urea must be excreted, and subsequently places a strain on the liver and kidney.

16
VITAMINS AND MINERALS

Nutrition is still an infant science. The incredible complexity of the literally thousands of biochemical interactions that occur every moment of your life promises to keep it that way—infantile.

That is not to say, however, that many of the biochemical functions of vitamins and minerals haven't been explored. Nor is it to say that some good, solid research information isn't available in assisting bodybuilders in their quest for superior nutritional advantage. The scope of this book prohibits an in-depth accounting of all of the various functions that are known about vitamins and minerals insofar as bodybuilding interests are concerned. However, some of the more noteworthy facts available are presented here in both table form and in text.

What Are Vitamins?

There are 23 substances that are classified as vitamins which are believed to be important in human nutrition. All vitamins are organic food substances—they are found only in living things. All are vitally important for proper growth and health, and all must be derived from external sources—the body cannot manufacture them (with a few exceptions that are not noteworthy because of the miniscule quantities involved).

Vitamins have no caloric value. Neither do they comprise any of the various bodily structures. They aid in building them, however, and do so by way of their constituency in many metabolically active enzymes in the body. They help regulate metabolism, convert fat and carbohydrates into energy, and assist in forming all tissues of the body.

Human requirements for each vitamin vary depending upon several factors. A few important factors are: climate, age, sex, body size, genetic predispositions, level of health, use of various drugs and other substances, and level of activity. It is widely held that one's nutritional requirements for any of the vitamins can be met through proper eating. Such is not the case when you consider the complexity of the above factors and couple them with the fact that many of the processed and precooked foods we eat nowadays are often far less nutritious than what we are often led to believe.

However, excessive vitamin intake cannot be assistive in promoting health either—the excess vitamins are either stored or excreted. In fact some vitamins (fat-soluble ones) can be toxic in great quantities.

The fat-soluble vitamins (Vitamins A, D, E, and K) are measured in either international units (IU) or U. S. Pharmacopeia Units (USP). The water-soluble vitamins, including vitamins C, the B-complex vitamins, and the bioflavinoids are measured in milligrams.

What Are Minerals?

There are 17 substances that are in organic and inorganic combinations which are collectively referred to as the nutritional minerals. Cumulatively they comprise approximately 5 percent of the human body (by weight). The functions of minerals in growth and health are voluminous—catalysts in biological reactions, bones, teeth, hair, all bodily tissues, nerve impulse, heart and muscle vigor, hormonal and fluid balance, digestion, and mental functioning are but a few of their functions. All of the 17 minerals must be supplied in the diet—the body cannot manufacture them.

The only minerals for which nutritional requirements have been established are calcium, iron, iodine, and phosphorus. The so-called "macro-minerals" (present in large quantities in the body) are calcium, chlorine, potassium, phosphorus, sodium, magnesium, and sulfur. They are traditionally measured in milligrams because of their abundance. However, the rest of the essential minerals are measured in micrograms because only "traces" of them are found in the human body (hence the name "trace minerals").

It is important to note that a deficiency in any one of the essential minerals causes the others to be relatively useless despite their abundance in the body. The biological functions of minerals are all interrelated to a large degree, and all must be supplied together. As with vitamins, the tremendous complexity of interactions and functions of the essential minerals makes it difficult to pinpoint exact daily requirements. The same factors that dictate vitamin requirements (age, sex, activity, etc.) are operative with the minerals. Moreover, normal intake of food appears to be somewhat less than an adequate insurance that your requirements are being met. Supplementation is therefore as advisable with minerals as with vitamins.

Bodybuilders' Vitamin and Mineral Requirements

Misguided nutritionists loudly protest that athletes in heavy training need not engage in "megadose" vitamin or mineral therapy. Just as loudly voiced are the opinions of the vitamin and mineral pushers—the manufacturers and distributors—who have financially vested interest in ensuring that the myth of megadose requirements is indeed justified.

So, who is right? In my humble opinion, neither of these two extreme opinions are justifiable, neither from practical experience nor from scrutiny of the research literature.

The factors which tend to support the notion that supplementing is advisable for championship-bound bodybuilders are as follows:

- Many of the drugs and other non-drug preparations that bodybuilders use to enhance anabolism (muscle development) often cause a corresponding increase in vitamin and mineral requirements.
- Many of these same substances cause certain vitamin and mineral balances to skew, necessitating supplements.
- The very act of strenuous (and stressful) training under loads that mortal man was not designed to bear are known to increase the nutritional needs of bodybuilders beyond what increased caloric intake can provide and still allow the bodybuilder to maintain a body fat ratio that is low enough to justify the title of bodybuilder.
- The devitaminizing and demineralizing effects of prolonged shelf life, soil depletion, additives, pesticides, bleaching, precooking under intense or prolonged heat, and processing, all but ensure that ingested foods will be less than nutritionally adequate.

The Best Sources of Nutrients for Bodybuilders

Carbohydrates
Whole grains
Fruits
Vegetables

Fats
Margarine
Vegetable oils
Whole milk and milk
  products
Nuts and seeds

Protein
Meats, fish, and poultry
Soybean products
Eggs
Milk and milk products
Whole grains

Vitamin A
Liver
Eggs
Yellow fruits and
  vegetables
Dark-green fruits and
  vegetables
Whole milk and milk
  products
Fish-liver oil*

Vitamin B^1
Brewer's yeast
Whole grains
Blackstrap molasses
Brown rice
Organ meats
Meats, fish, and poultry
Egg yolks
Legumes
Nuts

Vitamin B^2
Brewer's yeast
Whole Grains
Blackstrap molasses
Organ meats
Egg yolks
Legumes
Nuts

Vitamin B^6
Meats
Whole grains
Organ meats
Brewer's yeast
Blackstrap molasses
Wheat germ
Legumes
Green leafy vegetables
Desiccated liver*

Vitamin B^{12}
Organ meats
Fish and pork
Eggs
Cheese
Milk and milk products

Vitamin B^{13}
Root vegetables
Liquid whey

Biotin
Egg yolks
Liver
Unpolished rice
Brewer's yeast
Whole grains
Sardines
Legumes

Choline
Egg yolks
Organ meats
Brewer's yeast
Wheat germ
Soybeans
Fish
Legumes
Lecithin*

Folic Acid
Dark-green leafy
  vegetables
Organ meats
Brewer's yeast
Root vegetables
Whole grains
Oysters
Salmon
Milk

Inositol
Whole grains
Citrus fruits
Brewer's yeast
Molasses
Meat
Milk
Nuts
Vegetables
Lecithin*

Laetrile
Whole kernels of
  apricots, apples,
  cherries, peaches,
  and plums

Niacin
Lean meats
Poultry and fish
Brewer's yeast
Peanuts
Milk and milk products
Rice bran
Desiccated liver*

**Para-Aminobenzoic
Acid**
Organ meats
Wheat germ
Yogurt
Molasses
Green leafy vegetables

Pangamic Acid
Brewer's yeast
Rare steaks
Brown rice
Sunflower, pumpkin,
  and sesame seeds

Pantothenic Acid
Organ meats
Brewer's yeast
Egg yolks
Legumes
Whole grains
Wheat germ
Salmon

Vitamin C
Citrus fruits
Rose hips
Acerola cherries
Alfalfa seeds, sprouted
Cantaloupe
Strawberries
Broccoli
Tomatoes
Green peppers

Vitamin D
Salmon
Sardines
Herring
Vitamin D-fortified
  milk and milk products
Egg yolks
Organ meats
Fish-liver oil*
Bone meal*

175

The Best Sources of Nutrients for Bodybuilders (Continued)

Vitamin E
Cold-pressed oils
Eggs
Wheat germ
Organ meats
Molasses
Sweet potatoes
Leafy vegetables
Desiccated liver*

Vitamin F
Vegetable oils
Butter
Sunflower seeds

Vitamin K
Green leafy vegetables
Egg yolks
Safflower oil
Blackstrap molasses
Cauliflower
Soybeans

Bioflavonoids
Citrus fruits
Fruits
Black currants
Buckwheat

Calcium
Milk and milk products
Green leafy vegetables
Shellfish
Molasses
Bone meal*
Dolomite*

Chlorine
Table salt
Seafood
Meats
Ripe olives
Rye flour
Dulse*

Copper
Organ meats
Seafood
Nuts
Legumes
Molasses
Raisins
Bone meal*

Fluoride
Tea
Seafood
Fluoridated water
Bone meal*

Iron
Organ meats
   and meats
Eggs
Fish and poultry
Blackstrap molasses
Cherry juice
Green leafy vegetables
Dried fruits
Desiccated liver*

Magnesium
Seafood
Whole grains
Dark-green vegetables
Molasses
Nuts
Bone meal*

Chromium
Corn oil
Clams
Whole-grain cereals
Brewer's yeast

Cobalt
Organ meats
Oysters
Clams
Poultry
Milk
Green leafy vegetables
Fruits

Manganese
Whole grains
Green leafy vegetables
Legumes
Nuts
Pineapples
Egg yolks

Molybdenum
Legumes
Whole-grain cereals
Milk
Liver
Dark-green vegetables

Phosphorus
Fish, meats, and poultry
Eggs
Legumes
Milk and milk products
Nuts
Whole-grain cereals
Bone meal*

Potassium
Lean meats
Whole grains
Vegetables
Dried fruits
Legumes
Sunflower seeds

Selenium
Tuna
Herring
Brewer's yeast
Wheat germ and bran
Broccoli
Whole grains

Sodium
Seafood
Table salt
Baking powder and
   baking soda
Celery
Processed foods
Milk products
Kelp*

Zinc
Pumpkin seeds
Sunflower seeds
Organ meats
Mushrooms
Brewer's yeast
Soybeans

*Denotes the supplemental form.

Vitamin Requirements & Supplement Availability

Vitamin	Supplement Availability	RDA	Recommended for Bodybuilders*
A (IU)	fish-liver oils carrot oil lemon grass Vit. A palmatate** Vit. A acetate**	5000	up to 25,000
B^1 (thiamine) (mg)	yeast or rice bran thiamine hydrochloride** thiamine chloride** thiamine mononitrate**	1.2	up to 100
B^2 (riboflavin) (mg)	yeast or bran riboflavin**	1.5	up to 60
B^6 (pyridoxine) (mg)	yeast or bran pyridoxine hydrochloride**	2.0	up to 150
B^{12} (cobalamin) (mcg)	yeast or rice bran termentation concentrate cobalamin cyanocobalamin	3.0	up to 500
B^{13} (orotic acid)	orotic acid	—	unknown
Biotin (mcg)	yeast D-biotin**	300	300
Choline (mg)	soybeans yeast choline bitartrate**	900	900
Folic Acid (mg)	yeast pleroyglutamic**	0.4	up to 5
Inositol (mg)	soybeans corn or yeast	1000	1000
Laetrile	apricot kernels amygdalin	—	1 gram each meal (max)
Niacin (mg)	yeast or bran niacinamide** nicotinic acid** niacin**	16	up to 100

Vitamin Requirements & Supplement Availability (Continued)

Vitamin	Supplement Availability	RDA	Recommended for Bodybuilders*
Pantothenic acid (mg)	yeast calcium D-pantothenate**	10	up to 100
Para-amino-benzoic acid (PABA) (mg)	yeast para-aminobenzoic acid**	—	up to 100
Pangamic acid	apricot kernels pangamic acid** calcium pangamate**	—	10 mgs.
C (ascorbic acid) (mg)	rose hips acerola cherries citrus fruits green peppers ascorbic acid**	45	up to 4000
D (IU)	cod liver oil irradiated ergosterol** calciferol**	400	up to 5000
E (IU)	vegetable oils wheat germ mixed tocopheryl d-alpha tocopheryl dl-alpha tocopheryls**	15	up to 1200
F	unsaturated fatty acids essential fatty acids	—	2-5 tbsps. vegetable oil per day.
K (mcg)	alfalfa menodoine**	500	500
Bioflavinoids (Vit. P)	rutin hesperidin flavons bioflavinoids in combination with Vit. C	—	Ingest in conjunction with Vit. C

* Your specific needs may vary from these recommendations. Factors such as age, sex, body weight, metabolic rate, and activity level make exact predictions impossible. It is assumed that you are in extremely heavy training.

** Synthetic source.

178

Mineral Requirements & Supplement Availability

Mineral	Supplement Availability	RDA	Recommended for Bodybuilders
Calcium (mg)	calcium lactate	800	up to 2,000
	calcium gluconate		
	calcium pantothenate		
	dolomite		
	bone meal		
	Di-cal phosphate**		
	eggshell calcium		
	oyster shell calcium		
	liquid calcium		
Chloride	(in combination with other minerals)	—	up to 10 grams
Cobalt	(in combination with other minerals)	—	up to 5 mgs.
Copper	copper sulfate	—	up to 5 mgs.
Chromium	(in combination with other minerals)	—	
Fluorine	(in combination with other minerals)	—	
Iodine (mcg)	sea kelp	110	up to 150
	sea salt		
	seaweed		
	potassium oxide**		
Iron (mg)	dessicated liver	10	up to 15
	yeast		
	molasses		
	ferrous fumerate**		
	ferrous gluconate**		
	ferrous sulfate**		
Magnesium (mg)	dolomite	350	up to 1,000
	magnesium palmatate**		
	magnesium sulfate**		
	magnesium gluconate**		
Manganese	manganese gluconate**	—	up to 10 mgs.
Molybdenum	(in combination with other minerals)	—	
Phosphorus (mg)	bone meal	800	up to 4,000
	calcium phosphate**		

Mineral Requirements & Supplement Availability (Continued)

Mineral	Supplement Availability	RDA	Recommended for Bodybuilders
Potassium (mg)	potassium gluconate** potassium chloride**	5,850	up to 10,000
Selenium	(in combination with other minerals)	—	
Sodium (mg)	sodium chloride**	6,900	up to 10,000
Sulfur	(in combination with other minerals)	—	
Zinc	zinc gluconate** zinc sulfate**	—	up to 1 mg.

* Your specific needs may vary from the tabled recommendations. Factors such as age, sex, body weight, metabolic rate, and activity level make exact predictions impossible. It is assumed that you are in extremely heavy training.
** Synthetic source

180

There are, of course several other scenarios which could be generated along similar lines. But, just as compelling are the reasons why megadosing isn't the answer. It's expensive, potentially harmful (in the case of certain vitamins and minerals, excessive intake can cause severe side effects), and it isn't necessary by all reasonable scientific evidence. Those who insist on megadosing do so generally because they feel that it offers them an insurance policy of sorts. So be it. I haven't the strength to argue these people down, and their lack of improved performance capabilities will, eventually, prove to them the error of their ways.

Elsewhere in this book, you will find information relating to the needs of bodybuilders during training, and particularly during the precontest phase insofar as achieving a balanced and nutritionally effective diet. The tables on pages 175-180 will give you the best natural sources of all of the vitamins and minerals, and describe not only the recommended daily allowances (RDA) published by the National Academy of Sciences, but the daily allowances typically recommended by nutritionists who have worked closely with bodybuilders and other hard training athletes. Implicit in this dual approach is the notion that if you are sedentary (as the average non-training American is), then the RDA listing may be appropriate providing you are of average age, size, activity level, metabolic rate, etc. But if you are in hard training, then you need more. It's really that simple. In other words, adjust your vitamin, mineral, and caloric intake as the variables described above dictate.

17
STOKING THE BODYBUILDER'S FURNACE

Years ago, when the Egyptians dominated the Olympic weightlifting scene, their dietary habits were incorporated into the training regimen of the rest of the world. When the Japanese won the team honors in swimming, it was learned that an important component of their training diet consisted of spinach. The result? A mighty surge in the futures market for spinach sales. Such examples are endless in the world of sport, and bodybuilders are perhaps more commonly prone to dietary excesses than most other athletes.

Are you confused about how you as a serious bodybuilder can improve your performance and appearance through sound nutritional practice? No doubt you are, and it's not surprising considering the shroud of myths and misinformation regarding how best to fuel your body for peak performance. The subject of dietary requirements for bodybuilders has been written about almost ad nauseum, yet the confusion remains.

Why?

I suspect that, in large measure, confusion over how best to fuel your body stems from the fact that you have listened to many different opinions on diet, and in the process have neglected to look at the **similarities** in these dietary regimens—all you have seen are the differences! Let's discuss some of the more important questions that often arise in bodybuilders' conversations relating to proper diet. The important similarities will become clear and will help you toward your own bodybuilding goals.

What Should a Bodybuilder's Sources of Energy Be Comprised Of?

Bodybuilders, like everyone else, burn three nutritive dietary fuels: **fats, carbohydrates,** and **protein. Alcohol** and **simple carbohydrates** (i.e., table sugar) are non-nutritive fuel sources dear to the hearts of many, but they should not be used by the serious bodybuilder in anything but small quantities.

During periods of high fat consumption together with low carbohydrate intake, a by-product of incomplete fat metabolism, called **ketones,** is used as a fuel source. During all-out exercise, when oxygen is not in sufficient supply to the muscles, **lactic acid** begins to accumulate, and is used as fuel by the cell's mitochondria (the oxygen power plants inside muscle cells).

In What Proportions Should These Energy Sources Be Used by Bodybuilders?

There is some controversy surrounding the exact amounts of fats, carbohydrates, and protein bodybuilders should eat. The closest approximation can be determined from examining some of the effects of over- or underindulging in each. Most nutritionists generally recommend that the average person follow the "1-2-3 rule of thumb"—that is, twice as many calories from fats as from protein, and three times as many calories from carbohydrates as from protein. However, long years of experience, as well as some recent research evidence offered to bodybuilders from the scientific community, seems to indicate that a ratio closer to 2-1-3 would be more appropriate for protein, fat, and carbohydrate, respectively.

The particularly rigorous anaerobic nature of a bodybuilder's training precludes the need for greater amounts of fat, and increases the need for greater amounts of muscle-repairing and muscle-building protein.

I like to use an analogy to explain what happens when an improperly balanced diet is followed. Imagine yourself trying to light a log in your fireplace. The log, like fat, is a concentrated energy supply, and will not ignite easily. You then put some twigs under the log and try again. The twigs are like glucose (carbohydrates), igniting easily, thereby providing the impetus to light the log. To keep the log burning brightly and to prevent it from producing too much smoke (similar to how inefficiently burned fat produces ketones, a toxic substance that can be used as fuel when fat intake is too high and carboyhdrate intake is limited), continual use of kindling is required.

Bodybuilders, like weightlifters, sprinters, and other anaerobic (without oxygen) sport athletes, burn primarily glucose. Long-distance athletes burn primarily fat for energy, on the other hand. Glucose, like kindling, requires less oxygen, burns easily, and doesn't last long. Fat, like the log, burns longer (it's a more concentrated energy source), and requires more oxygen. This is precisely why bodybuilders need less fat in their diet than other athletes.

During periods of inactivity or rest throughout the course of a bodybuilder's day, however, fat becomes the primary source of energy. As much as 90% or more of a bodybuilder's energy is derived from fat during rest. During the workout, however, carbohydrates become the predominant fuel source, accounting for up to 70% or more of the fuel used for energy. This general ratio of fat/carbohydrate fuel source reverses itself as the length of a training session increases and also as the severity (intensity) of the training decreases. Long, submaximal training sessions, however, call for a better supply of complex carbohydrates for fuel.

Can't Protein Be Used as Fuel?

Yes, but only during periods of fasting. When a bodybuilder's carbohydrate and fat intake is too low, as it might be during precontest fasting, the energy needed to sustain his or her training efforts must come from someplace. Ingested protein is converted to glucose and used as fuel. However, since the brain is a voracious glucose user (up to 66% of all circulating glucose), the body then gears up for the fuel crunch by cannibalizing its own muscle tissue!

So, the foolish bodybuilder who reduces calories by eating a high protein/low fat/low carbohydrate diet is actually engaging in a self-defeating cycle. The reason so many bodybuilders feel dragged out, dizzy, or weak on such diets is that the glucose from the previous protein meal, together with the glucose that was converted from the breakdown of muscle tissue is used up rather quickly, thereby starving the brain of its fuel!

For any fitness enthusiast or serious bodybuilder, the only purposes to which ingested protein ought to be put are muscle growth and muscle reparation. When it is forced to act as fuel for energy, the path leading to destruction (literally) is being trod.

What Is the Best Way to Diet Down for a Contest?

184

Bodybuilders are finally getting the big picture! It used to be standard procedure for bodybuilders to "bulk-up" in the off-season, and then diet down for contests, using all manner of bizzare and counterproductive dietary methods. In the past few years, however, the more successful bodybuilders have learned that the best method is to remain within a reasonable distance of their competition body weight and to keep their precentage of body fat to a minimum by eating balanced meals and supplementing wisely. Then, just before the contest, they avoid any faddish diets and simply reduce their caloric intake a bit to bring their muscularity to a razor edge. At this stage of contest preparation, the bodybuilder's intake of fats, carbohydrates, and protein are generally kept at about the 2-1-3 ratio for protein, fats, and carbohydrates.

How Can an Obese Person Lose Fat?

The dietary regimen and training regimen for fat people wishing to trim down is quite different from the one recommended for the advanced bodybuilder—or from the average (slightly overweight) person, for that matter.

Fat people must, at all costs, avoid maximally taxing type exercises, such as those requiring greater than 80% effort. Vigorous exercise, you will recall, burns glucose, not fat! Slow, steady exercise at a pace near 60%-70% of maximum effort is best for the obese for two reasons: First, it burns fat, second, the exercise will create a slow return of the body's ability to mobilize fat for energy, and reduce the fat-depositing capacity that has been allowed to run rampant. Long periods of **moderate** exercise coupled with some serious calorie counting is the key for combating obesity.

Can the Average Person Benefit from the Bodybuilder's Dietary Regimen and Training Approach?

Most certainly! Bodybuilders are perhaps the fittest people on the face of the earth when you consider all of the various components of fitness—not just the typically referred to cardiovascular fitness. Their life-style of vigorous exercise, however, cannot be matched by the average person—it takes years of dedicated work to achieve this kind of fitness. The average person ought to include all four of the basic forms of exercise—stretching, aerobics, anaerobics, and sports activities—rather than engaging in the highly specialized training of the competitive bodybuilder. But the dietary regimen of bodybuilders is an excellent method of dieting for all fitness-conscious people. Again, however, the needs of some athletes, particularly those involved in aerobic sports such as running long distances, require greater amounts of fat in their diet because fat is a more efficient fuel source than what may be afforded by the bodybuilder's diet.

During explosive movements, and high intensity movements with short duration, muscle glycogen is the chief source of muscle fuel. The remainder of the fuel needed for this kind of energy output (about 30% of the total) is derived from free fatty acids in the blood (supplied by the mobilization of triglycerides—stored body fat) and blood-borne glucose.

Blood glucose is derived from the liver during periods when energy demands are not being adequately met by muscle glycogen stores or when glucose requirements are exceptionally high as it might be during prolonged aerobic training. Two different processes are involved in the manufacture of glucose by the liver—**glycogenolysis** and **gluconeogenesis.** The first process involves the breaking down of glycogen into glucose, and the second involves the manufacture of glucose from lactate or amino acids.

As bodybuilders, you should be aware that exceptionally long workouts require energy demands be met by the free fatty acids and intramuscular triglycerides— only initial energy demands during the first ten minutes of heavy training are met by intramuscular glycogen. The recommended 2-1-3 ratio of protein, fats and carbohydrates will give you all the necessary fuel to carry you through even the most grueling bodybuilding training regimen. The added benefit, of course, will be noted in the lowered body fat percentage over time.

Should This 2-1-3 Ratio Be Carried Right Up to the Day of the Contest?

For maximum contest appearance, in which vascularity, definition, and size maintenance are important, some last-minute alterations in this recommended bodybuilder's food ratio ought to be implemented.

The recommended sequence of precontest dieting can best be summed up with the following points:

- Reduce your caloric intake about 4-6 weeks prior to the contest to get your body fat level down to minimum levels.
- You should not have to vary from the recommended 2-1-3 ratio of protein, fat, and carbohydrate intake during this precontest calorie reduction.
- Neither should you have to lose more than 5-10 pounds—you should always be within striking range of being in top shape for contests year round.
- Engage in some mild aerobic exercise (such as bicycle riding) during the precontest phase of calorie reduction.
- One week prior to the contest, engage in a glycogen depleting (very exhausting and prolonged) exercise session such as cycling or running. This should involve about sixty to ninety minutes of such exercise.
- For the next three days, eat only protein and fat, leaving carbohydrates out of your diet to a large extent.
- The following three days should involve returning to a diet consisting of the recommended 2-1-3 ratio of protein, fats, and carbohydrates.
- During the last seven days, engage in no aerobic activities—just train with the weights for size, definition, and Iso-Tension posing, as the Weider Iso-Tension Principle proposes.
- As you did during the off-season and precontest phases of your training, continue to eat at least five or six meals per day, keeping them small, and counting your calories. You should not gain weight during the last seven days.

Following this regimen will ensure that on the day that it counts, the day of the contest, your body will possess the vascularity and definitive muscularity that is the hallmark of the champions.

18
ANABOLIC STEROIDS

The eminent Dr. James Wright in the September issue of **Muscle & Fitness** (1980), made the point that drug use for a normally healthy athlete may enhance his/her performance, but is doubtful whether those same drugs will make them any healthier. This, says Wright, is one of the principle values of sport. He goes on to make the point that in this day and age, sports have become more than merely a vehicle for promoting fitness and health (whether it be physical, mental, or social). Perhaps a fourth ethic is emerging, where the intent of sport is to win, but not at the expense of, or disregard for, truth (perhaps a reapproachment of the second and third ethical points of view). Wright ended his article by saying:

> In the interest of minimizing drug abuse and reducing the hazard to the user and society, it is our responsibility to educate readers about all potential effects, both desired and undesired, associated with these drugs. In other words, it is our responsibility to give them the truth."

The terms, "use," "misuse," and "abuse" have been used in clinical circles regarding drug administration. Generally accepted clinical definitions for these terms are as follows:

Drug use: When the intended or sought-after effect(s) of a drug are obtained with a minimum of hazard

Drug misuse: When a drug is taken such that the hazard is significantly increased

Drug abuse: When a drug is taken such that the hazard is greatly increased, or such that the individual is no longer capable of functioning normally or coping with his/her environment adequately.

188

So, the **modus operandi,** then, for this chapter is to point out prevalent methods of drug **use,** given the present state of the art and science. It should be clear that whether a bodybuilder uses, misuses, or abuses drugs, desired effects may be achieved—it is the undesired effects (hazards) that must at all costs be minimized. Practically any physician will tell you that the most efficient way to use drugs (for any purpose) is to get the most out of the least. This is often hard to do, and the undesired side effects must be minimized to a point where they pose no real threat to the individual.

Anabolic Steroids

In his book, **Anabolic Steroids and Sports,** Dr. James Wright has meticulously cited all of the relevant literature on the topics of what steroids are and how they work in athletes. It is not the intent of this chapter to duplicate the efforts of Dr. Wright. In his latest book, **Anabolic Steroids and Sports, Volume II,** all you ever wanted to know about steroids' effects in chemical structures, and factors influencing steroid effects can be obtained.

The intent of this chapter is to bring the scientific literature and practical experiences offered through case histories of steroid users to a practical and usable level. It is not the intent to assume a position for or against the use of drugs in sport—this is a decision which must be rationally approached by each individual personally and in consultation with his or her medical doctor.

To understand what anabolic steriods actually are, a few terms must be defined first. The word **metabolism** refers to all bodily functions involving the production of, maintenance of, or destruction of tissue and energy. The building processes (or **myotropic** processes) are referred to as **anabolism,** while the breaking-down processes are referred to as **catabolism.** Thus, **anabolic** effects, insofar as steroids are concerned, are those effects involving the synthesis of protein for muscle growth and reparation.

There are many different hormones in the body. Collectively, **hormones** are regulatory chemicals produced by various organs, glands, or tissues, whose purpose is to coordinate such bodily functions as growth, tissue repair, reproductive cycles, and other aspects of physical and mental processes. The male hormone **testosterone** has two primary functions. The first is to stimulate the development and maintenance of male secondary sex characteristics (such as facial hair, deep voice, the distribution and amount of body fat, and other characteristics associated with masculine features). This is referred to as the **androgenic** function of testosterone. The **anabolic** functions of testosterone include the development and maintenance of the characteristically larger musculature of males.

Thus, we can now define the term **anabolic steroids.** They are synthetically derived chemical compounds which mimic the anabolic effects of testosterone while, at the same time, minimize the androgenic effects. This minimizing of anabolic effects was accomplished by manipulating the structure of the basic hydrocarbon molecule of testosterone in various ways. The extent to which the anabolic-androgenic ratio has been altered is referred to as the **therapeutic index.**

Therapeutic Indexes of Anabolic Steroids

The traditional method used for establishing a therapeutic index for a synthetic anabolic steroid is to compare the growth of a rat's **levatorani** muscle with that of his **seminal vesicles.** The growth of the muscle is said to represent the anabolic effect of the test drug, while the growth of the seminal vesicles are representative of the androgenic effect. The standard against which the test steroid's effects are compared is the extent of growth stimulated by testosterone. Thus, if the levator ani muscle growth is twice that of the standard, and the seminal vesicle growth only half that of the standard, the therapeutic index is determined as follows:

$$2 \div \tfrac{1}{2} \times 4 \ (TI)$$

However, problems arise with regard to the usefulness of such an index. For example, if the test drug had four times the anabolic effect of the standard, and the same androgenic effect, the therapeutic index would be the same.

$$4 \div 1 \times 4 \ (TI)$$

Needless to say, test drug number one would be useful in cases where the androgenic effects needed to be minimal, whereas if the androgenicity of the drug wasn't a factor (and it almost always is), then test drug number two would be the choice since the anabolic effects are superior.

Additionally, there is little in the way of solid research evidence to indicate that therapeutic indexes of drugs calculated by animal studies are applicable to humans, be they patients, normal individuals, or athletes. And, lastly, even if there existed a table of therapeutic indexes derived from studies on humans, factors such as diet, training, variable drug doses, variable administration schedules, and (perhaps most importantly) inter- and intraindividual variability of drug response all but nullifies the usefulness of such indexes.

But they're all we have in the way of research findings. Most athletes tend to weigh the personal experience factor more heavily when choosing an anabolic steroid. The usefulness of the therapeutic index is, at this point, relatively meaningless for use by athletes using anabolic steroids. It should not be used as the sole determiner in steroid selection.

Steroid Protein Activity Index of Anabolic Steroids

One of the most important attributes of anabolic steroids is their ability to stimulate protein synthesis. This is accomplished partly by the fact that the body tends to "save" nitrogen (the primary constituent of proteins) when anabolic steroids are used. The extent to which a particular anabolic steroid causes nitrogen retention is known to be a reasonably good index of the protein metabolism capacity of the steroid. In other words, a good estimate can be derived as to a steroid's efficiency in promoting protein metabolism through the use of the SPAI (steroid protein activity index). It is computed as follows:

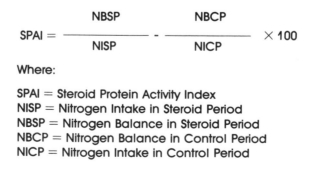

$$SPAI = \frac{NBSP}{NISP} - \frac{NBCP}{NICP} \times 100$$

Where:

SPAI = Steroid Protein Activity Index
NISP = Nitrogen Intake in Steroid Period
NBSP = Nitrogen Balance in Steroid Period
NBCP = Nitrogen Balance in Control Period
NICP = Nitrogen Intake in Control Period

Thus, the rate or extent of nitrogen retention during the time steroids are being used is compared to the extent of nitrogen retention during the period when no steroids are being used.

It appears that some use can be derived from the combined use of the TI and the SPAI. If both indexes are relatively high, then there appears to be reasonable cause to have a closer look at the drug—it may be that it will be the safest and most efficient for you, but it may be too that unwanted side effects are beyond what is tolerable for you as an individual—only careful experimentation can answer this question for you.

191

How Steroids Work

Once into the bloodstream via oral, pellet implant, sublingual, or injected routes, anabolic steroids find their way to individual muscle cells where they exert their activating influence on the genes responsible for protein synthesis. In much the same way that naturally occurring testosterone works, they physically attach themselves to specific receptor sites within the cell, and stimulate the DNA to direct the cell's ribosomes to manufacture greater amounts of protein.

Concurrent with the administration of anabolic steroids, however, there must be sufficient vitamins and minerals available via food intake or supplements. Many vitamins are thought to be synergistic with anabolic steroids (i.e., they "help" or "facilitate" the steroid in effecting protein synthesis). Too, there appears to be reason to believe

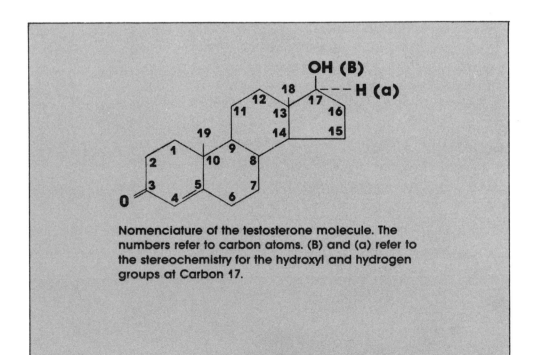

Nomenclature of the testosterone molecule. The numbers refer to carbon atoms. (B) and (a) refer to the stereochemistry for the hydroxyl and hydrogen groups at Carbon 17.

that a **need** must be present in the organism before protein synthesis will occur. The need is apparent in clinical use of steroids in cases such as anemia or malnutrition for greater protein synthesis. But in healthy athletes the need is **created** through extremely heavy training. Let me restate this point—anabolic steroids will be nigh unto useless in promoting increased strength or muscle size without proper nutrition, sufficient amino acids (protein), and extremely heavy, regular bouts of weight training. These points will be discussed again later.

192

Not all of the anabolic steroid molecules reach the cell receptor sites, however. Most float around in the bloodstream until they are broken down in 17-ketosteroids by the liver (hydralized), or broken down while in the bloodstream (changed to estrogens or aromatized). These by-products are believed to be responsible for many of the side effects of anabolic steroids, although in unknown ways. At any rate, to slow the rapid inactivation of the anabolic steroids by the liver, scientists soon discovered that the addition of an alkyl substituent at the 17th carbon position (see figure on page 191) of the steroid molecule greatly increased the life of the molecule. However, again, this alteration is also believed to be responsible for a number of the unwanted side effects often accompanying steroid use.

Reported Side Effects from Anabolic Steroid Use

By now, most athletes who have used steroids have heard of the side effects associated with the drug. Gym talk and steroid package inserts seem to be the chief source for such information, or—quite possibly more commonly—personal experience over years of self-administering the drug has attuned the user to the more personally unwanted effects.

Some of these hazards of steroid use are listed here, although in no particular order of import or severity.

Liver Function Alterations

Carbohydrate metabolism, protein metabolism, lipid (fat) metabolism, and the elimination, detoxification, or inactivation of substances such as urea, bacteria, hormones (e.g., anabolic steroids), and other noxious materials, are all functions of the liver. Lab tests to detect disruption of these functions will be discussed later in this manual. Among athletes using steroids, the long-term effects of such liver function disruptions are unknown; the short-term effects have proven to be minimal and reversible upon cessation of steroid use. However, toxic hepatitis can be brought about by the continued use of steroids and diuretics (amacide).

Cardiovascular System Impairment

Blood clotting factors are sometimes disrupted. The metabolism of glucose, triglycerides, and cholosterolis is impaired, potentially leading to atherosclerosis (plaque build-up in the arteries). Also, resting blood glucose levels and glucose tolerance can be reduced (dangerous for diabetics and prediabetics). Increased insulin secretion can contribute to atherosclerosis as well.

Another potentiating factor for atherosclerosis is the increased cortisol levels. Oral Steroids appear to render the liver relatively incapable of breaking cortisol down, thereby increasing the concentrations of cortisol in the blood. An interesting hypothesis related to this increased cortisol level is that, since cortisol is the body's major stress hormone, athletes are able to train harder. This may be the edge athletes report oral steroids to have over injectable steroids, enabling them to train harder and possibly make better gains in strength and size with oral compounds.

While blood readings on these factors return to normal following discontinuance of steroid use, the long-term effects of such changes remain unclear. In as much as cardiovascular disease is by far the leading cause of death in the United States, the effects that anabolic steroids have (directly and indirectly) on the cardiovascular system is seen by many to be the most serious and potentially hazardous of all the reported side effects.

Hypertension (High Blood Pressure)

Elevated blood pressure over a prolonged period is known to create a potential for a host of cardiovascular diseases. Anabolic steroid use is quite frequently accompanied by considerable increases in blood pressure. Fluid/electrolyte balance is though to be related to hypertension. Many athletes (perhaps a majority) report mild to severe edema (water retention) when on steroids. The exact nature of this side effect is not known, although it is speculated to be a result of the steroid's effect on the adrenal cortex.

Hormones secreted from the adrenal cortex play an important role in maintaining an equitable electrolyte balance in the body. As with blood and liver function, blood pressure readings usually return to normal upon discontinuance of steroid use, but the use of anabolic steroids over a long period of time remain a question. It may be that the increased body size causes the heart to work harder. Steroids are known to increase both potassium and nitrogen levels, which may increase blood pressure.

194

Reproductive Process Alterations

When steroids are administered via oral or injected routes, normally secreted testosterone is no longer needed in the same amounts. FSH (follicle stimulating hormone), which are secreted by the pituitary gland, are reduced when sufficient testosterone is present. The result is testicular atrophy and sperm count reduction.

In animals, prolonged FSH and ICSH reduction has been known to cause disruption in the ability of the pituitary gland to produce these gonadotropins. In any event, this effect, as well as the shrinkage of the testes and reduction in testosterone and sperm production, are reversible upon discontinuance of steroid use.

Libido (sex drive—the ability to achieve an erection, to be more specific) appears to be altered variably or not at all. Libido changes (increases or decreases) appear more frequently with larger doses of anabolic steroids. Normalcy is achieved with discontinuance of the drug.

Increased Aggressiveness

An extremely common effect of steroid use (particularly steroids with a relatively high androgenic component) is increased aggressiveness. Testosterone is known to be a major contributing factor in the higher level of aggressiveness in men than women. Also, studies show that prisoners who were committed for crimes of violence had significantly higher levels of testosterone than those committed for nonviolent crimes. Steroid users have been known to become highly violent and aggressive when on high doses of steroids, particularly those whose androgenicity is high and also just before contests when steroid use is unusually high.

The social and psychological ramifications of such behavior changes has been known to be severe indeed—broken families, broken friendships, and a host of other socially deplorable circumstances have arisen in these instances of steroid abuse. The heightened aggression problem is seen to be one of the most dangerous side effects associated with steroid misuse. While aggression levels return to normal upon discontinuance of the drug, the residual effects all too often linger on if only in the memories of the user's loved ones.

Development of Breast Tissue in Males

Called **gynecomastia**, breast tissue under the nipple is often accompanied by tenderness (soreness) to the touch. There appears to be a varied response in this regard, with certain steroids causing it and others not. Most commonly the syndrome arises with high doses of steroids, particularly those with a high androgenic component. The nipples return to normal upon discontinuance of the particular drug causing the problem. However, nodules sometimes appear which may need to be surgically removed.

Virilizing Effects

The androgenic effects of steroids (or "virilizing" effects) include such functions as growth of seminal vesicals, penis and prostate, thickening of the vocal chords (deeper voice), increased amounts of body and genital area hair, oily skin (causing acne), and increased (or initial kindling of) sexual drive, and are generally increased by the use of steroids in adolescents. So too is another possible side effect—that of premature ossification of the long bones (possibly resulting in slightly stunted growth in height).

Women (particularly younger women) can experience similar symptoms, including clitoral enlargement and interrupted or irregular menstrual flow. While menstruation returns to normal after discontinuance of the drug, the other virilizing effects remain—**they are not reversible.**

Some athletes have reported an increase in chest hair growth and even claim that loss of scalp hair diminished or stopped upon usage of steroids. A thickening of facial hair has also been empirically observed by male steroid users.

Susceptibility to Connective Tissue Damage

While not shown in any controlled scientific studies, experience seems to show that if steroids are used by beginners in the weight training world, their strength and muscle size increases far more rapidly than the attendant tendons and connective tissues. This is believed to be due to the relatively poor blood supply in such connective tissue as compared with that of muscle tissue. With the vastly increased strength of the muscle, extreme exertion (as is often the case in many sports—particularly in powerlifting) can and often does cause connective tissue to rupture.

It is generally felt by athletes that a solid year or two of heavy training should precede any use of anabolic steroids in hopes of bringing the strength ratio of the muscle and tendons to a more equitable balance. Then, another year of heavy training before maximum exertion is applied is recommended.

Degeneration of Tissue

Many old-time users of anabolic steroids (especially testosterone) who have begun to experience more than normal numbers of injuries have speculated that their increased susceptibility to injury is due to their prolonged use of testosterone. The Russians believe that this increased susceptibility is due to a decreased viscoelasticity in the muscle, although no scientific data are available to substantiate this claim. Whatever the cause for such increased propensity for severe muscle tears may be, it is nonetheless a fact—it may be the result of prolonged steroid use or it may not be.

Some electromyographic studies indicate that steroid-produced size increases result in "abnormal" tissue. It may be that such tissue is weaker structurally.

Increased Susceptibility to Infection, Weight Loss, and Strength Loss Following Discontinuance of Anabolic Steroid Use

This syndrome is suggested to be the result of what scientists call **negative nitrogen balance.** After getting off the drug, the body is not yet back to normal in testosterone or gonadotropin secretion, and more than normal nitrogen is lost, particularly if one persists in heavy training during this time. With a negative nitrogen balance, sufficient protein cannot be synthesized to affect recovery.

Joint Soreness and Stiffness

Upon discontinuance of anabolic steroids, severe joint pain and stiffness is often experienced. The cause of this problem is not known, but it is suggested by some that it is caused by excessive training during the negative nitrogen balance period (which can last as long as three months). The most serious consequence of joint pain is that it disrupts one's training. Gradually decreasing the dosage of the steroid before cessation is recommended by some experienced bodybuilders to combat joint soreness.

Other Side Effects

Many other possible side effects have been reported both in literature as well as by word of mouth (case histories). While most are either rare or as yet unobserved in healthy athletes, they bear mention. Hepatitis (dirty needle), cramps, cancer, headaches, nausea and gastrointestinal upset, tendancy for nosebleeds, drowsiness, feeling of well-being, disrupted thyroid function, loss of appetite, increased appetite, intestinal irritation (blood in stool), dizziness, and, in some cases, reduction in lean body mass (loss of muscle—possibly due to poor nutrition while dropping weight for a contest).

Of all the potential side effects from using anabolic steroids, the two that appear most frequently, from the standpoint of both scientific reason as well as practical experience, seem to be: the potential for steroids to disrupt cardiovascular function, particularly in the long run, and the often acute levels of aggressivity displayed by the drug abusers. There seems to be conclusive evidence that high-density lipoproteins are markedly decreased when using some anabolic steroids, a significant factor in the increased risk of coronary problems.

Anabolic steroid manufacturers list the following contraindications: pregnancy, nephrosis of the kidney, bilary obstruction, liver damage, and prostate or breast cancer. Extreme caution is advised by the pharmaceutical houses for those with a history of coronary or heart disease, diabetics, and those with renal or hepatic problems (i.e., kidney or liver problems).

While only a **fool** would disregard such contraindications and cautions (let alone some of the other listed side effects possible from steroid use) only an **alarmist** would be disturbed by the seemingly endless horror stories and yarns spread around concerning the "deathly perils" of steroid use. The truth seems to be (and only **seems** to be) that steroids are, in the short run, relatively safe for athletes to use providing care is taken with regard to the factors just listed and the manufacturers' listed cautions and contraindications. Even relatively high dosages of steroids over a relatively extended period of time have not shown irreversible harm done to normal and healthy athletes (with the exception noted among women). Given the current state of the art of steroid use in sports, it seems that after careful screening (performed by your physician), the risk-to-benefit ratio is heavily in favor of steroid use. The long-term effects of steroid use are not known and remain the prominent calculated risk of the user.

It is certain that the clandestine and backward way in which steroids are typically misused is perhaps the most prevalent reason for any side effects to present themselves as health threats. Open and frank discussion on the matter of anabolic steroid use is seen by many to be the single most potent, combative technique in alleviating the potential hazards.

The first bit of true advice that I can offer is to find a medical doctor in whom you have confidence (he or she **must** be an expert in sports-medicine), and if the doctor is willing to work with you on your steroid program, **welcome** the opportunity—and **share** your experiences with the rest of the sports world! If you can monitor possible side effects, this would be helpful, even if the doctor would not prescribe the steroids.

The Beneficial Effects-from Anabolic Steroid Use

In therapeutic cases anabolic steroids have been used to combat anemia and as replacement therapy for patients whose hormone level is subnormal or who are unable to adequately digest proteins, are underweight, or have protein deficient states associated with various infections (gastritis, colitis, or enteritis). They have also been used to assist in the formulating of bone matrix among patients suffering from osteoporosis.

In some cases anabolic steroids have been used to combat certain aftereffects of radiation therapy. They have also been used by physicians to improve appetite, improve psychological disposition, and promote healing (administered before or after surgery). In certain cases, anabolic steroids have been administered to adolescents to stimulate growth. Relatively high doses have been administered to women suffering from breast cancer (up to 300 mg. per week).

Therapeutic doses have ranged from as low as 2 mg. per day for a few weeks to as high as 2 mg. per kg. body weight each day for as long as several years! While many factors are generally considered by physicians in determining appropriate dosages, the risk-to-benefit rule of thumb prevails. The side effects from steroid use are weighed against the severity of the disease and a decision is made regarding dosage and time (with other factors also considered).

But normal and healthy athletes have adapted the uses to which anabolic steroids have been put in therapeutic settings to facilitate sport performance. After a quarter century of experimenting, generally handed down by word of mouth, a few athletes have learned the best administration and dosage schedules to follow in order to maximize their performance while minimizing the risks associated with such use. In some quarters of the athletic world, anabolic steroid use has become highly sophisticated—a blend of scientific application and many years of self-experimentation (often bordering on drug abuse) have yielded to these athletes a knowledge of the drug (in a practical sense) that far transcends that of most physicians.

Still, a vast majority of athletes using anabolic steroids have very little (if any) comprehension as to how to go about maximizing the benefits while minimizing the risks. The vast majority of athletes are guilty of misuse and/or abuse because of ignorance. Their ignorance is understandable, since very little understandable information has been given them, and most athletes "in the know" won't talk! They know anabolic steroids work, so they take them.

Some of the most prevalent uses to which anabolic steroids have been put by athletes are as follows.

Increased Strength

The contractile elements of a muscle cell (called myofibrils) are increased in number through heavy training and appropriate dietary regimen. Anabolic steroids, owing to their primary function of stimulating protein synthesis, assist in this regard since the myofibrillar elements are comprised of protein (actin and myosin). Some strength can be gained through **tissue leverage** resulting from increases in cellular fluid (sarcoplasm) and general edema (water retention). This strength is temporary, however, particularly if body weight must be lost to make weight for a contest.

Increased Muscle Size

The myofibrillar growth and increased sarcoplasmic content (spoken of above) are the chief factors responsible for muscular size increases. The same preconditions prevail, however, to maximize size increases—heavy training and adequate nutrition must be present.

Reduction in Pain from Arthritis/Tendinitis

Such use was (and is) one of the clinical uses of anabolic steroids. Many athletes claim relief of pain from tendinitis while on steroid therapy.

Reduction in Percentage of Body Fat

While diet and training appear to be the primary factors in reduced levels of body fat, there also appears to be some body fat reduction over and above what normally might be expected when using anabolic steroids. It is speculated that increased respiratory quotients is the cause for faster losses of body fat than normal.

Increased Respiratory Rate (and Endurance)

There is evidence to suggest that mitochondria (the organelle within muscle cells responsible for various oxidative functions among other things) are increased in number. This would have the net effect of increasing the cell's capability of utilizing oxygen during heavy training, thereby improving endurance. Possibly more explanatory, however, is the fact that cortisol levels in the blood are increased, thereby giving greater endurance. Cortisol is a stress hormone produced in the adrenal gland.

Increased Vascularity

It is not clear what causes this, but it does occur. It is suggested that the increased blood pressure that often accompanies steroid use is the main factor. Vascularity is one of the much sought after attributes of top caliber bodybuilders.

Improved Recovery Time after Injury or Training

The fact that anabolic steroids promote synthesis and/or retard nitrogen excretion explains why improvements in recovery time follow-

200

ing injury or surgery and particularly following heavy training, is observed. This, of course, relates to less training time lost.

Increased Capability to Do More and Heavier Reps and Sets

This increased capacity is thought by some to be the result of an increased capacity to resynthesize creatine phosphate (CP), an important, fast-energy substrate in the muscles. Without sufficient CP, the muscle very rapidly fatigues (lactic acid concentrations become intolerable). There is substantial scientific evidence supporting this contention, and it appears that CP synthesis is a side benefit of alkylation of (oral) steroid molecules. The increased cortisol levels in the blood are probably more responsible for increased endurance than is the CP theory, however.

Increased Aggressiveness

Increased aggressiveness/hostility was listed as a dangerous side effect, but many bodybuilders regard it as a beneficial effect. It is believed that increased aggressiveness causes one to work out harder and to put more effort into moving the heavy weights. While this may be true for some, experience dictates that the desire to win and to excel is far more potent a motivator than pharmaceuticals in this endeavor.

It must be pointed out that, while empirical evidence is often very strongly supportive of many of these reported effects of anabolic steroid use in sports, very little of the scientific literature is. The use of such steroids, then, must be classified as an inexact science at this point owing to the sparseness of truly objective data that would support the listed beneficial effects.

Thus, the methods of use, dosages used, and the exact steroids to be taken are factors that must be, in "guesswork" fashion, decided upon. Indeed, it is clear that a vast majority of athletes using steroids are forced to guess. They simply have no understandable source of information to guide them. The final section of this chapter points out some of the more important factors to consider when choosing dosage, methods of administration, cycles, and types of steroids. Such information is presented in the spirit of educating steroid users and potential users as to methods of minimizing hazards and maximizing beneficial effects of steroid use. The information is not meant to be, in any way, a stamp of approval on the methods and considerations listed—too little is known at this point to be so bold as to categorically state that "this" is the best way, or that hazards are not present. Before progressing to this final section, however, some down-to-earth information about blood tests is necessary.

Blood Test Results—How to Read Them

The table on page 203 lists the various blood (serum) constituents that are typically included in blood tests prior to steroid administration or steroid therapy. "Normal" ranges for each of the constituents are listed, but very little data are available that would indicate some of them to be classified as normal for the athlete engaging in heavy weight training. Extreme stress (such as that imposed through weight training) as well as muscular hypertrophy (increased muscular size) tends to elevate some of the readings—greater than "normal" ranges are therefore appropriately applied to athletes, but these altered ranges have not been established as yet by any scientific studies. In particular are the typically high LDH and SGOT levels among athletes undergoing stressful training. It is not uncommon to have readings of 10%-20% above the "normal" ranges for these two serum enzymes, the elevated readings stemming from metabolic stress—not from steroids.

But, let's take a look at each of the important blood readings in a more systematic way. I shall endeavor to explain the significance of each relative to athlete's interests both while using steroids as well as off steroids. Hopefully then, you will begin to see the usefulness of blood monitoring in minimizing the hazards of steroid use.

Calcium

While increases or decreases in plasma calcium can signal many different factors, of significance to the athlete is the fact that frequent use of diuretics (such as Lasix) can cause a decrease in calcium. Abnormally high calcium concentrations can be caused by ingestion of high doses of vitamin D. Anabolic steroid use does not seem to be a factor.

Clinically Normal Ranges for Selected Serum, Whole Blood, or Plasma Constituents*

Item	Normal Ranges	Item	Normal Ranges
Calcium	8.5–10.5 mg/dl	CPK (Creatinine Phosphokinase)	55–170 U/L (male)
Inorganic Phosphates	2.5–4.5 mg/dl		30–135 U/L (female)
Glucose (Fasting Level)	70–110 mg/dl	Alkaline Phosphatase	30–85 mU/dl
BUN (Blood Urea Nitrogen)	10–26 mg/dl	LDH (Lactic Dehydrogenase)	100–225 mU/dl
Uric Acid	2.1-7.8 mg/dl (male)	SGOT (Serum Glutamic-Oxaloacetic Transaminase)	8–33 U/ml
	2.0–6.4 mg/dl (female)		
Cholesterol	150–300 mg/dl		
Total Protein	6.0–7.8 gm/dl	SGPT (Serum Glutamic Pyruvic Transaminase)	1–36 U/ml
Bilirubin	0.1–1.2 mg/dl		
Triglycerides	10–190 mg/dl		
		Testosterone	246–1328 mg/dl (male)
			30–120 mg/dl (female)
		Sodium	136–142 mEq/L
		Potassium	3.8–5.0 mEq/L

*Depending upon the source for these normal ranges, the values can fluctuate as much as a few porcentage points, indicating tho inexact nalure of the estimates of "normalcy."

Inorganic Phosphates

Since phosphorus and calcium are working partners in most metabolic functions, increases or decreases in one will cause a commensurate change in the level of the other. Of note to the weight-training athlete is that elevations in blood phosphorus may be associated with hyperthyroidism and elevated secretions of human growth hormone. Anabolic steroids appear to be a non-factor.

Fasting Glucose

Users of anabolic steroids should be aware that such drugs can often significantly alter blood sugar tolerance. Normal to extremely elevated blood glucose levels can be a signal of a diabetic or pre-diabetic state. Too, lowered blood sugar (hypoglycemia) can signal liver disease (rare).

BUN

Urea is the byproduct of protein breakdown in the liver. It is excreted in the urine. High Blood Urea Nitrogen (BUN) levels can signal renal (kidney) failure. Of significance to the athlete is that unusually high intake of protein can cause a slight to moderate elevation of BUN, as can excessive protein catabolism.

Uric Acid

Elevations in uric acid can signal gout, renal failure, or congestive heart failure. For the athlete, perhaps the most important considerations are that hyperuricemia may be the result of fasting (starvation diets) or diuretic use. Anabolic steroids appear not to alter uric acid concentrations.

Cholesterol

With noncommittant elevations in bilirubin and alkaline phosphate, hypercholesterolemia can signal liver disease. Anabolic steroids can often cause elevations in cholesterol while causing a decrease in high density lipoproteins. This in turn increases the risk of atherosclerosis (coronary artery disease).

Total Protein

Through a process of electrically charging the serum solution (electro-phoresis), blood proteins tend to layer themselves, thereby making it possible to determine precise ratios. The normal ratio of albumin to globulin is 3.2-4.5 gm/dl and 2.3-3.5 gm/dl respectively. Elevated globulin and depressed albumin (i.e., a reversed A/G ratio) can be suggestive of chronic liver damage.

Bilirubin

While a normal level of total bilirubin rules out any significant impairment of the excretory functions of the liver, an elevated total bilirubin level can be (and often is) indicative of obstructive jaundice. Bilirubin is a byproduct of hemoglobin metabolism, and is excreted by the liver.

Triglycerides

Like cholesterol, the triglycerides can be related to coronary artery disease. Electrophoresis is used to distinguish the different classifications of hyperlipidemia. Cholesterol, triglycerides, and phospholipids are classified as lipids, and circulate in the blood while bound to protein— thus the term **lipoproteins.** Of note are type 2 in which there is elevated cholesterol and mildly elevated or normal triglycerides, and type 4 in which the cholesterol is normal and the triglycerides are elevated. These types may signal coronary disease.

CPK

There are many causes of elevated Creatinine Phosphokinase (CPK) including: intramuscular injections, vigorous exercise, skeletal muscle disease, cerebral and myocardial infarctions, and muscle hypertrophy. It appears to be normal for weight-trained athletes to have significantly elevated CPK values, although in the presence of other symptoms or blood reading such elevations should be checked out.

Alkaline Phosphatase

When there is an extremely elevated alkaline phosphatase reading with elevated liver function tests, liver disease is generally indicated. If the alkaline phosphatase reading is high without a concurrent elevation in liver function tests, bone disease may be indicated. Anabolic steroids have been reported to decrease alkaline phosphatase, even after the steroids have been discontinued.

SGOT

Serum Glutamic-Oxaloacetic Transaminase (SGOT) is an enzyme which catalyzes the conversion of amino acids and vice versa. It is found in the heart, liver, skeletal muscle, kidneys, and bone. Damage to cells causes elevated SGOT readings, and the exact site of damage can generally be determined via other elevated readings of tests. It is not unusual for SGOT levels to be elevated among athletes in heavy training since skeletal muscles undergo considerable trauma (strains, bruises, etc.) Readings generally peak within 36 hours following injury and return to normal within six days or so. Repeated trauma over days will tend to keep the SGOT level elevated.

SGPT

Serum Glutomic Pyruvic Transaminase (SGPT) is liberated upon damage to liver cells. In the absence of cardiac or other muscle injury, extremely elevated SGOT and SGPT are often indicative of hepatocellular damage (anabolic steroids can cause such hepatocellular damage). Generally, elevated alkaline phosphatase, cholesterol, and bilirubin accompany such liver damage.

Testosterone

Anabolic steroids mimic normally occurring testosterone, thereby inhibiting its secretion. It is not uncommon for testosterone levels to dip to levels well below normal while using steroids (male and female). This effect is almost always reversible following discontinuance of the use of anabolic steroids.

Sodium and Potassium

Electrolytes in general can fluctuate in the body depending upon many factors (environment, various drugs being used, certain disease entities, etc.). Of significance to the athlete is the fact that the use of steroids as well as extreme heat (sweating) can cause mild to severe electrolyte imbalances. Diuretic use also causes loss of electrolytes as can anti-inflammatory drugs (e.g., Butazolidin). Since electrolytes play a major role in muscle function, loss of strength is not uncommon upon use of such anti-inflammatants and diuretics.

I strongly urge each bodybuilder who is using, or planning to use, anabolic steroids or other drugs to have a complete blood workup done, and seek out a competent sportsmedicine physician to assist you in interpreting the results. The preceeding listing is only meant to inform such users or potential users of some of the hazards and pitfalls in interpreting blood tests—many of the readings are related in complex ways.

Furthermore, since many of the blood constituents can vary considerably from day to day (depending upon drug dosages and other factors), it is important to have such a test performed **multiple times,** particularly during a heavy cycle of drug use as might be the case just prior to a contest. The effects of most steroids are both time and dose related and can cause variable fluctuations in many of the blood readings over a very short period. Of course, this involves money. So does purchasing drugs, and **so does illness related to drug abuse.**

So as not to sound like an alarmist, however, it is significant to note that cessation of drug use will prompt recovery to normal levels within weeks (time ranges from 2 to 6 weeks generally). Furthermore, there is scientific evidence that blood readings are not elevated significantly (and where they are, they're returned to normal quickly) during an intermittantly applied descending dose pattern of injectable anabolic steroids. More will be said concerning dose schedules in the next section of this chapter. The point is, as it has been throughout this chapter, that **proper** use of steroids can certainly reduce the hazards— only a fool would turn a deaf ear to what science and experience have to offer.

What the Research Shows

There is substantial research on certain aspects of steroid use. It is important that users and potential users pay heed to this knowledge. It is in the best interests of maximizing benefits and minimizing hazards. It can all be said in one paragraph.

To minimize the risks and still maximize the benefits of anabolic steroid use in training, use an intermittent pattern of descending dosage of injectable steroids. Orals should be used sparsely as they are more toxic to the liver and manifest more severe (most are 17 alpha-alkylated) side effects. Orals should be reserved for periods just before competition if the androgenic component is high, and sparsely during off-season training if the anabolic component is high and the androgenic component is low. In both cases the SPAI should be high. When side effects begin to manifest themselves to any level of intolerance, discontinue the use of that drug. Monitor blood readings as often as possible, particularly during the first 3–4 weeks of steroid usage. Always consult a sportsmedicine physician and have him or her monitor your blood and general health before and during steroid use. In all cases, adequate nutrition and weight training should accompany steroid use.

There it is, folks—all in a neat and tidy nutshell. Now there won't be any more steroid abuse, right? While I ask this question with tongue in cheek, these guidelines will indeed minimize the hazards of drug abuse. However, as many bodybuilders are aware, greater than safe doses of oral steroids seem to work a bit better than the previously discussed "safe" method. It is unfortunate that proponents of such drug abuse believe that the extra bit of strength or size gained by way of such abuse is worth the risk. For, if they were indeed scientific about it, they'd find that over time the difference would vanish. It's not **years** of time either—it is probably only a matter of a few **months** before the relatively safer method described will allow one to achieve all the strength and size that is desired. And, experience shows that the gains made over time are relatively more long-lasting (possibly as a result of the body growing accustomed to the increases as well as the individual's lifestyle changes to accommodate it more effectively) than are the gains made by the more risky method of high oral intake and to hang with the side effects.

Diet and Nutrition

During periods where weight gains are desired, your caloric intake should be increased to about 500 calories more than what you expend each day, and the principal source of those extra calories should be a complete protein source (one that has all of the essential amino acids). Each meal should consist of a variety of essential nutrient sources (i.e., the four basic food groups—whole grains and cereals, vegetables and fruits, meat and eggs, and dairy products). Where your diet is deficient in certain nutrients, supplementation is advised. In fact, it's probably advisable to take a good brand of vitamin/mineral/enzyme supplement since the food you'll eat probably won't contain as much as you'll need to maximize gains while on steroids. It is also advisable to eat at least four or five meals a day, the total number of calories adding up to 500 above those expended. **Five hundred** is the best estimate since the biosynthesis of muscle, although speeded up from the steroids, cannot progress indefinitely before excessive amounts of fat begin to appear around the midsection. Ingesting slightly more protein calories than needed, together with heavy training, will ensure that muscle is being put on rather than fat. About one pound per week is what most athletes can expect to gain in muscle for the first few weeks of a steroid cycle. Once off the steroids, however, caloric intake should be reduced to maintenance levels.

In cases where no weight increases are desired, ingesting as many calories as you expend will ensure that your percentage of body fat will diminish (providing that you're weight training).

Athletes whose percentage of body fat is already low (i.e., below 5 or 6 percent) and who still **insist** on using steroids should beware that the only place left to go is up in body weight. Little in the way of increased strength will be attainable if you maintain your body weight and use steroids when your body fat level is already low. Generally a descending cycle (as mentioned earlier) of very low dosage is sufficient to maintain strength and size after having achieved the desired size and percentage of body fat.

209

Methods of Steroid Use

Some of the nomenclature that has become prevalent among body-builders using steroids includes words like **stacking, blending,** and **staggering.** Other words or phrases are **cycling, descending dose pattern, ascending dose pattern, plateau, steroid bounce, tapering,** and **shotgunning.** These words were born essentially out of practical experience rather than any scientific text. There are many examples of scientific research **supporting** the contentions of athletes who have reported their observations, but precious little research has **proven** them to be true. It is my opinion that in cases where large numbers of steroids users have reported the same phenomena, at least a modicum of credence ought to be given to that point of view, regardless of the lack of scientific support. But, let's take a look at these concepts that have sprung up among the steroid-using generation of athletes around the world, and offer a bit of information relative to each.

Stacking

Stacking refers to the practice of using more than one anabolic steroid at a time. Many long-time users of steroids feel that a synergistic effect can be achieved by doing this. **Synergy,** in this context, means that the desired action of one drug is aided by the other—sort of a helper if you will. Many drugs—not just steroids—exhibit this kind of synergism when used in combination with another substance. There appears to be no best method of stacking, presumably because everyone responds differently to various combinations of steroids, both from the point of view of desired effects as well as from the onset of unwanted side effects. In fact, what seems to work best for you may change overnight due to plateauing of one or both drugs. It is generally felt by these same long-time users that the best place to start in finding the best drugs to stack is with an oral and an injectible, but this method doesn't fit into the scheme of improving the risk-to-benefit ratio. More on that later.

210

Plateauing

When the steroid doesn't seem to be affording the user with the desired gains in strength or size, it can be safely predicted that the steroid is no longer working maximally. It is believed that this kind of **plateau** in progress is caused by the steroid receptor sites shutting down. The first place one ought to look, however, is at his or her training program and diet. Increasing the overload (if undertrained) or decreasing it (if overtrained), or limiting your caloric intake can often be the culprit responsible for the plateau in progress, as can insufficient nutrients in general (e.g.,vitamins or protein). If the problem is indeed receptor site shutdown, then no amount of additional steroid should work to overcome the plateau. If a prudent cycling program of anabolic steroid use is followed, however, plateauing should never become a problem—you won't be on that drug long enough for it to happen generally. Again, more on that later, when a model drug program is outlined that may assist in minimizing risks and maximizing benefits.

Staggering

To avoid plateauing on a drug, or to avoid plateauing on two (stacked) drugs, long-time users have often opted to get off the drug(s) and go on another. It is felt that this allows the system to pick up where the last one left off. This practice works for some, but not for others. It may be that hitting a plateau incited the user to double his efforts, or to change his workouts—or even to eat more (some drugs cause a reduction in appetite, and switching to another may bring it back, thereby allowing further improvement in size or strength). In any event, it doesn't seem likely that one steroid uses different receptor sites than another, so the receptor shutdown theory doesn't seem to hold water. No one knows for sure what mechanisms are at work in allowing such **staggering** of drugs to push an athlete past a plateau, or if indeed it does.

Tapering

Research clearly shows that abrupt discontinuance of anabolic steroid use is not the best (safest) method to get your system back to normal. It's better to slowly reduce your dosage over a period of 4-6 weeks (the longer the cycle, the longer it takes to **taper** off effectively). Again, however, there seems to be a safer alternative—building the taper into the cycle to begin with.

211

Shotgunning

Taking a host of drugs in the hopes that what one misses the other will get has been a popular method of steroid use (or abuse) in the past. There is no sound rationale for this line of reasoning, either in the scientific literature or in the practical world. It simply doesn't work that way. While there are obviously differences in anabolic steroids, the aspect that athletes are interested in—namely the nitrogen-retaining aspect for muscle growth—works basically the same for all anabolic steroids. The receptor sites are the same, the RNA and DNA is the same, and the protein-manufacturing ribosomes are the same. Or so it seems, given the present state of the art.

Dosages

Anabolic steroids come in many forms, and the dosage generally depends upon what steroid you're about to use. Each steroid has what is referred to as a **half life.** This is a term that relates to the length of time the drug remains active in the body before being broken down (aromatized or hydralized). Athletes using anabolic steroids have, over the years, developed a somewhat dangerous belief that more is better. This is not always true, and it certainly isn't true for anabolic steroids, when one begins to weigh the ever-present risks against the potential benefits.

For example, take a look at the figure on page 212. As the benefits derived from the use of steroids begin to wane (level off), the side effects continue to spiral upward, becoming more and more measurable. The point at which beneficial effects plateau (marked with an "X") is the point at which tapering off the steroids should begin, and it is also the point at which dosage should be regulated. This point will

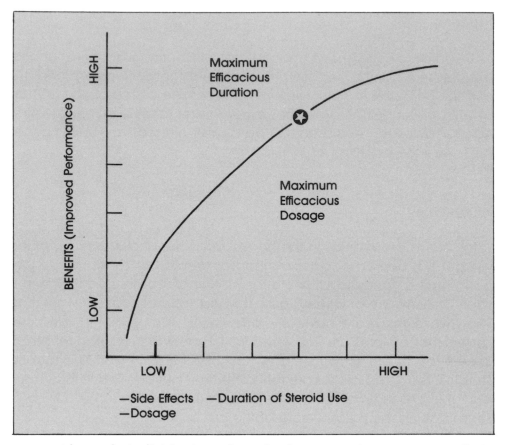

vary with each individual and each drug in unknown ways. Only experimenting will tell just how. Keeping accurate training reports and monitoring side effects both visually as well as through blood tests will afford the astute athlete sufficient information in order to regulate dosage and duration efficiently, particularly if physician-assisted.

It is generally common among athletes engaged in heavy weight training (particularly bodybuilders) to regulate steroid use on the basis of the formula:

1 mg. per kg. body weight per day

This would constitute a relatively high **dosage**—two or three times that amount is not unheard of in some circles, although in my experience little benefit in terms of improved performance is to be expected from such high doses. Certainly the side effects become far more pronounced with this dosage, and the risk-to-benefit ratio is certainly not in the best interests of the athlete's health.

Cycling

Cycling refers to the practice of manipulating dosage and duration in concordance with your training or competition schedule. Many, many different cycles have been used over the years, and it would be impossible to begin to relate them here, much less the rationale behind each (if indeed one existed). Instead, I shall attempt to present a method of cycling which has been used rather successfully in the past in terms of maximizing the benefits while minimizing the hazards of steroid use. The cycle has been adapted successfully to bodybuilding, weightlifting, and powerlifting. It has also been used rather extensively by many athletes in sports such as football, track, and field, and others.

Observe the figure on page 214. Notice that the cycle lasts for six weeks with a two or three week break between cycles. Over the six weeks of steroid administration, the dose continually diminishes. This practice allows the body to gradually return to normalcy—testosterone production never wanes to extremely low levels and blood readings generally remain in the "normal" range. Yet, over time (months), the benefits derived are of the type that experience has shown to be longer lasting. Short or infrequent heavy dosage cycles produce gains but they are fleeting, as most of the gains in size and strength come from water or fluid retention and tissue leverage. Long-term cycling allows for a more pronounced increase in the myofibrillar elements of the cell, which are the actual contractile elements in muscle tissue. The strength derived from this method of training and cycling generally is far longer lived, and reaches a greater level as well.

Experience has shown that most bodybuilders "plateau" on most steroids within six or seven weeks. The shorter cycle presented here therefore circumvents this problem—and the necessity to engage in exotic stacking or staggering programs.

Notice, too, that the primary amount of steroid should be in injectable form. This is advisable because injectables display far fewer negative side effects than do the oral 17 Alpha-alkylated steroids. There are some anabolic steroids that, despite being orally administered, are less toxic on the liver because of their lower androgenic rating. As stated earlier, scientists have been able to manipulate the chemical structure of the basic testosterone molecule such that it will last longer in the system before being hydralized or aromatized. Some orals are quite good in the sense that they are either not of the 17

Off–Season and Pre–Season Cycling: For 100 Kg. Athlete

Period (off–season)	Oral (e.g., Anavar, Maxibolan, or Winstrol)	Injectable (e.g., decadurabolin or primobolan)	HCG
weeks 1 & 2 (begin with blood test)	50 mg/day	300 mg/week	
weeks 3 & 4 (blood test)	25 mg/day	200 mg/week	
weeks 5 & 6	0	100 mg/week	
weeks 7 & 8	0	0	2cc every 2 days

Weeks 9–16 Repeat Cycle In Its Entirety

(pre-contest)	orals*	injectable*	other
week 6	20 mg D-bol/day	100 mg/week	All athletes supercompensate
week 5	40 mg D-bol/day	200 mg/wk	with added protein, vitamins, and elec-
week 4	20 mg D-bol/day 50 mg Anadrol/day	300 mg/wk	trolytes if diuretics are to be used prior to competition
week 3	100 mg Anadrol/day	300 mg/wk	Begin use of "cutting-up"
week 2	50 mg Anadrol/day 10 mg Halotestin/day	400 mg/wk	preparations (bodybuilding)
week 1	50 mg Anadrol/day 20 mg Halotestin/day	None required	Last Day: begin diuretics

FOLLOWING CONTEST USE AN OFF-SEASON DESCENDING DOSE PATTERN TO "NORMALIZE" BODILY FUNCTIONS.

*Use Primobolan injections and a low androgenic oral (e.g., Anavar) the last three weeks if cutting body weight is going to be a problem.

Alpha-alkylated variety (e.g., Maxibolan), or they have superior strength-producing effects in comparison to their androgenic effects (e.g., Anavar).

During off-season cycling, these low risk orals should be the only ones used, the more androgenic orals reserved for precontest preparation or the waste basket. During the precontest phase of your training, a 6-8 week (no more), ascending-dosage pattern can be followed to maximize contest readiness. I consider this kind of cycle to be the maximum-risk method of anabolic steroid use, and should be reserved only for important contests no more than two or three times each year. The orals of choice in this kind of program would be Dianabol (no longer available in oral form, but is still available in its generic form, methandrostenolone), Anadrol 50, or Halotestin. Both Halotestin and Anadrol 50 are extremely androgenic and should be used with extreme caution or not at all.

Other Anabolic Steroids

There are some foreign drugs that are showing some promise, but are not on the U.S.A. market as yet (not legally anyway). Some of the more noteworthy are Proviron (Germany), Steranabol (Italy), Anabolicum (Italy), Nilevar (England and France), and Formebolonum (Italy). More appear each year, and each appears to have one advantage or the other over the rest. Thus far, few anabolic steroids have emerged that are clearly superior in their anabolic effect. The few that show such superiority have been found through long years of experience on the part of athletes, with only a few scientists guiding the way.

Most long-time users of anabolic steroids have shown a decided preference for Anavar (strength), Maxibolan (size), Methanprostenolone (strength and size), and Winstrol (size). Of the injectables, there appears to be a preference for deca-durabolin, primobolan, and various testosterones (principally cypionate). The sublingually administered or pellet implant steroids have not become popular in the U.S. or elsewhere.

Testosterone

Little has been said regarding the use of the various forms of testosterone thus far. That's because I don't believe that they are worth the trouble. Of course they work, but if your goal is developing strength or size over the long term (as it justifiably should be if you believe that this is the safest way to go), then there is no place for the toxic testosterones.

Anabolic steroids were developed because they were proven to be better (less androgenic) than the testosterones. Aside from the increased aggressiveness caused by testosterone there is no proven advantage to using them except, perhaps, to your bank account (the testosterones are generally cheaper). As for the aggressiveness aspect, self-motivation and determination weigh heavily enough for increased aggression under the weights—it needn't be taken home or among friends.

There is a common belief among bodybuilders that testosterone is needed for its androgenicity to "balance" the more anabolic drugs. It's felt that some sort of synergistic effect is produced above and beyond what can be produced with anabolic steroids alone. This is, in my opinion, a myth. If androgenicity is important, many anabolic agents have sufficient androgenic characteristics to assist in that aspect. But, frankly, there is no scientific evidence that this kind of balancing is efficacious. It certainly isn't in keeping with the basic principle of augmenting the risk-to-benefit ratio.

Conclusion

The use of anabolic steroids and other drugs has become a deeply rooted way of life in sports around the globe. That they work has become self-evident to all athletes wishing to gain strength and size, and has even become rather prevalent in endurance sports for increasing muscular endurance. Attempts at legislating against them have only served to exacerbate the problem of drug abuse. It is my conviction that education is the only way that such drug **abuse** in sports can be minimized. It will probably never be eliminated—it is certain that the **use** of drugs never will.

What little research into the use of anabolic steroids in sports that exists has clearly demonstrated some very helpful guidelines in minimizing the risks involved while keeping the benefits at a level that will be useful to athletes. These guidelines have been presented in this chapter.

The methods of steroid use presented here are not my own—they are examples of what's being done in the sport world. I do not condone such practices. But I do urge all bodybuilders now using or about to use drugs of any sort to find the most efficient way of doing so. This will always involve educating yourself on the drugs to be used, seeking competent sports physicians' advice, and minimizing risks while maximizing benefits.

19

AMINO ACIDS
AND GROWTH HORMONES

There isn't a bodybuilder alive who isn't familiar with the critical importance of protein in developing massive muscles. In fact, most bodybuilders have looked into the subject deeply enough to recognize the term **amino acid.** For those of you who haven't, amino acids are what protein is made of. In fact there are over 200,000 **different** protein molecules in your body which are comprised of from about 20 amino acids for the simplest protein molecules to over 100,000 amino acids for the most complex protein molecules!

In this chapter I will explore some of the major uses to which amino acids are put by the body, and pay special attention to those functions which are of greatest importance to bodybuilders and other athletes in heavy training. There is a new age dawning, friends, and as science marches on so too does its effect on all spheres of sport. As more of the incredibly complex story behind amino acids is uncovered by the **Sleuths of Academe,** the lot of the scientific bodybuilder will become more difficult. For, to maximize your training efforts you will need to become practicing biochemists as well as athletes.

What Are Amino Acids?

Amino acids are organic compounds that have both an amino (NH_2) and a carboxyl (COOH) radical in their molecular structure. The amino acids found in protein are categorized into two groups, **essential** amino acids and **nonessential** amino acids. Of course, all of the amino acids are essential for metabolism and growth, so the terms used to classify them are a bit misleading. The essential amino acids are those which either cannot be manufactured by the body or are manufactured only in small amounts by the body and have to be derived from food. In other words, it is essential that these amino acids are sought outside the body and injested. The nonessential amino acids can be manufactured by the body in sufficient quantities; it is not essential to find other sources.

Tyrosine, a nonessential amino acid, is derived from **phenylalanine**, an essential amino acid. It cannot be manufactured by the cells, but since it depends upon the presence of phenylalanine it is not classified as an essential.

Two of the essential amino acids, **arginine** and **histidine**, are said to be essential only for children (prepubertal), but not for adults.

To complicate the picture, there are certain amino acids not found in protein which have found their way into the pharmaceutical handbags of many bodybuilders and other groups of athletes. One in particular is **L-3-4-dihydroxphenylalanine** or **L-Dopa**. L-Dopa is a potent stimulator of human growth hormone (hGH), but has some rather severe side effects (see Chapter 20).

Another hGH-stimulating amino acid that is not found in protein is **5-hydroxytryptophan**. Because of these serious side effects, **arginine** and **histidine** (the children's essentials) are frequently substituted because they are virtually safe as well as effective in hGH stimulation. So too are **lysine, cysteine, tryptophan,** and **ornithine**, a derivative of arginine.

The growth hormone stimulation effect is well known to both scientists and athletes alike, and has opened up a whole new field of nutritional supplementation. The practice of stimulating the pituitary gland to secret more hGH promises to be the wave of the future in all strength sports.

The accompanying table lists all of the amino acids, including both the essential and nonessential ones, as well as those not found in protein but used for their hGH-stimulating effects.

Protein molecules cannot be manufactured by the body unless all of the required amino acids are present. In fact, all of the essential amino

The Amino Acids

Essential Amino Acids	Nonessential Amino Acids	Non-Protein Amino Acids
threonine	glycine	L-3-4-dihydroxyphenyl-alanine*
lysine*	alanine	5-hydroxytryptophan*
methionine	serine	**Other amino acids**
arginine*	cysteine*	ornithine*
valine	aspartic acid	
phenylalanine	glutamic acid	
leucine	hydroxylysine	
tryptophan*	cystine	
isoleucine	tyrosine	
histidine*	proline	
	hydroxyproline	

* Amino acids with substantial stimulatory effects upon hGH release

acids must be at the site of protein synthesis before any of them can act. This means that every single meal you eat must contain all of the essential amino acids in sufficient quantities to effect protein synthesis. If some are not present when needed, those that are either get stored in cells until needed or are degraded by the liver and used as energy or stored as fat.

What Do Amino Acids Do?

About three quarters of your body's solids are comprised of proteins. These include **structural proteins, enzymes, genes, oxygen-transporting proteins, muscular-contractile protein,** and many other types that perform specific function throughout the body.

The function of the amino acids which comprise these many different bodily proteins are incredibly diverse. Of particular interest to body-builders are the hGH-stimulating effects of certain amino acids and, of course, the muscle-building functions. However, because the amino acids are involved in practically all aspects of bodily function, their diverse nature makes them collectively important to life itself.

Tracing the path of ingested proteins as they pass through the gastrointestinal tract, into the bloodstream, and ultimately to the site where they are needed is both interesting and informative. The journey lends us clues that we can use to increase the efficiency of many bodily functions including muscle development and improved metabolism.

Through it all, however, it is wise that you remember the critical importance of general nutrition to the entire process. The vitamins, minerals, and other nutrients play an important role in the processes of metabolism. The interrelatedness of all nutrients, including the amino acids, should not be taken lightly, for unless the proper metabolic climate exists within the body, growth and development cannot occur.

Protein enters the stomach. Once in the stomach, protein is acted upon by the enzyme **pepsin**, which splits them into **proteoses, peptones,** and **large polypeptides.** Pepsin is particularly important because the collagen in the fibrous tissue of meat can only be broken down by this enzyme, exposing the rest of the meat to the action of other enzymes.

Partially digested proteins enter the small intestine. The proteoses, peptones and large polypeptides enter the small intestine where they are acted upon by the pancreatic enzymes **trypsin, chymotrypsin,** and **carboxypolypeptidases** and converted mainly into small polypeptides, plus a few amino acids.

Finally, the small polypeptides are digested into **amino acids** when they come into contact with the walls of the small intestine. The wall cells contain **peptidases** (enzymes) that effect this final stage of digestion.

The amino acids are transported through the walls. Getting through the walls of the small intestines and into the portal blood is no easy trick! Four different transport systems are required: one for **neutral** amino acids, one for **basic** amino acids, one for **acidic** amino acids, and one specifically for the amino acids **proline, hydroxyproline,** and **glycine.** The first three transport systems are activated by the relative pH of each amino acid. For example, any substance with a pH below 7 is an acid; above 7 is a base. Substances with a pH of 7 are considered neutral (neither an acid nor a base).

The walls of the small intestine are lined with receptor sites onto which both an amino acid and a sodium ion must attach before the carrier transports them across the cell membrane into the portal blood. The energy to cause the movement of the carrier from one side of the cell membrane to the other is believed to be the difference in sodium concentrations on either side. In other words, the amino acids would not get into the portal blood unless the sodium concentration on the intestine side was greater than inside the cell. The sodium then can diffuse through the cell wall, "dragging" the amino acid carrier with it. The animo acids then build up inside the cell until the concentration of amino acids is increased sufficiently to force them to diffuse through the opposite wall and into the portal blood system.

The amino acids are distributed throughout the body. Once in the bloodstream the amino acids are quickly transported throughout the body. A small number of the amino acids are used immediately, depending upon the current needs of the various tissues. Within 10 minutes, all of the amino acids are either used in protein synthesis or stored. Excess amino acids are degraded by the liver through a process called **deamination,** and then used as energy or stored as fat.

Amino acids are stored mostly in the liver, the kidneys, the intestinal mucosa, and the blood, or inside the cells as intracellular proteins.

Immediately after the amino acids enter the bloodstream their concentrations rise, but only slightly because of the rapidity with which they are used or stored. During the course of the day, the stored amino acids are systematically reclaimed and are transported by the blood to needy sites. Several grams of proteins can be transported each hour in the form of circulating amino acids.

These are important bits of information to all bodybuilders because muscular growth depends upon the efficiency with which the amino acids can get to the tissues in need of them. Tissue proteins, for example, depend upon **hGH** and **insulin** to be formed, while circulating amino acids are increased in concentration by **adrenocortical glucocorticoid hormones.**

Proteins are synthesized. As all bodybuilders know, the amino acids that are essential in the diet cannot be formed by the body. The remaining amino acids can, and depend on the presence of the appropriate **alpha-keto acids.**

For instance, **aline,** one of the nonessential amino acids, depends upon the alpha-keto acid **pyruvic acid.** Pyruvic acid is formed in large quantities in the body during the utilization of glucose. Then, through a process called **transamination,** the amino radical is transferred to the pyruvic acid, and the keto oxygen is transferred from the pyruvic acid to the donor of the amino radical. Alanine is the product. The other nonessential amino acids are formed through a similar transamination process.

Once the appropriate amino acids are present in a cell the needed protein is synthesized very quickly. However, tremendous energy is required to effect the **peptide linkages** in the protein molecule, and this energy comes from **adrenosinetriphosphate** (ATP). An incredible 500-4,000 calories of energy is required for each peptide linkage!

Your genes determine exactly which proteins are needed and in what quantities. The genetic code is transferred from the cell's **DNA** to a **messenger RNA** through a process called **transcription.** The messenger RNA then carries the code to the cell's **ribosomes** where proteins are manufactured. In the ribosome, **transfer RNA** delivers the appropriate amino acids during the protein synthesis process. There is a different transfer RNA for each of the twenty amino acids that are incorporated into proteins. Inside the ribosome, **ribosomal RNA** promote the peptide linkages that bind the various amino acids together into protein molecules.

The exact structure of each protein molecule, the precise number required, and the locations at which they're needed are all regulated by the activity of hundreds of bodily enzymes and their influence upon the cells' DNA genes. In some cases, especially with the formation of ATP—the substance necessary for muscular contraction—the entire process thus far described is carried out within a very few seconds!

Improving the Effectiveness of Amino Acids

The single most important question you, as a bodybuilder, can ask yourself is, "How can I improve the anabolic processes of my body so that muscular strength and size is increased and body fat is reduced?" The answer lies in all that's been explained thus far in this chapter—and two potent hormones called **somatotropin**, or **hGH**, and **insulin**.

Here are some of the most important functions of hGH:

Enhancement of amino acid transport through the cell membranes. hGH enhances the passage of amino acids into the muscle cells, thereby increasing their intracellular concentrations, one of the important "triggers" for protein synthesis.

Enhancement of protein synthesis by the ribosomes. hGH has a direct influence upon the ribosomes, causing them to produce more muscle building proteins, regardless of whether high concentrations of amino acids are present.

Increased formation of RNA. hGH stimulates the transcription process in the cells' nuclei, forcing them to produce greater numbers of messenger RNA, which in turn promotes faster protein synthesis.

Decreased catabolism of protein and amino acid. At the same time there is an increase in protein synthesis, there also is a decrease in the breakdown of protein and the utilization of protein and amino acid for energy. This occurs because there is a rapid mobilization of large quantities of free fatty acids from stored fat which are used for energy rather than the protein. Of course, this makes more amino acids available for the increased protein synthesis that is going on simultaneously.

Decreased utilization of glucose for energy. For the same reasons cited in the paragraph above, glucose is spared from use as energy.

This causes a rise in blood glucose that in turn stimulates greater secretion of insulin. Insulin greatly potentiates the action of hGH. While severe overstimulation of insulin secretion can cause serious metabolic disturbances, a slight increase in insulin can be quite beneficial on three important counts: Insulin increases the active transport of amino acids into the cells. Insulin accelerates the translation of messenger RNA codes for increased protein synthesis. Insulin increases the transcription of DNA in the cell's nuclei to form greater quantities of messenger RNA, which in turn leads to still further protein synthesis.

Insulin is nearly as important as hGH in promoting growth. Furthermore, neither hGH nor insulin alone will cause very significant growth. Yet a combination of both of these powerful hormones will cause very significant growth!

There are several ways that you can stimulate the pituitary gland and pancreas to secrete greater than normal amounts of hGH and insulin respectively. Of course, each of these two hormones can be administered in the form of an injectable drug, but this practice is both unnecessary and potentially dangerous. Instead, stimulating greater secretion rates by **natural** means has been shown to be extraordinarily effective in promoting muscular growth, not to mention increasing tendon, ligament, and connective tissue strength as well as reducing body fat.

Several amino acids are powerful stimulators of hGH release. The most notable ones (that are also totally safe) are **arginine**, arginine's cousin **ornithine, cysteine, tryptophan, histidine**, and **lysine.**

As for insulin, you needn't worry about its secretion because the hGH's action in sparing glycogen from use as energy causes greater than normal insulin release concurrently. Both hGH and insulin will be acting together anabolically, greatly enhancing muscle growth and development.

The Method of Amino Acid Use Is All-Important

If there was no **need** in the body for all the extra protein that hGH and insulin was forcing to be manufactured, it would be summarily broken back down by the liver and restored or used for energy. Simply taking the aforementioned amino acids randomly, then, is a worthless endeavor.

Scientists working in concert with the Weider Research Clinic have found the answer to maximizing the anabolic efficiency of these incredible amino acids. Certain biochemical agents must be present to assist in converting them to the form in which they can exert their stimulatory effect upon the anterior pituitary gland. Also, the entire process must be performed in the proper atmosphere, which involves the presence of essential vitamins, minerals, and—importantly—**stress.** It is stress which creates the need for anabolism.

Having all of these nutrients, stress factors, and amino acids available at the exact time the insulin and hGH are exerting their influence on protein synthesis makes the entire process very scientific indeed! It must be done in a very precise fashion to maximize the effectiveness.

The Weider Research Clinic has determined that it is theoretically possible to replicate the anabolic effectiveness of ingested or injected anabolic steroids through this nutritional process! The **initial** anabolic action of the nutritional process is believed to be equivalent to over 50% of that of anabolic steroids, and over the course of several months actually can equal the anabolic effectiveness of anabolic steroids!

Let me reiterate an important point: nutritionally stimulating a powerful anabolic climate within the cells of the body must be done using a precise method of supplementation and administration.

There is a wealth of scientific information which shows that hGH release will take place more efficiently during periods when there is a great need for anabolism in the body. Such a time exists after training, particularly after severe training of the type bodybuilders typically undergo. Scientists now know that exercise tremendously increases your need for many of the amino acids, including those which stimulate hGH release. In fact, up to 90% of the MDR of leucine, an essential amino acid is oxidized during an exercise period lasting two hours. A similar situation exists during the early morning hours when you have "fasted" for several hours during sleep.

We also know from scientific research that all of the amino acids essential to growth as well as the vitamins and minerals that act as catalysts in the process must be there at the critical time. These facts have led the Weider Research Clinic scientists to the following daily regimen for maximizing an anabolic climate in the muscles and other tissues of the body:

Morning: Normal meal supplemented with a multivitamin pack and protein powder fortified with a teaspoon of free form amino acids.
Lunch: Normal meal fortified with two teaspoons of free form amino acids.
Immediately before workout: About 1 gram arginine and ornithine, and a light meal fortified with 2 teaspoons of free form amino acids.

224

Also, supplement with magnesium, methionine, potassium, calcium and niacinamide—catalysts in the process of hGH stimulation.
Evening meal: Same regimen as morning meal.

Drugs have proven to be both a blessing and a curse for man. They have the potential to be one of the most important sources for improving man's health and well-being, but they also have the capacity, when abused, to cause severe illness or death.

Whenever it is possible, **natural** means of improving your health and well-being are recommended. For bodybuilders, this relates specifically to building muscle mass, and from where I sit, I must conclude that there may be a better way to do this than using anabolic steroids. The answer lies in the **natural** stimulation of anabolism, and **amino acids** hold the key to this process.

20
L-DOPA

226

Many years have passed since the first daring and resourceful athlete laid what he thought was his life on the line and popped a single Dianabol tablet. For him, it was perhaps the winning edge. For sport, it was the dawning of a new era.

When the practice of steroid doping caught on, the scientific community flexed its mighty muscle but, for whatever reasons, failed to convince the athletes using them that they shouldn't. The athletes, you see, had seen the dog tracks in the snow (only a fool would deny the existence of a dog after having seen its tracks). The steroids were working, and the reported dangers seemed overstated. The scientific community had lost much of its credibility, and now all are paying the price.

With each new drug restored to by athletes in the maniacal quest for performance supremacy, there comes a loud and ominous bellow from the scientific community. But having cried wolf before, their warnings generally fall on deaf ears. The latest craze being perpetrated in the bodybuilding world is the use of an amino acid not found in protein called **L-Dopa.**

After careful analysis of the facts available in the research literature, and consultation with several renowned biochemists, I must conclude that this potent drug has no place in legitimate sport. Further, the ominous warnings of the medical community ought to be heeded in this instance because there are indeed some rather serious immediate effects stemming from the use of L-Dopa that far exceed the relatively mild ill effects of anabolic steroids.

In fact, there are other substances which have as profound an effect on growth hormone secretion (the purpose for which L-Dopa is used by unsuspecting bodybuilders) as does L-Dopa. And, without the serious ill effects! This fact alone should render its use obsolete! But, let's explore in more detail what L-Dopa is, what it does, what the side effects are, and what it doesn't do.

What Is L-Dopa?

Some of the amino acids found in protein are valine, leucine, threonine, arginine, lysine, histidine, and phenylalanine. Amino acids not found in protein are 5-hydroxytryptophan and L-3-4-dihydroxy-phenylalanine (L-Dopa). Arginine, histidine, and lysene, according to the research literature, are the three protein amino acids that significantly stimulate the secretion of hGH (human growth hormone) from the anterior pituitary gland. L-Dopa and 5-hydroxytriptophan are also well known stimulators of hGH.

L-Dopa is commercially available as **Aldomet** (pure L-Dopa) and **Sinemet** (L-Dopa combined with **carbidopa**, a substance that prevents the early breakdown of L-Dopa). The intended use of L-Dopa, from a medical point of view, is to combat the symptoms of **Parkinson's disease.** Parkinsonism is characterized by a fine, slowly spreading muscular tremor, muscular weakness, and rigidity theoretically resulting from the depletion of dopamine in the extrapyramidal centers of the brain.

What L-Dopa Does and the Price You Have to Pay

L-Dopa does not directly stimulate the release of hGH. Instead, the conversion of L-Dopa to dopamine in the brain appears to be the stimulating factor. Dopamine acts as a neurotransmitter which mediates the release of hGH-releasing factor, which in turn stimulates the secretion of hGH from the anterior pituitary.

Pure L-Dopa (e.g., Aldomet) is highly inefficient in this regard since about 75% of the ingested substance is broken down before it ever penetrates the blood-brain barrier to be converted to dopamine. Much of the remainder of ingested L-Dopa is rendered ineffective due to the inhibitory effect of vitamin B_6 on L-Dopa. Thus only a minute amount of L-Dopa ever performs the intended function of hGH secretion.

To circumvent the unwanted breakdown of L-Dopa, and the reverse effects stemming from the inhibitory action of vitamin B_6, Sinemet is often used (L-Dopa in combination with carbidopa). Unfortunately, Sinemet isn't too smashing a substitute when you consider the fact that **dyskinesis** (defective voluntary movement patterns) is caused even with very low doses!

There are several adverse reactions that are common with L-Dopa use. In fact, every bit of research into the effects of L-Dopa lists some of them as **frequent**, which means that they occur most of the time. These include: **anorexia, nausea, vomiting, abdominal distress, flatulence, dyskinesis, orthostatic hypotension, muscle twitching, grinding of teeth, weakness, numbness, fatigue, headache, confusion, nightmares, insomnia, anxiety, agitation, psychotic episodes with paranoid delusion, hallucinations, severe depression** and **hypomania.** Blood values are significantly altered, and the incidence of malignant melanomae are increased.

The list is extensive and terribly frightening. What is most distressing is the fact that many of these undesirable side effects are **frequently** observed! Bodybuilders using this substance, commonly in combination with anabolic steroids and exogenous hGH (somatotropin), run further risks of complex interactions creating (potentially) devastating side effects.

Bodybuilders with drug mentalities are often wont to throw caution to the wind—some form of macho response to their thwarted egos, I suppose—and forget in the process that there is a better way.

An Alternative That's Healthy—and Just as Effective

Anyone familiar with the research literature on methods of inducing greater secretory activity in the pituitary knows that there is very little difference between L-Dopa and arginine insofar as their ability to stimulate hGH secretion is concerned. Glycine, the simplest of all amino acids, is also an excellent hGH stimulator. Further, exercise followed by arginine or glycine administration seems to be a more effective method of stimulating hGH secretion than using these substances alone.

Neither will cause your urine to darken or turn red as a result of the presence of potentially dangerous metabolites (as happens with the use of L-Dopa). Neither will have a reverse action in response to the presence of vitamin B_6 either. (When using L-Dopa, you must eliminate B_6 from your diet to allow L-Dopa to be effective.) hGH-stimulating amino acids of these types are safe and healthy to use. L-Dopa is not, and neither is it more effective. There seems to be little in the way of scientific argument that supports the use of L-Dopa for its hGH-stimulating effects.

There is, in fact, considerable evidence being compiled that shows the combination of free-form amino acids, proper vitamin and mineral supplementation, and scientific bodybuilding procedures to be as much as 60% as effective as anabolic steroids in producing initial muscular growth. This percentage will decrease over time to zero. In other words, the initial anabolic effects of steroid use may be 40% greater than healthful living in producing muscular gains, but this difference disappears over time because of a ceiling effect on your muscle-growth capabilities.

In my experience, fully 90% of all bodybuilders and powerlifters I know have already plateaued in strength and muscle size. Those who are using steroids would be well-advised to switch to sound nutritional supplementation at this point because they cannot expect gains from their drug use to be any better than those which can be derived from proper supplementing with free-form amino acids, vitamins, and minerals.

As far as I'm concerned, using L-Dopa is a dead issue, simply because I am convinced that there is a better way that is not-so-coincidentally far safer and healthier. There is every reason to believe that as the science of nutrition advances, methods of supplementation will be developed that will be more effective than the use of any such dangerous, or potentially dangerous, drugs in bodybuilding and strength development.

21

OTHER DRUGS
AND PRACTICES SOMETIMES
USED BY BODYBUILDERS

There are virtually dozens of other drugs used (most often indiscriminately—which constitutes misuse or abuse) by athletes in their quest for improved performance. All are drugs and therefore can be potentially dangerous. The standard caution must be offered—get thee to thy physician! Your sportsmedicine physician is generally your best bet in determining whether you are a healthy candidate for whatever drug you feel you need to take. It is only a fool who would take a drug that some other athlete says is good—it is best to find out for sure, or at the very least to get a more informed opinion.

Other Drugs Often Used by Bodybuilders

In the quest for that winning edge—the advantage over one's opponent—many bodybuilders opted to dig deeper into their pharmaceutical grab-bag. Probably the most frequent users of these other drugs are the bodybuilders, although weightlifters, powerlifters, and other athletes do as well. The tables on pages 231-233 list many of these ergogens, classifying them into two categories: ingested and injected ergogenic aids, and other practices and substances (non-injected and non-ingested).

Efficacy Listing of Injected and Ingested Substances Often Used as Ergogenic Aids

Ergogen (listed alphabetically)	Increased Performance While in Competition			For Precontest Training Increased Recovery or Therapy		
	Yes	No	Questionable	Yes	No	Questionable
adrenaline (epinepherine)	SE		Z			SEZ
alkalies		SZ	E	SEZ		SEZ
*alcohol		EZ	S	SEZ		
anti-inflammatants (Butazolidin)	SEZ			SEZ		
amino acids beyond the normal daily requirement		SEZ		SEZ		
*anabolic steroids (Dianabol, etc.)		SEZ		SEZ		
antiestrogens (Novadex, Clomid, Teslac)		SEZ				SEZ
asparates		SZ	E	SEZ		
B-12 injections			SEZ			SEZ
barbiturates		SEZ		SEZ		
blood doping		S	EZ	SEZ		
beta blockers		SZ	E	SZ		E
camphor			no responses			
*caffeine	SE	Z				SEZ
*central nervous system stimulants (strychnine, etc.)	E		SZ			SEZ
digitalis		SZ	E	SEZ		
**diuretics	Z	E	S	SEZ		
ether		SEZ		SEZ		
**electrolytes	SEZ			SEZ		
glycogen loading	E	S	Z	SEZ		
gelatin		SEZ		SEZ		

Key: S = strength; E = endurance; Z = muscular size or bodybuilding
* drugs banned by the IOC in international competition (or other sport groups have banned these and other drugs as well); caffeine and alcohol are banned on a discretionary basis in certain sports of the IOC.
** diuretics are often used to cut water weight in order to make weight for contests in boxing, weightlifting, powerlifting, and wrestling. Bodybuilders use diuretics and other drugs to "cut up" or achieve greater definition for contests. Electrolyte replacement is a must.
Note: Some of the efficacy ratings listed depend upon whether certain preconditions or concommittant conditions are met. For example, certain ergogens don't work unless heavy training or adequate nutrition is implemented. Further, some are extremely dangerous and should be administered only under expert supervision, while others should **never** be used owing to extreme danger.

Efficacy Listing of Injected and Ingested Substances
Often Used as Ergogenic Aids (Continued)

Ergogen (listed alphabetically)	Increased Performance While in Competition			For Precontest Training Increased Recovery or Therapy		
	Yes	No	Questionable	Yes	No	Questionable
glycine			SEZ			SEZ
human chorionic gonadotropin (HCG)		SEZ				SEZ
lecithin		SEZ			SEZ	
liver extracts		SEZ			SEZ	
levidopa (ex. Sinemet)		SEZ				SEZ
marijuana		SEZ			SEZ	
minerals or vitamins (supplements)		SEZ		SEZ		
nicotine		Z	SE		SEZ	
nitroglycerin		SZ	E		SEZ	
*narcotic analgesics (ex. morphine)	E	SZ		E	SZ	
*psychomotor stimulants (ex. amphetamines)	SE	Z			SEZ	
phosphates		SEZ			SEZ	
pain killers (analgesics)	SEZ			SEZ		
periactin (antihistamine)		SEZ			E	SZ
sulfa drugs		SEZ			SEZ	
somatotrophic hormone (STH)		SEZ		SEZ		
sugar		SEZ			SEZ	
*sympathomimetic amines (ex. ephedrine)	E	Z	S		SEZ	
wheat germ		SEZ			SEZ	
**wydase	Z	SE			E	SZ
yeast		SEZ			SEZ	

Key: S = strength; E = endurance; Z = muscular size or bodybuilding

* drugs banned by the IOC in international competition (or other sport groups have banned these and other drugs as well); caffeine and alcohol are banned on a discretionary basis in certain sports of the IOC.

** diuretics are often used to cut water weight in order to make weight for contests in boxing, weightlifting, powerlifting, and wrestling. Bodybuilders use diuretics and other drugs to "cut up" or achieve greater definition for contests. Electrolyte replacement is a must.

Note: Some of the efficacy ratings listed depend upon whether certain preconditions or concommittant conditions are met. For example, certain ergogens don't work unless heavy training or adequate nutrition is implemented. Further, some are extremely dangerous and should be administered only under expert supervision, while others should **never** be used owing to extreme danger.

Efficacy Rating of Non-injected and Non-ingested Ergogenic Aids
(Substances & Practices)

Ergogen (listed alphabetically)	Increased Performance While in Competition			For Precontest Training Increased Recovery or Therapy		
	Yes	No	Questionable	Yes	No	Questionable
acupuncture	SE	Z		SEZ		
analgesic balms		Z	SE			SEZ
cold (wet or dry)		Z	SE	SEZ		
carbon dioxide	SEZ			SEZ		
disinhibition conditioning	SE		Z	SEZ		
DMSO			SEZ	SEZ		
electrostimulation		SEZ		SEZ		
heat (infrared, wet or dry)			SEZ	SEZ		
hypnotism	E		SZ	SEZ		
manipulation (chiropractic or naturopathic)	SE		Z	SEZ		
massage or vibration			SEZ			SEZ
music		SEZ		SEZ		
motion pictures		SEZ		SEZ		
meditation	SEZ			SEZ		
noise (loud and explosive)	SE	Z		SEZ		Z
Pavlovian disinhibition	SE		Z	SEZ		
oxygen	E	Z	S	E		SZ
transcutaneous electrical nerve stimulation (TENS)		SEZ		SEZ		
ultraviolet light		SEZ				SEZ
ultrasound		SEZ		SEZ		

Key: S = strength; E = endurance; Z = muscular size or bodybuilding
Note: Some of the ergogenic practices listed here may work or be beneficial only if certain preconditions or concommittant conditions are met. Further, some can be dangerous and should only be administered under expert supervision.

These tables should adequately provide an idea of the effectiveness, as well as the variety, of substances and practices going on in the sports related to bodybuilding. There are a few drugs, however, used in conjunction with anabolic steroids that merit further explanation.

Periactin (an antihistamine) is often used conjunctively with anabolic steroids to increase appetite. Many steroids tend to diminish one's appetite, and would be relatively useless without finding some way to increase caloric intake. Periactin makes you very drowsy, particularly for the first 4-5 days of use, but the drowsiness generally subsides and the appetite becomes nothing less than voracious. Avoid this drug, as it has been known to result in some rather severe conditions such as asthma and glaucoma.

Sinemet is an anti-Parkinsonian drug which reportedly is used by some athletes in an attempt to increase the amount of human growth hormone secreted in the body. It causes vomiting and nausea, but probably little (if any) of the desired result has ever been noticed. (See Chapter 20.)

Human chorionic gonadotropin (HCG) is a frequently used drug in assisting steroid users' testes to begin producing testosterone again after a cycle of anabolic steroid use. It appears to work, but should be used near the end of a tapering off period, and not for more than about three weeks. Dosages can range as high as 2cc per day for that short period of time—longer will cause the pituitary gland to discontinue production of gonadotropin. This drug is used by some "fat farms" in the belief that it assists in mobilizing fat deposits. There is no scientific evidence of this and I don't believe there is any empirical evidence either.

Clomid, like HCG, is used to stimulate testosterone production once tapering from steroid use is begun. However, its action is on the pituitary (stimulates gonadotropin release) and not on the testes directly. It also works, but is not as effective as HCG. Again, as with HCG, a two-or-three-week cycle on Clomid is sufficient.

Somatropin (somatotropic hormone or STH) has become the state-of-the-art strength and size drug in the free world. It is extracted from the pituitary glands of cadavers and monkey carcasses, and makes all tissues of the body grow. Acromegalia and diabetes are the chief side effects but have not been observed if the drug is used as clinically prescribed (e.g., for six weeks and not more than 1 cc every other day). Somatropin is a potent fat mobilizer, it increases the thickness of ligaments and tendons (thereby reducing risk of injury), and it causes substantial muscular growth and strength increases. It is best used in conjunction with anabolic steroids and a high-calorie/high-protein diet. Soon there will be a synthetic growth hormone on the market— one that has had the deleterious side effects cloned out. It is the belief among many weightlifters and bodybuilders that the record books will be completely rewritten with the use of this drug. Other countries of the world either have had, or are currently developing, various growth hormones. Before this drug is recommended under any circumstances, however, far more practical research needs to be carried out.

Exoboline is a German drug that reportedly is effective in facilitating protein synthesis. Since it is not a steroid (it is related chemically to vitamin B_{12}) it is not detectable in steroid tests—neither is it illegal in international competition. Small amounts are available in the United States, and there promises to be more as time goes by. It is relatively safe, having few, if any, side effects.

235

Wydase is used clinically as a **spreading** agent for other drugs. It is used almost exclusively by bodybuilders in the belief that It assists in reducing (temporarily) subcutaneous fat. Assumedly it does this by causing mobilization of the fluid in fat cells—they return to normal in a short period of time.

Another drug akin to Wydase (used by bodybuilders) is **Thiomacase.** It, too, is reported to cause a thinning of subcutaneous deposits, allowing the bodybuilder to appear more cut-up and hard. Both Wydase and Thiomacase are typically used just prior to a contest (within the last two weeks), and are injected subcutaneously in various points around the body depending upon where the fatty deposits are. Side effects appear to be minimal or nonexistent, although no scientific tests are known to have been done to determine this.

PART IV
PSYCHOLOGY
22
MOTIVATION

"C'mon, let's go train!"

"Naw, got a date."

"But, you **have** to train because my car isn't running and I need a ride to the gym!"

And so it goes in the typically mundane world of the bodybuilder. Hundreds of similar scenarios could be constructed to get the point across that there are more motivating forces in your life than just getting to the top in the bodybuilding world. Sex, friendship, will to excel, obligation—these are the competing factors from the above scenario. There are, of course, a great number in any bodybuilder's life, and the exact course of action taken at any given time depends upon the relative strengths of the many competing factors operating at the same time. Your job, if bodybuilding greatness is paramount in your life, is to ensure that the incentive to train—to become the greatest—is the strongest of all the competing factors in your life.

This is no easy task, even if you are already highly motivated to excel. The demands upon you as a bodybuilder are great, and involve so many factors—such as diet, sleep, medical assistance, money, scientific training, and much more—that it's a safe bet that no athlete has ever achieved the ideal state of training because of the competing factors in his or her life which often detract from training.

There is a very healthy amount of scientific research behind motivation in sports. Much of it pertains directly to you as a bodybuilder. Many bodybuilders and aficionados (coaches and exercise physiologists) of the sport see **motivation** and **incentive** as the **primary problem** in achieving peak bodybuilding performance.

What Is Incentive?

David Birch and Joseph Veroff, two internationally prominent psychologists, teamed up in 1966 to write what is widely regarded as one of the most definitive attempts at defining human motivation. They identified seven major incentive systems that collectively account for almost all of man's goal-directed behavior. Through an extensive review of the research on motivation to that date, they postulated that a motive, the incentive itself, will direct a person's **immediate** goal-oriented activity only if that motive is the strongest of all other competing motives. Birch and Veroff's incentive systems are as follows:

- Regulating bodily experiences (**sensory incentive system**).
- Reacting to new stimuli (**curiosity incentive system**).
- Evaluating their own performance (**achievement incentive system**).
- Withstanding the influence of others (**power incentive system**).
- Operating on their own (**independence incentive system**).

Bodybuilders, like any other class of athletes, need to train. They need to carefully regulate their diet, and they must also tend to other aspects of contest preparation that transcend the confines of the gym. They are therefore subject to the above-listed incentives, and the one that is the strongest wins. The important job of regulating these incentives so that the appropriate one surfaces as the strongest at the right time can be a real challenge. It is a challenge that only the most disciplined bodybuilder can meet.

But it can and **must** be done if championship status is your long-range goal. And that brings up an interesting point of discussion. Implicit in Birch and Veroff's paradigm of goal-directed behavior is the notion that long-range goals can only be achieved if short-term (immediate) goals are regulated effectively.

The above notion bears repeating: You cannot expect to become all that you can become unless you set short-term goals and manipulate your life to the extent that you systematically achieve each one. Each immediate goal must be fully realized, and the sequential attainment of these immediate goals will, if thought out carefully, lead you down the path to championship status. A closer look at each of Birch and Veroff's incentive systems will illustrate how you can effectively manage your day-to-day goal orientation.

Sensory Incentives

Tasting, hearing, smelling, seeing, and feeling are the main sensory experiences for man. And, perhaps the most negative of all for bodybuilders is feeling pain. Pain acts in a negative manner because it generally causes an **avoidance** response. In the gym, under heavy iron, pain is commonplace. You put up with it because you know the outcome will be more pleasant than the temporary discomfort. But, in truth, don't you shy away from exercises because of an avoidance reaction to what you know will be painful? If you're normal you probably do; more often than you would like to admit.

Hunger is another negative sensory experience that all bodybuilders have experienced. So hunger, like pain, is often avoided. Other sensory experiences (both positive and negative) are common to bodybuilders as well. The pumped sensation, physical effort, fatigue, and tension are examples. Top bodybuilders learn how to make these sensory experiences work for them rather than against them. They learn how to make them positive rather than negative incentives.

Curiosity Incentives

Curiosity plays a major role in children's pursuits of new activities, and the same basic curiosity stays with most adults albeit in the form of an incentive to optimize stimulus complexity. That is what the research shows. Relating this concept to bodybuilding is quite simple and straightforward. Continually engaging in a boring, simple, training regimen can become a negative incentive over a short period of time. Get into the **science** of bodybuilding! Make it challenging! Alter your routine periodically; take advantage of what science has to offer— avoid boredom!

Achievement Incentives

Sport psychologists are generally in agreement that the incentive to achieve in sports is probably the "master" incentive. Relative to bodybuilders' interests, two important achievement orientations show up. The first and most common is the drive **to enjoy** success. The second is the drive **to succeed.** In the first case, a bodybuilder who experiences success (at the local contest level, for example), is spurred on to greater things. Even after attaining the Olympia, he (or she) continues because the orientation is to continue to experience success.

The incentive to succeed, perhaps the most devastating from the standpoint of the fans at least, is the drive a bodybuilder displays in getting to the top and then quitting. This drive to succeed is immediately quenched upon achieving success, and further participation is no longer meaningful to the bodybuilder. He or she has finished his or her task.

There appear to be three main categories of achievement incentives in sport: competence, a sense of effectiveness, and masculine identity. **Competence** in bodybuilding is generally judged on the basis of comparison with others in the group, and success is dependent upon what the individual's goals are. So, while related, competence to win at any given level in bodybuilding may not signal success. It is important to keep your goals clear, and to avoid the pitfall of winning or losing, which can cloud your own judgment of your level of competence.

Your **sense of effectiveness** can be modified by success and failure. It is important for you, particularly if you are a beginning bodybuilder, to know your own level of competence and to set your sights on long-range goals through successfully achieving short-range goals. In this way, your own sense of effectiveness will remain positive.

The sport of bodybuilding, like most sports in our culture, achieved the popularity it has because it afforded the participants a chance at improving their **masculine identity.** Girls in our culture have been told for generations that successful women are not achievement oriented—they must learn to do the things women do. Boys, on the other hand, have been told that achievement is closely linked with masculinity, and that success as a man depends heavily upon their fostering a masculine image. For good or bad, this age-old stereotype is changing, and more and more women are entering the sport arena (including bodybuilding) expecting the **feminine** image to be enhanced. Boys and men, of course, continue to participate for reasons associated with the masculine image they were brought up believing to be important.

Affiliation Incentives

The need for reassurance is perhaps the strongest incentive for a person to train with another person. The need to feel a measure of self-worth and social acceptance is generally offered by others with whom you train. Forming this kind of a "mutual admiration" arrangement is good, and fosters greater achievement incentive as well.

It is a well-known paradox in sport psychology that those of us who are unable to love or like another person are those who seek affiliation the most, whereas those who are loved or liked the most are those who do not depend on affiliation for a source of reassurance or feelings of self-worth. Most good coaches know this, and try to accommodate the person who needs affiliation as well as the person who doesn't. As a bodybuilder, you should try to remain aware and sensitive to the needs of your training partner(s) because ultimately their achievements will reflect on your own. If you're in it together, then work together!

Aggression Incentive

In its purest form, aggression is defined as being present when the intentional destruction or injury of another person occurs or is sought. Of course, such aggression has no place in sports, and in fact is rare in bodybuilding. Rather, a form of "instrumental" aggression is operative, where behavior is intensified to achieve a particular goal. Frustration, resentment, or pain are typical causes for negative forms of aggression to appear in the gym. A more instrumental (and positive) approach to training aggressively can be fostered by simply keeping your short-term goals in mind, and pursuing them vigorously.

Independence Incentives

The need some bodybuilders feel to "do it on their own" is referred to as independence. However, a complex interplay of situational factors often occurs that tend to modify this behavioral pattern. Independent bodybuilders often interrupt their concentration or independence incentive when they feel a need to be evaluated—as in a contest. Also, curiosity incentives often replace independence incentives when the bodybuilder is confronted with a different (competing) incentive. Highly independent bodybuilders tend to lose interest in the sport more easily than those who have a greater affiliative incentive. In addition, highly independent athletes who continually fail (in their own self-evaluation) eventually seek assistance from others, allowing their achievement incentive to come to the fore. If they were more attuned to their needs, such assistance could have been available to them long before failure became such a problem.

Power Incentives

Bodybuilders have whopping egos. This has become a cliche in bodybuilding and not without just cause. And it is precisely because of their egos that certain problems arise. The need to exert influence over others and the need to remain insensitive or unreceptive to the advice of others is, by definition, a power incentive. Personality clashes in the gym can be frequent, and they arise very frequently from two bodybuilders' attempts to not only resist being influenced by the other, but trying to impose themselves on the other.

Perhaps a more pervasive example of the power incentive operating in bodybuilding is when, for reasons of peer acceptance, familial acceptance, or public acceptance, a person engages in the sport. When your motivation is such that you bodybuild because others will have a higher opinion of you, you do so because of a power incentive. Status, recognition, or prestige are powerful motivators, and if that's your bag, so be it. It's one of the realities of life that is neither good nor bad. But being dependent upon some form of social evaluation must ultimately cease—self-evaluation is also critical, and must be fostered for continued success and perhaps especially for continued enjoyment in the sport.

The Interplay of Incentives

Your ability as a bodybuilder can be likened to a machine. But the power that makes it work is **motivation!** Although seven different incentive systems were treated in this chapter, you must bear in mind that they are not independent—they often work both for and against one another in determining your course of action. While skill, ability, or genetic predisposition are important factors in your bodybuilding success, the intangible which makes them work in winning is **motivation.** Just as there can be no performance without ability, there can be no performance without motivation.

Judge yourself on the basis of these seven incentive systems, and know yourself better. Doing so will help you to more fully understand the way toward achieving your long-term goals in bodybuilding.

How to Sustain Your Motivation

- Perhaps the most effective means of ensuring continued motivation in bodybuilding is to set short-term goals. Your short-term goals should ultimately lead you to your long-range goal, but be prepared to cope with occasional setbacks on the way.

- Know yourself. Learn about the major motivating forces in your life, and adjust them to complement each other rather than acting negatively or continually competing with one another.

- The most effective way to regulate the competing motivators in your life is to establish a schedule for training and avoid interrupting influences.

- Learn how to make pain a positive factor in training—key on the end result rather than the temporary discomfort.

- Feel the exhilaration of the pumped sensation, the joy of effort, and the enjoyment of all-out training fatigue—they are signals of goal attainment.

- Make your training a challenge in itself! Allow the fascinating complexity of the art and science of bodybuilding to totally captivate your interest. Get into it! Construct and reconstruct your regimen as your knowledge of the sport grows. This will help you to avoid boredom and also to get the most out of your training for faster goal attainment.

- Be aware that achieving success is important, but also understand that for **continued** success, you should also learn to **enjoy** success.

- Remember that success is what **you** say it is—not what someone else says it is! You can foster a sense of competence, effectiveness, and masculinity or femininity by realizing that **none** are dependent upon winning or losing on the posing platform.

- You may wish to train alone or with a partner, but always remain receptive to assistance and self-assured of your own self-worth. In so doing you will find it easier to avoid failure. If you can avoid failure, you have, by definition, succeeded. And, success begets success.

- Foster aggressiveness in training. There is no room for weaklings in any sport, and the best way to achieve training objectives in bodybuilding is to train with a vengeance.

- There is a fine line between having a strong ego and being narcissistic. If you feel the need to influence others in the gym, do so by example rather than by flapping your jaw. And, if you feel the need to squelch others because you perceive them as a threat to your own power position, remember that you may learn something by listening for a change. Foster a strong ego, but restrain your overbearance.

23

BRIDGING THE
MIND-BODY GAP

Your quest for excellence has followed a tortuous path. Fraught with pain, disappointment, and minimal rewards save the fleeting gratification offered by your reflection in a dirty mirror in a dimly lit gym, your quest nevertheless remains undaunted. Are the physical hardships you have overcome as a bodybuilder the major source of your dedication or lack of it? Or is the source largely psychological in nature? Your performance in the gym and on stage in competition is most certainly affected by a delicately equilibrated harmony of both mind and body.

The Ideal Performance State

The very fabric of your personality can be greatly affected by your own appearance. Bodybuilders, after all, take pride and find solace in looking good. Over time, your psychological state can affect your appearance. Poor workouts, lack of dedication, shoddy onstage performance, or an inability to endure the physical hardships of strenuous training can obviously affect your appearance as well. The ideal performance state, whether during training or in competition is affected by this interplay. It is therefore of critical importance that you, as a bodybuilder, learn the secrets of modifying your behavior in order to create this ideal performance state.

Your Internal Climate

Your mental state (how you feel) is inextricably related to how you perform. Sport psychologists have studied this interplay of athletes' performance levels and their internal (psychological) climates and have uncovered some guidelines for optimizing athletic performances through controlling one's mental state.

Dr. James Loehr, a psychologist at the U.S. International University, describes the ideal performance state as being comprised of two critical psychological states: high energy and pleasant feeling. The range of possibilities that exist for these two criteria are presented below. Included are the kinds of feelings that accompany each state.

Ideal performance state: High energy/pleasant feelings (alert, energetic, lively, stimulated, vigorous, enthused, high team spirit).

Second-best performance state: High energy/ unpleasant feelings (nervous, fearful, anxious, angry, frustrated, upset, vengeful).

Third-best performance state: Pleasant feelings/low energy (tired, fatigued, weary, exhausted, out of gas, low desire).

Poor performance state: Low energy/unpleasant feelings (bored, disinterested, annoyed, irritated, seriously lacking motivation).

Dr. Loehr believes that these traits are fundamentally the same for all athletes across all sports. Loehr found in his research of champion caliber athletes that for them to consistently perform at optium levels they must have achieved substantial control over their emotions to the extent that they are able to instantly catapult themselves into their own ideal performance state. In his research, Dr. Loehr was able to identify twelve distinct feelings athletes must be able to call upon during performance of their respective sports. These twelve feelings have very strong applicability to bodybuilders as well.

Physically Relaxed: Muscle tension resulting from nervousness can affect your onstage performance, and it can also result in performance decrements in your training. Try to foster the ability to relax your muscles and to be "loose."

Mentally Calm: Identified by Dr. Loehr as the second most important attribute leading to top performance, a mentally calm feeling during training and posing is generally accompanied by the ability to concentrate. Conversely, a racy and fast mental state is often associated with an inability to concentrate.

Low Anxiety: The greater the pressure you feel, the lower your performance level will be according to the data from Dr. Loehr's research. Champion bodybuilders generally meet pressure situations head on, and feel challenged and pressure free.

Energized: Together with calmness, being positively energetic stands out as being the most important attribute of champion caliber body-builders. The source of their energy is not anxiety, fear, anger, or frustration according to Loehr, but rather **joy!** Loehr's data clearly linked joy with enjoyment, determination, challenge, intensity, and power.

Optimistic: Peak performances are accompanied by feelings of optimism and positiveness. Pessimism and negative feelings, on the other hand, hinder peak performance.

Enjoyment: Enjoying yourself during training or competition is essential to staying relaxed and calm, controlling anxiety, and sustaining high energy levels. How can you put forth maximum effort if you hate what you're doing?

Effortless: When you have mastered the mind—when you have bridged the gap between mind and body—the task at hand feels easy despite 100% effort being applied.

Automatic: When your efforts become guided by instinct, logical or analytical thought processes fade in favor of a spontaneous and free-floating process. The old axiom **paralysis by analysis** seems to apply in bodybuilding as well as other sports.

Alert: Most top performances are accompanied by a remarkably heightened awareness, particularly with regard to bodily and situational factors. Physical and environmental "signals" are not a source of distraction, but rather serve as data input for heightened awareness and performance increments.

Mentally Focused in Present: The ability to block irrelevant signals from cropping up into the conscious during your performance stems largely from a mixture of calmness and high, positive energy according to Dr. Loehr. Only those stimuli that are directly related to the task at hand are allowed to filter into the top athletes' minds.

Self-Confident: Being a top performer, whether in your training or in competition is closely associated with a belief that you are the best, and that you are in control. You must be able to transform potentially threatening situations into positive challenges and remain calm and poised in adversity.

In Control: Top bodybuilders control the situation, they are not controlled by it. This control comes from within and is often called **inner strength.**

"Attempting to perform well in the presence of the wrong emotional climate is in many ways analogous to planting a seed in frozen soil," says Dr. Loehr. "The potential of the seed cannot manifest itself until the conditions of temperature, moisture, and so on are optimal." And so it is with human performance. As a bodybuilder, you cannot expect your efforts in the gym to be anything but submaximally beneficial, or your onstage presentation to be anything but below par without the right mental attitude. Your feelings and emotions create an energy and a force that trigger both psychological and physical arousal.

Arousal stemming from fear, anxiety, anger, or frustration invariably have debilitating effects on your efforts. On the other hand, the kind of arousal that is stimulated by being challenged, inspiration, enjoyment, or power create the ideal performance state.

Controlling Your Mental State

You have the capabilities of controlling your mental state. You are not a piece of floating debris atop the sea of life's experiences. You are not subject to the whims of tide, wind, and storm. You are, in a very real sense, the master of your own destiny. But you have to learn the secrets to achieving the kind of mastery over your mind and body it takes to become a champion. They don't come naturally. They are not innately bestowed upon any of us. The twelve mental characteristics of championship performers are won through hard training, constant vigilance, and an absolute resolve to excel.

Here are some techniques you can use to accelerate such control:

Awareness Training

You must learn to relate your feelings with the corresponding performance level. The critical relationship between the mind and body will become self-evident when you are able to recognize the correlation. Recognition can be enhanced by a simple device, your training log. You should write how you feel after all your heavy sets and after your workout. Whether your workout was particularly success-ful or it was dullsville, write it down. Next to it, write how you feel, using the twelve items as your guide. A simple technique is to rate your feelings on a scale of 1-5 for each of the twelve mental factors. (See page 248 for chart.) Great workouts would be comprised of mostly ones and twos, while poor workouts would reflect mostly fours and fives. Strive always to foster situations and feelings that are conducive to achieving ratings of one or two on each mental attribute.

Emotional Rehearsal Training

During the day when you're resting, try to visualize your best, most

Rating Your Emotional State

Rate your own emotional state by circling the number that most closely matches your own feelings on each of the following twelve emotional responses.

great workout	1 2 3 4 5	poor workout
physically relaxed	1 2 3 4 5	physically tense
low anxiety	1 2 3 4 5	high anxiety
highly energetic	1 2 3 4 5	low energy level
high optimism	1 2 3 4 5	low optimism
enjoyed myself	1 2 3 4 5	did not enjoy myself
effortless training	1 2 3 4 5	great effort was expended
responded instinctively	1 2 3 4 5	had to deliberate
very alert	1 2 3 4 5	very dull
not bothered by external factors	1 2 3 4 5	easily distracted
very confident	1 2 3 4 5	totally lacking confidence
in control of situation	1 2 3 4 5	no control of situation

Total Score Interpretation

12–24: Ready to train for the Olympia Crown!

25–48: You need to get to know yourself better and to control your emotional response to your training.

49–60: Either quit, get out of the gym for a few days of emotional relaxation, or seek professional help!

productive workouts or contest performances. Remembering your emotions during those times and then attempting to cause them to appear by "willing" them to do so is a technique that will help you to achieve the right frame of mind and emotional climate you will need to become a champion.

Prior to contests, and especially prior to each workout, isolate yourself for a few minutes, and call up these favorable mental states. You can do it because you do indeed have control over your mind and your emotions. It is not dissimilar to actors learning how to cry with real tears; you must exercise your mental control just as you exercise your muscles.

Autogenic Training or Progressive Relaxation

Tension recognition is the key to progressive relaxation techniques of strengthening the mind-body link. A wealth of scientific information exists that clearly indicates that neuromuscular function and mental states are directly related. Thus, the now widely recognized fact that emotional control follows muscular control. Bodybuilders who are able to control their emotional states are better able to extract maximum benefit from their training efforts because of this important mind-body energy transfer capability.

Autogenic training is similar to progressive relaxation training in that both emphasize biofeedback techniques in keying on each muscle in sequence to master tension control. However, autogenic training takes it a step farther by advocating a form of self-hypnosis. The power of suggestion forms the crux of self-hypnosis techniques, and with it the ability to adjust the activation levels of individual muscles is facilitated.

Personality Factors Identified by Cattell (Cattell's 16-PF) and How Bodybuilders Compare with the Average Person[*]

Factor	Description	Bodybuilders' Score	Average Person's Score
A	sociability	5.68	5.5
B	intelligence	5.86	5.5
C	emotional stability	4.86	5.5
E	dominance	6.55	5.5
F	surgency	3.91[**]	5.5
G	conscientiousness	4.41	5.5
H	adventureousness	4.45	5.5
I	realism	4.55	5.5
L	suspicion	7.05[**]	5.5
M	imaginativeness	6.05	5.5
N	shrewdness	5.36	5.5
O	insecurity	6.55	5.5
Q1	willingness to accept change	6.27	5.5
Q2	self-sufficiency	5.86	5.5
Q3	self-control	5.68	5.5
Q4	tension	5.50	5.5

[*] Data based on research performed by Dr. Ellington Darden, reported in *Research Quarterly*, Vol. 43(2), p. 142-147, 1972.

[**] These are the only scores in which bodybuilders scored significantly different when compared to the average person. Other differences in the two sets of scores were not statistically different, but are interesting nonetheless.

The ability to concentrate on single muscles during training, and the ability to bring out the most in muscular appearance when posing are both enhanced using this kind of mind-body awareness technique. Your powers of concentration are honed to a fine edge with autogenic training.

250

Personality Awareness

Knowing yourself (how you react to people and to situations) is extremely important for any person wishing to maximize his or her performance capabilities in the world of sport and elsewhere. There has been sparse research into what the optimum personality profile for champion bodybuilders ought to be. However, some guidelines are available from the research literature, and it will behoove those aspiring to championship status to look closely at their personalities— and make the appropriate adjustments. "I am what I am" temperaments should change to "I am what I want to be" instead. For again, you do have control over your own destiny, and that includes your personality!

24

TENSION CONTROL
AN IMPORTANT INGREDIENT
IN BODYBUILDING SUCCESS

"Hey, gimme a spot, will you?"

"Get off my back! Can't you see I'm training?"

"Sheesh! Sorry I asked!"

This kind of attitude is common in most gyms I've ever been in, and the kind of tension present at the time such a flare up occurs can be cut with a knife! Typically, the guy who wants you off his back is getting ready for a contest, and uses this fact as an excuse for not wanting to help. It would break his concentration. But your asking had already done that, hadn't it? And, was he really concentrating in the first place? I suspect that he wasn't—or at least not as well as he could've been had he remained a little more calm. Tension, you see, reduces an athlete's ability to concentrate.

Stress: Functional or Dysfunctional?

Perhaps the upcoming contest made him uptight. Perhaps it was the excessive doses of steroids he was using. Or, it might be that an overactive psyche prompted the outburst. Chances are, it was a combination of factors. And, he isn't the only one who suffers from such tension. All athletes experience the same kind of tension to some degree. The stress it produces has both psychological and physical ramifications that aren't always conducive to peak performance.

Sport psychologists M. Vanek and B. Cratty described four different periods that an athlete may experience tension (or stress), and presented some important concerns that should be tended to during each. **Long-term tension** (weeks or months prior to a contest), **prestart tension** (days before a contest), **start tension** (just before competition), and **post tension** (following the contest). Bodybuilders' performance onstage can, of course, suffer as a result of too much start tension. However, the final few weeks prior to a contest, and the long-term tension that they often experience, is of far more vital concern since **appearance** will suffer greatly as opposed to merely presentation appeal. Some advice for bodybuilders plagued by such disruptive tension levels is available from the research literature, and is presented later.

First, let's differentiate between functional and dysfunctional stress. Some stress is inevitable and certainly desirable for proficient training; the issue here is to control the dysfunctional effect and enhance the functional one. Perhaps the clearest (though not entirely scientific) description of the kind of stress, or arousal, that is appropriate for different classes of athletes was presented by Dr. Joe Oxendine, another sport scientist, in 1970 (see table on page 253).

Of course, the arousal levels Oxendine spoke of refer only to that which should ideally be present at the time of competition. Long-term tension is not spoken of in his scheme. If tension levels arose that even remotely approached blind rage (as it did with the guy who wanted people off his back during his training), it seems rather obvious that it would be dysfunctional. On the other hand, making it through a particularly heavy set of squats may indeed require that a bodybuilder "psych" himself into a mental state that is close to level two or three on Oxendine's scale.

Powerlifters of the highest caliber approach platform lifting with an outward calm. Inside, however, in the confines of the subconscious mind, there trickles primordial jungle instinct. These trickles become raging torrents of emotion as they escape into the conscious. So intense are the resultant emotions that there is no room for any other thoughts—surrounding noise, other people, the weight on the bar, and even pain are all but mere shadows of reality. Single-minded effort predominates.

Bodybuilders rarely, if ever, find themselves in a situation where venting such extreme arousal is necessary. Instead, **controlled** emo-

Optimal Arousal Levels for Some Typical Sport Skills	
Level of Arousal	**Sport Skill**
5 (blind rage)	football blocking/tackling powerlifting running 220 and 440
4 (extremely excited)	sprints long-distance running shot put wrestling judo broad jump swimming races
3 (moderately excited)	basketball skills gymnastics high jumping boxing
2 (aroused)	baseball pitching and batting fancy diving fencing football quarterback soccer skills
1 (slightly aroused)	archery bowling field goal kicking golf putting and short irons basketball free throw
0 (normal state)	DAILY ACTIVITIES

tions—mild arousal—are called for when performing heavy training sets. This type of control is necessary if your aim is to concentrate on the training effect.

Furthermore, on the platform, a bodybuilder's level of arousal should probably not exceed the level one position on Oxendine's chart, except in rare instances where a particularly difficult pose or some kind of gymnastic movement is called for in the posing routine. In such cases, a level two or three would certainly be more than adequate.

Bodybuilders Have No Need for High Levels of Arousal

It's nice to be ''into'' what you're doing during training and on the platform, but being ''into'' your training and being **consumed** by it are not the same. Functional stress for a bodybuilder is whatever level of arousal it takes to maximize the efficiency of your heavy training without jeopardizing your concentration—or that of others around you.

There is rarely, if ever, a need for bodybuilders to display the kind of intensity of emotions that our example bodybuilder did in the opening paragraph of this chapter. There are several research studies which give clues as to how you can control emotional discharge during the weeks prior to competition. The key is to make the stress levels that contest anticipation often causes work **for** you rather than **against** you.

Techniques of Controlling Emotional Arousal and Stress

Too much tension alters various physiological functions in the body. Psychologists refer to the class of bodily changes that accompany stress as the ''fight or flight'' syndrome. They include:

- elevated heart rate
- elevated blood pressure
- localized pooling of blood (primarily to the arms and legs)
- rise in oxygen consumption
- release of sugar stored into the bloodstream
- increased recovery time requirements (for lactate removal)
- decreased reaction time
- decreased skin resistance
- decrease in alpha brain waves
- stepped up secretion of adrenaline
- muscular tenseness throughout the entire body
- general inhibition of performance capability in movements requiring skill or dexterity
- a momentary facilitation of gross bodily movement, generally followed by a decrement over several minutes of extreme arousal

For bodybuilders, almost all of these physical symptoms can be devastating. The tense muscles include not only those that are being exercised, but also include their antagonists. This kind of dysfunctional response robs you of maximum training effect because you are less capable of achieving maximum overload or concentrated effort in the desired muscles.

The other physical symptoms of overarousal serve to prematurely fatigue you, and the lost adrenaline can take up to several weeks to replace if overarousal is your normal training state for even a few days.

All of this adds up to one very bad condition—it invites overtraining, and **fast!** It is in your best interest to constantly remain aware of these physical responses, and to guard against their becoming dysfunctional. There are a few other methods other athletes have used successfully to control long-term tension, especially Eastern European athletes. The table below lists the most common methods, and the desirable physical changes that research has shown each to cause.

Physical Changes Resulting from Various Relaxation Techniques*

Physiological Stress Factors	Programmed Relaxation	Autogenic Training	Hypnosis	Transcendental Meditation	Zen and Hatha Yoga	Relaxation Response Technique
oxygen consumption	no research	no research	decreased	decreased	decreased	decreased
respiratory rate	no research	decreased	decreased	decreased	decreased	decreased
heart rate	no research	decreased	decreased	decreased	decreased	no research
alpha waves	no research	increased	no research	increased	increased	no research
skin resistance	no research	increased	increased	increased	increased	no research
blood pressure	no research	inconclusive	inconclusive	no change	no change	no research
muscle tension	decreased	decreased	no research	no research	no research	no research
reaction time	no research	no research	no research	increased	no research	no research

* Adapted from Benson, H. *et. al.* "The Relaxation Response", *Psychiatry*, 37 (1974): 37-46.

Programmed Relaxation

Edmond Jacobson, a Harvard professor during the early part of this century, devoted his entire career to researching the link between one's emotions and skeletal muscles. He has presented strong research evidence that by controlling tension levels in the skeletal muscles, a person was more able to control various emotional states, including stress.

The technique he described in his now famous book, **Progressive Relaxation**, is quite simple. While lying down, alternately contract and relax a muscle with decreasing intensity until the contraction is barely perceptible. This procedure should be followed in various ways (described by Jacobson) and with a variety of body parts. Bodybuilders and other athletes have used this method quite successfully for relieving muscular tension, and because of its simplicity and relatively innocuous nature, it is one that you should try any time you're feeling tense or under stress. Jacobson recommends doing this on at least a daily basis and over several months in order to effect a complete re-education of the nervous system.

256

Autogenic Training

Originally a German technique (developed by Oscar Vogt during the 1920s), autogenic training was fully researched and systemized during the 1950s by J. H. Schultz, a German psychiatrist and neurologist. Autogenic training is in widespread use in the Soviet Union and other Eastern European countries, because the athletes and coaches there understand the great importance of being psychologically prepared as well as physically prepared.

The Soviet athletes make extensive use of autogenic training techniques during the precompetitive period. Basically the training technique is based upon six psychophysiological exercises, to be practiced lying down with eyes closed:

1. Focus on a feeling of heaviness in the limbs.
2. Focus on a cultivation of a sensation of heaviness in the limbs.
3. Try to feel your heart beating, and focus on slowing it down.
4. Focus on your breathing rate, and while concentrating on it, reduce the number of breaths taken.
5. Focus on your upper abdomen, and visualize a sensation of warmth.
6. Cultivate a feeling of coolness on your forehead.

Schultz cautions that the participant must simply ''let it happen.'' Do not try to force the feelings described above with any intensity or compulsion. Each of the six exercise-induced states described above should be added to the previous one. Do not shift away from one to the other. The previous states should be retained when going to the next.

As you can see from the table on page 255, autogenic training can induce profound changes in tense or stressed athletes that are quite beneficial.

Hypnosis

There are two cautions that have to be given in regards to hypnosis.

First, it can be dangerous for anyone other than an expert in the techniques used and the psychodynamics of the subject and circumstances. Secondly, the research done on the effect of hypnosis on sport performance paints either a bleak picture or one clouded with alternative explanations and ambiguities. It would be presumptuous for you, as a bodybuilder, to expect hypnosis to improve your training by way of stress reduction.

However, the possibility is there, and bears mentioning. Dr. Warren Johnson, a sports psychologist at the University of Maryland reported his 1961 research on the effects of hypnosis on strength, power, and endurance in **Research Quarterly.** Of twelve subjects tested, only one showed test score improvements after both hypnotic and posthypnotic suggestions. But what improvements! Their subject, a professional football player who was an ardent weight trainee, was able to press a forty-seven pound barbell 130 times before hypnosis. After hypnosis however, and in subsequent tests, his scores were 180, 230, 333, and 350 respectively! He reported that his entire outlook on what his capabilities were had changed as a result of his hypnosis, and that he had a new idea about his potentialities. He was inspired to go on to set personal records thereafter.

This same kind of faciliatory response to barbell pressing was noted by Dr. Bill Morgan, a sport hypnotist at the University of Wisconsin. There appears to be potential for hypnosis to improve training efficiency, but to what degree or with what outcome is unclear at best.

Transcendental Meditation

Transcendental Meditation (TM for short) effectively elicits a relaxation response (see previous table). It has no mystical overtones steeped in black magic or inexplicable pseudoscientific phenomena. Instead, it is a rather simple-minded approach to reducing stress, improving mental alertness, and improving sport performance.

What seems to throw people off (or, **turn** them off, as the case may be) is the repetition of the mantra. The mantra is usually a Sanskrit or Tibetan phrase that is repeated over and over during the period of meditation. Actually, the sound (the mantra) is nothing more than the stimulus that elicits relaxation. That sound eventually disappears and the mind experiences subtler levels of thought. Finally, by "transcending," the mind arrives at the "source" of the thought. While in a comfortable seated position with eyes closed, the process of transcending the outer stimulation of sound and tactile sensory messages around

The Four States of Consciousness

	AWARE	NOT AWARE
THOUGHT	AWAKE	DREAMING
NO THOUGHT	TRANSCENDENTAL MEDITATION	DEEP SLEEP

258

you and from your own body, the conscious mind is brought into contact with your creative intellect. The result is that you emerge fresh, without muscular tension and ready for action.

There is no doubt that TM physical and psychological effects can benefit an athlete's performance, and that your training in bodybuilding particularly over several weeks, will be improved.

Let's look at the research for confirmation of these beneficial effects. Dr. Keith Wallace, a UCLA physiologist, collaborated with Dr. Hebert Benson, a cardiologist at Harvard Medical School, and Dr. Archie Wilson of the University of California Irvine Medical School to determine the physical changes that accompany TM states. In all, thirty-six meditators were studied. They found that metabolic rate was reduced in all subjects, with oxygen consumption dropping by an average of 18%. Also, blood lactate levels dropped nearly three times faster than the normal resting decline rate, and stayed down even after the meditation was over! Galvanic skin resistance to electrical current rose 250% during meditation, indicating that although deeply relaxed they were in an entirely wakeful state. A fact also confirmed by their increased alpha brain waves.

What have you got to lose? Give it a shot! Chances are, you'll feel rejuvenated and train harder than ever, with less distraction and with greater physiological benefit.

Yoga

Yoga is similar to TM, except that physical techniques are used in place of the mantra. Similar results in the research literature have been observed regarding the beneficial physiological effects of yoga exercises. Like TM, yoga is reported to be a powerful relaxation aid, but is not associated with causing drowsiness or sleep. The previous table on page 255 shows the physical effects of yoga for athletes, and body-builders can find potential use for this technique of stress reduction.

Relaxation Response Techniques

In 1974, H. Benson and his colleagues studied the results that TM and various other relaxation techniques had on the body, and attempted to develop a method that would replicate these effects but would be easier for athletes to use. Their efforts were not without rewards; the method they arrived at indeed has proven to be remarkably similar to TM and other techniques in eliciting a relaxation response.

There are, according to Benson, four distinct similarities between all of the more successful relaxation techniques:

1. **A mental device** (a sound, an exercise, etc.) used for the purpose of minimizing one's attention to other distracting stimuli.
2. **A passive attitude** (don't force it—let it happen) that allows you to not be detracted by external stimuli.
3. **Decreased muscle tone** (comfortable position) from minimal muscular work.
4. **Quiet environment** (little, if any, detracting stimuli present) and closed eyes.

Benson's technique can easily be incorporated by any athlete without expert instruction or time-consuming preparation or effort. There is some research evidence that his method does indeed create the same kind of relaxation response as the other methods do, and should be given due consideration particularly because of its ease of acquisition.

When to Use Relaxation Techniques

Many techniques may be used to reduce stress. A day off, a day at the beach, or just believing in a particular method may work. Research over the years has been relatively conclusive, however, that the techniques mentioned in this chapter—programmed relaxation, auto-genic training, hypnosis, TM, yoga, and the relaxation response tech-nique—definitely work on both a physical as well as on a mental level in eliciting the relaxation response.

As a bodybuilder, your chief aim is to approach your workouts with none of the physical or mental aberrations that result from stress or anxiety. Only in this way can you ever hope to achieve maximum efficiency from your workouts over time. This is particularly true for bodybuilders entering the precompetitive stage of their training. Great pressure can be disruptive of training efforts in very well-known physiological ways including the propagation of an overtrained state.

Scientists who have studied these relaxation techniques have recommended using them at least once or twice a day for twenty-minute periods. Over the course of several weeks great attitudinal as well as physical changes take place in most instances.

Whatever technique you use for relaxation, remember that your individual response to training and competition may require greater or lesser levels of arousal, so try to gauge your efforts by careful self evaluation. Find your own optimal level of arousal, and work to achieve it when your training requires it. Avoiding overtraining both from the physical and mental aspects is the first and most important step toward creating a keen sense of **motivation.** And, the greater your motivation to succeed in bodybuilding, the greater your chances of success. Perhaps the most efficient method of ensuring this state of affairs is to **relax!**

25
CONTEST PREPARATION

"Oh, the Gift the Giftie Gie us, to see ourselves as others see us." The Scottish poet Robert Burns might have made a great head physique judge. His stinging epithet rings true especially in today's bodybuilding scene. Of course, come contest time every physique competitor sees himself a bit differently than the head judge. What do they know anyway?

Unfortunately, no one has ever had a monopoly on contest preparation knowledge. It is difficult, if not downright impossible, to patent an exact formula for physique perfection. Hitting the so-called "peak" at the dawn of the prejudging hour is the single most difficult aspect of bodybuilding competition. This chapter, however, is dedicated to the thought that I can improve your odds at hitting the perfect peak.

Preparation Time

Allotting an exact time for specific contest preparation is all but impossible. Dedicated bodybuilders can only narrow the timespan to between six and twelve weeks. Most competitors emphatically insist that preparing in anything less than six weeks is suicidal. And sticking to a strict diet for longer than twelve weeks is also suicidal. Suffice it to say, this loose time period represents the bodybuilder's twilight zone. The signpost up ahead reads, "the body's energy and will can either collide or merge harmoniously." Contest preparation is a peculiar arrangement of training, dieting, posing, and drugs (at least in the case of most male competitors). I make this modern-day assumption without any gift of clairvoyance, only an admittance of having been around, so to speak. It's safe to assume that most present-day competitors (a majority of women excluded) are probably cycling calorie intakes, training characteristics (load, exercises, sets, and reps), and steroids. Establishing general guidelines, most competitors select a contest at least six months down the pike, train heavily and intelligently, and eat a lot of good food. Eating and training thusly, as the body inherently demands, it is absolutely impossible for any male to begin the contest preparation phase any less than fifteen pounds off his best contest weight. Trying to maintain a weight differential any less than this is not healthy, not size-producing, and definitely not fun. No one expects a bodybuilder to resemble Orson Welles in the off-season but to ensure the energies concomitant with heavy weights you must consume your necessary quantities of good food regularly. I say this, knowing only too well that the degree of muscularity, separation, and definition required to **win** a major contest today, lay just south of absurdity. And the trend is getting steadily worse. The day of competitive anorexia may be upon us. But so it is, and so you must!

The Conquest of the Body

First comes the body! If you could pose like Ed Corney but were actually built like the chairman of the board, even the music "My Way" couldn't bale you out. But, built like Arnold or Sergio, with a routine no more graceful or delicate than a crow's digestive system and you would win a lot of contests. And so the conquest of the body begins. Clearly, peak perfection of the body is at least 50% dietary. Weight training for the shape and mass, and pushing yourself away from the table for the cuts. As the big day approaches, fat and extraneous water must be shed efficiently. And I shall suggest how.

Low Fat and Calories vs Low Carbs

In years past, and even today, many bodybuilders prefer the beefsteak, eggs, and water routine prior to a contest. The problem with this high-protein, low-carbohydrate diet is the loss of energy, loss of concentration, loss of muscle mass, and just plain braindrain. Occasionally, the loss of memory that accompanies this diet is comparable to smoking dope for eight years straight. Nevertheless, with the use of judicious stimulants (caffeine, etc.) you can make it to the contest leaving no doubt that you can get ripped to shreds. And about as massive as a shred, too. Good-bye "me mate" and so long pleasant demeanor along the way.

However unpleasant carbohydrate-limiting diets are, they are effective for putting together a contest-ready body. I say this in deference to the opinions of the pseudo-medical community, and the opinions of nutritionists and potbellied physiologists. Those same guys insisted the earth was flat. Depending upon one's degree of muscularity as the contest approaches, if you reduce carbohydrate intake down enough, the body switches to fat and protein for fuel. Such a tight precontest diet might appear as shown on page 264.

The low-carbohydrate diet is usually calorie restricted too (which accounts for about 99% of its effectiveness). Only, don't tell anyone that fact if they have just suffered through this diet!

The Low-Fat Thing

Lately, many competitors are enthusiastically exposing balanced fat, protein, and carbohydrate diets but with very low emphasis on fats since they yield more calories per gram than any other foodstuff. And all this time you thought sugar was so bad! The low-fat diet works well, but does not seem to work for everyone (logic notwithstanding). Unfortunately, the low-fat, low-calorie diet also contributes to muscle loss and braindrain. Muscle loss appears to be inevitable whenever calorie balance is **not** maintained. Fats cause physical and mental satiety like no other food. This is the reason that most competitors crave pizza and buttery foods after shows rather than a pure confectionary.

The underlying hope of the low-calorie diet is that you can consume an occasional delight such as a pizza slice, even in the contest phase as long as your average daily caloric intake falls below your caloric expenditure. Low-fat diets are healthier than low-carbohydrate or extremely high-protein diets. Most bodybuilders today follow well-balanced, low-fat diets, gradually cutting calories while increasing aerobic activities. You would want to lose anywhere from one to three pounds per week. The last week will drop off five pounds (give or take a couple) because some of this is last-minute water loss. My opinion is that more success can be gained through low-fat diets. Such a diet might be constructed as shown on page 264.

Low-Carb Diet

Pre-AM training	Midday meal	Post-Training meal
2 poached eggs	Small salad	Broiled fish
¼ lb. lean meat	Drained tuna in water	Egg whites
Coffee	Distilled water	Mineral water
10 leaver tabs.—vitamins & minerals		

Low-Fat Diet

Pre-AM training	Midday meal	Post-Training meal
Bowl of shredded wheat—skim milk	Tuna sandwich—no spread or diet spread	2 fruits
2 dry toast	2 pieces of fruit	Baked potato
¼ lb. Turkey		Fish or deskinned chicken
Vitamins & Minerals		

The Miracle of Frosted Flakes

With approximately ten days to go before a contest, you will want to practice some simple carbohydrate loading. This is a method of ridding yourself of interstitial body water and bringing out muscle separation, striations, and vascularity. For three days most of (but not all) your carbs are eliminated and very hard and long workouts are performed. This depletes your glycogen stores. Then to supercompensate the muscle glycogen stores, you should consume almost exclusively carbohydrates for the next four days. In addition to bringing out muscle striations and vascularity, this will give you very effective energy. Carbohydrates are consumed but only in limited quantities throughout the day, so as to not retain water. As the contest approaches there is a gradual shift from long-chained complex carbs to short-chain carbs. A sample, last-week diet follows:

Sat./Sun./Mon./Tues.—High protein, low fats, near-zero carbs, hard training.

Wed./Thurs.—Baked potatoes, rye toast, low-fat cottage cheese.

Friday—Non-spiced noodles, pasta, fruit (light, but intensely carbed, meals).

Sat. A.M.—Three hours before competition . . . fruit slices on frosted flakes and a small sweet roll or small scoop of ice cream.

At this point water retention in the gut and under the skin should not be a problem if you haven't been pigging out. Do not use the Frosted Flakes as an excuse to sugar load. If you do that you'll bring water into the gut. I would stress trying to find the diet combo that works best for you. Try the glycogen-loading routine once or twice well before a critical contest to determine exactly how you react to it.

Precontest Training Changes

These days everyone is an expert on the best ways to train prior to a contest. There are really two schools of thought. Some argue that sets and reps must be increased, as well as stepping up the training pace. The idea is to burn calories and pull out the cuts. You may also start double splitting your workouts approximately six weeks prior to the show. Training weights fall, and you use strict form and work for a fast, quality pump. This same school of thought also stresses aerobic training prior to a contest, to include jogging, fast walking, and low-intensity bike rides. The underlying premise is to move the body into a fat-burning metabolic state. The scientific advocates of these methods will note that your RQ (resting quotient) is greater in the early morning. This means that the CO_2 exhumed relative to the CO_2 consumed is slightly higher, meaning that fat is contributing in a greater fashion to energy production, if the subsequent workout is aerobic. Caffeine, remember, is that good, old friend of your kidneys. Use it moderately.

The other school of thought has as its primary tenet the notion that the biggest problem before a contest is the loss of muscle mass. What is the cause of muscle loss? The drop in training weights that inevitably occurs prior to competition. (This may or may not be true . . . equal blame has to fall upon the simple reduction of calories.) To prevent loss of muscle mass, continue to train heavily for lower reps and do **not** do aerobics! To bring out the cuts, keep carbohydrates fairly high and lower overall calories instead. This method is less of a crash course and must be pursued over a longer time span. The old standard is to never lower calories beyond 1,200 to 1,500 since the deficit will become too great and the body will burn its own muscle mass.

In either case, successful dieting is difficult and remains an art that must be mastered. Either way **will** work, it is really a matter of finding which method suits your metabolism (and lifestyle) best. The key to bringing your body to its fullest peak is to train hard, avoid serious training injuries, and intelligently cycle your training, eating, and dosing (drugs, if used). Learn to diet correctly, safely, and over the proper time period of your body metabolism.

Posing Presentation

At today's level of bodybuilding competition, it does little good to have a tremendously developed body if you cannot display it properly. Bodybuilding is a unique sport in many ways. It is, after all, the only sport where the actual competition is not the same as the training itself. In golf competition, you play golf just as in practice. In tennis you play tennis. But in bodybuilding, you do not train with weights, you pose!

If you have even rudimentary coordination, it is not difficult to be an average poser. Ah! but to be a great, artistic poser, that is a bit more difficult. Posing is graceful, muscular dance perfection. It is powerful and dramatic projection. It is charismatic, masculine, confidence personified. Think of yourself as displaying not only strong body parts to the judges but displaying a **sense of being** to them also. Posing should be functional, but it also should be done with dynamic pizzaz! Posing practice should definitely be done more than just one week prior to the competition. At that late stage, you are often too energy-depleted to practice posing adequately. Posing positions, posture, and transitional moves, should be perfected during the off-season.

Compulsory Poses

Compulsory poses represent the meat of competition. Rounds one and two of the prejudging usually hold the key to victory. Mosts contests are pretty well nailed down after the prejudging phase. In my opinion, bodybuilders spend sufficient time on their full posing routine, but not enough time on their stances and compulsory presentation.

Muscularity Round: Compulsory Poses

The current rules for this round call for seven compulsory poses for men and five for women and couples. The men's compulsories include: front double biceps, front lat spread, side chest, back double biceps, side triceps, back lat spread, and front abdominal. Presently, women's and pairs include: front biceps right leg extended, side chest, back double biceps (left leg back), side triceps (leg back), and abdominal (hands over head). These are NPC and AFWB positions. The AAU organization requires more positions.

All of these static poses should be practiced and practiced with and without mirrors. You will find that the contest tension brings out better control and muscular striation. In this phase of competition, you may get called back out for endless comparisons. I suggest using some spontaneity and changing arm and leg positions in these comparisons. As mentioned earlier, because these morning rounds require constant isometric tensing and flexing you will be wise to ensure proper mineral and carbohydrate nutrients for energy and prevention of cramps. Of critical importance are the minerals calcium, potassium, magnesium, and some sodium chloride substitute. If you can get away with it, try to wear a judicious bit of lotion or oil in the prejudging rounds.

The Relaxed Round

In the relaxed round the general overall physique is assessed. This is defined as general body shape, symmetry, muscle balance, muscle mass, fullness when relaxed, overall proportion, skin tone, and appearance along with extras such as posture, looks, grooming, trunk fit, confidence, and general attitude. Essentially, four stances are graded. These are, facing the judges, left side presented to judges, back presented to judges, and right side presented to judges. Since a large portion of your overall score comes from this round, it behooves you to practice stances a lot. A minor twist, flex, or turn here and there can sometimes spell the crucial difference. Practice in front of mirrors, in front of friends, and in front of enemies. Get the complete picture. Remember too, although the judges ask for complete relaxation absolutely no one truly relaxes. So practice flexing and tensing a bit without trying to look like a jerk or a contracted robot. Flare the lats a trifle, tense the legs and abdominals, and lift the ribcage.

The Individual Routine

The coordinated muscular presentation of your body and mind comprises the final prejudging round. Your routine should reflect the ultimate synthesis of strength and grace, of form and function. The pertinent idea is to incorporate basic positions into a smooth, transitional flow. Beginners are wise to construct simplistic routines of perhaps ten good poses and not to jump right into the fancy Makkawy stuff. Transitions that show dramatic fluidity are essential. Think of good posing as modified, muscular ballet. Good posers control their bodies effortlessly and are able to relate well with the crowd. You should be able to be adaptive, hitting poses that "turn on" the audience. Keep in mind, however, that you are posing for the judges more than the crowd; make sure you show them your strong points.

Pose without straining, grimacing, or shaking. The job is to impress and not to humor or frighten. Hold your poses for a full two or three seconds so the judges all get a chance for assessments. Don't hold the poses so long or repeat them so often that everyone gets sick of you. A good, functional routine should not exceed 90 seconds.

Music, Trunks, and Oil

Your choice of posing trunks and music can be either helpful or harmful. The trunks should cover the glutes fully. In the case of the men, if you have a short torso you can wear skimpy trunks like Tim Belknap does. Others with longer torsos typically need more coverage to the appearance of a higher waistline. White trunks are great if you have a dark tan and small hips. Otherwise, light colors tend to illusively widen the hips. They also tend to divide the body into distinctive blocks instead of helping merge the body. Most competitors look good in darker colors and everyone looks good in basic black. If you're built like Sergio, you can successfully wear gold-sparkled trunks!

Women have a greater variety of styles to choose from. These suits can vary from original bedazzlers that Shelly Gruwell makes to the plain-jane two-piece. Women need suits that offer breast and glute coverage and provide minimum abdominal and back coverage. The suit should not be so tight in the upper body that it threatens to burst with movement that is too vigorous. Couples will want to wear matching suits although that is, at present, optional.

Try to find a recognizable piece of professionally taped music but do not use a song that gets beaten into the ground by the disc jockeys day after day. Of course, you must practice the final routine with the music. This is even more important with couples. Your best poses should be hit with dramatic points in the music, preferably at the front and end of your selection. Have your music recorded at the beginning of a blank cassette and have two copies.

Those Important Extras

Obtaining a nice, even tan, having your hair properly groomed, and possessing good skin appearance can be of crucial importance. Tanned skin tends to reflect light less than white skin, especially when oil is used. If you are fortunate enough to live in a sunny climate use that sun rather than artificial light. The sun has a drying effect, tending to draw subcutaneous water out from the tissues. Don't get a sunburn though, because that retains water under the skin. If you are sunning heavily always use a skin lotion to maintain skin lubrication. This will give the skin a nice glow by the time competition rolls around. Unfortunately, we cannot all live in California. If you cannot get natural sun, you will have to use either ultraviolet type-A tanning salons or use artificial tanning lotions. Tanning should be done in ten to fifteen sessions at thirty minutes each in an artificial booth.

Many competitors will use pills that contain **canthraxanthin** or a potent medication called **trisoralenelder.** The latter medication must be taken two hours prior to exposure and should not exceed the rec-ommended amount in days or dosage. Depending upon your skin type, you may still have to use some artificial coloring. I like **Vitiligo** stain (in other circles known as **dye-o-derm**). In my opinion, **Sudden Tan** is good but tends to run upon sweating. It makes a lot of people stain orange, and **Clinique** tends to give the physique competitor a dirty, chocolate look. These commercial preparations should be used three days before competition and not too heavily because they cut out definition.

Skin preparation also includes removal of body hair. Most women are old hats at this but many male competitors end up with uncomfort-able rashes because of shaving improperly. I have found that athletic training razors are best (the kind trainers use to shave ankles prior to taping) used with hot water and a light soaping. Some like to dry shave but I recommend against that in the groin area, an area particularly prone to skin irritation. Start shaving a minimum of ten days before the show. Since you look more defined shaved down, this will help reinforce sticking to your diet. Upon removal of the body hair ten days before a show, you will find a much easier time spot-shaving as the contest approaches.

Hair styles, beards, and mustaches are a personal preference. Just make sure all are well groomed the day of the show.

Everyone seems to prefer different types of oil for the evening pre-sentation. Baby oil is the standard but under bright lights tends to cause a distracting glare and reflection, especially if the lighting is not directly overhead. Indirect lighting will cause shadowing and, together with the oil reflection, it can reduce perception of cuts and striations. Have a friend apply your oil evenly. Other choices for oil include, **Nivea** skin oil, almond oil, and **Ban-du-Soleil** which gives the body a mild orange hue.

A problem for some competitors, especially those using steroids, is water retention. The best natural way to handle this is to begin a program of controlled dehydration during the last week. This is done through sodium restriction, fluid intake control, and sweating through aerobics and the use of a sauna. Water intake should be progressively lowered until over the last two days the only water taken in is a small swallow to down your minerals and vitamins. I say this assuming you are consuming almost exclusively long-chain carbohydrates the last two days. Since these foods contain about 75% water, some water is released into the system in this manner. The morning of the show you may eat lightly, and drink sparingly or not at all.

Prescription diuretics are dangerous substances that cause a lot of muscle flatness. Furosemide (**Lasix**) does not spare potassium and will draw an enormous amount of fluid from muscle tissue in most people. Potassium-sparing diuretics such as the **thiazide** group are less dangerous. At any rate, if you choose the diuretic route, use them on a Monday and Wednesday if you have a Saturday contest. By controlling water on Thursday and Friday you won't experience any water rebound until later. You will also want to increase your intake of electrolytic minerals (such as through effervescent potassium **K-lyte**) ten days before and up to the show. Others have used mild laxatives and/ or an enema two days before the show to clear the bowel and upper intestinal track. My opinion is that these two methods can be a hit-or-miss proposition. Clearly you should not rely upon them. Be especially observant of high-sodium foods that last couple of days before the show. Avoid airline food unless you've ordered a fruit plate. A nagging question of many competitors is the amount and type of foods to consume between the morning and evening show. Do not assume that the scores are all decided after the prejudging. I have personally observed several reversals and changes made during the evening. My advice is to eat lightly—perhaps a couple of baked potatoes and a couple pieces of fruit with minimum amounts of water or other liquids.

The Timing of the Pump

Many bodybuilders complain of not being able to achieve or sustain a good pump at the critical moments throughout the prejudging rounds. Usually this is a sign of inadequate nutrition immediately prior (last 72 hours) to the show. This is why carbohydrates are crucial the last week, otherwise you may end up flat as a pancake. Do not pump up too early or too vigorously. Try to pump up about five minutes before being called on stage for your first comparison. The use of niacin, chewed ten minutes before going on, in some people, causes mild skin vessel vasodilation and adds a bit of red hue to the body, however. Some people get blotchy and experience an uncomfortable itching with this agent, so be careful. Once on stage, the constant tensing and flexing will tend to maintain your pump. The same can be said at the evening show. Pump up five minutes prior to your routine but do not overpump. This may destroy some of your cuts, particularly in the thigh area.

The Posedown

The culmination of your bodybuilding efforts will come when you are able to win your class and participate in the posedown for the overall title awards.

The very combative posedown is geared toward the audience but many judges use it to determine the final placements. Therefore, the posedown should be your final trip to the bank, so to speak. It's your ultimate generation of energy. You should assume that you are posing directly for the title. Cultivate and practice your posedown display. Use a variety of your most powerful poses one right after the other. Keep posing until the judges request you to stop. Only then does the contest end.

A Final Word

Remember, winning a contest these days is a rough proposition. Complete contest bodybuilding, including specific preparation for the big day, is truly a complex science. Study and experiment. Learn, remember, and most of all, be patient. Building and refining your championship physique to peak on the day of the event is the ultimate challenge.

. . . to bodybuilding!

INDEX

273

275

276